Living in the Vineyard

D1279370

Listening for the
Voice of God

God Bless You!
Cyndy Lindblad
2018

CYNDY LINDBLAD

© 2017 by Cyndy Lindblad

All rights reserved. No portion of this book may be reproduced, stored in a retrieval system, or transmitted in any form or by any means—electronic, mechanical, photocopy, recording, scanning, or other—except for brief quotations in critical reviews or articles, without the prior written permission of the author.

© Cover Image: image copyright, used under license from Shutterstock.com.

Unless otherwise specified, Scripture taken from the New King James Version®. Copyright © 1982 by Thomas Nelson. Used by permission. All rights reserved.

DEDICATION

I would like to dedicate this book to my husband, Peter, my greatest advocate. Thank you for believing in me and never allowing me to give up on my dream. I love you so much!

To my mom, JoAnn Hansen., whom the Lord called home September 29, 2017. Mom was always so excited for me to call her and read each devotional I had written. Her encouragement and love kept me writing. Never did I dream she wouldn't see the book in its completion. Thank you, Mom, for telling me to never stop writing. Your belief in me made all the difference. I love and miss you so much!

And last but certainly not least, to my Lord and Savior, Jesus Christ! With each devotional written I have fallen more in love with You. May this book bring You the honor and glory You alone deserve!

"I am the vine, you *are* the branches.
He who abides in Me, and I in him,
bears much fruit; for without Me
you can do nothing."

John 15:5

And He said,
"Let me go, for the day breaks."
But he said,
"I will not let you go unless You bless me."

Genesis 32:26

It is hard to hang on tight
to God, and wrestle with
Him until morning,
when the night...
seems so long.

Wrestling with God

Genesis 32:26

And He said, "Let Me go, for the day breaks".
But he said, "I will not let you go unless You bless me."

Jacob was returning home, leaving behind the place of his father-in-law Laban. Throughout the journey, Jacob called on the Name of the Lord. Before meeting his brother Esau, Jacob sent his entire family ahead. It is here we find Jacob *wrestling* with God.

What did God say? *"Let Me go, for the day breaks."*
Jacob's reply, *"I will not let you go until You bless me."*

After reading this portion of Scripture, I thought, "How willing am I to wrestle with God until He blesses me? How long will I sit at His feet, cry out in desperation, or rest in His Word before becoming discouraged and letting go?"

Jacob wrestled with God throughout the night. We have all been there, when the darkness seemed to magnify our heartache. God does not leave us without hope. We may weep in the night, in the dark places of our soul, but with God there will come a morning when the sun will shine again.

> "Weeping may endure for a night, but joy *comes* in the morning."
> —Psalm 30:5

Then I thought, "What has been a burden on my heart for so long it has become a way of life with no hope for an answer? Have I lost my persistence in crying out to the Lord for a blessing?"

What about you? Perhaps it's a wayward child, a diagnosis that looks impossible, a financial burden too heavy to bear, or a difficult relationship? It is hard to hang on tight to God and wrestle with Him until morning, when the night seems so long. When we are in this place, may we draw strength from God's promise:

> *"Draw near to God and He will draw near to you."* —James 4:8

May we be like Jacob and cry out to the Lord, *"I will not let You go until You bless me,"* and with great anticipation watch for how the Lord will answer our prayer.

But He answered and said,
"*It is written, man shall not live by bread alone,
but by every word that proceeds
from the mouth of God.*"

Matthew 4:4

It is time we allow our Father
to fight our battles
and flee from temptation.

Lead Me Not Into Temptation

Matthew 4:1-4

Then Jesus was led up by the Spirit into the wilderness to be tempted
by the devil. And when He had fasted forty days and nights, afterward
He was hungry. Now when the tempter came to Him he said,
"If You are the Son of God, command that these stones
become bread. But He answered and said,
"It is written, man shall not live by bread alone,
but by every word that proceeds from the mouth of God."

Satan, believing Jesus would bow down to his bidding, did his best to tempt
Jesus. With this same determination, he tempts us today. Disguising temptation as harmless, he whispers, "What could it hurt this one time? Who will
ever know?" "This isn't gossip, this is a prayer request"—he helps us justify,
as we share a heartache shared in confidence.

What did Jesus do in the midst of temptation? How did He flee? He answered
with the Word of God:

> *"It is written, man shall not live by bread alone,*
> *but by every word that proceeds from the mouth of God." —Matt. 4:4*

What do we do when the Tempter comes to us? Do we try to reason with
him, explain why he is wrong? Do we sit and ponder his temptation, justifying
it as harmless? As we read Jesus' reply in the midst of His temptation it is
clear what we must do. We must answer the Tempter with the Word of God:

> No temptation has overtaken you except such as is common to man;
> but God is faithful, who will not allow you to be tempted beyond
> what you are able, but with the temptation will also make the way of
> escape that you may be able to bear it.—1 Cor. 10:13

It is time that we allow our Father to fight our battles and flee from temptation. As we call on Him, speaking the Word of God, He promises to give us
a way of escape that we may be able to bear it.

> For in that He Himself has suffered, being tempted,
> He is able to aid those who are tempted.—Hebrews 2:18

> Therefore submit to God. Resist the devil and he will flee
> from you.—James 4:7

*And Jesus, walking by the Sea of Galilee,
saw two brothers, Simon, called Peter, and Andrew, his brother, casting a net into the sea;
for they were fishermen.*

Matthew 4:18-19

As Jesus called
Peter and Andrew...
He calls us today.

Follow Me

Matthew 4:18

And Jesus, walking by the Sea of Galilee, saw two brothers,
Simon, called Peter, and Andrew, his brother,
casting a net into the sea; for they were fishermen.

Simon, called Peter, and his brother Andrew were fishermen on the Sea of Galilee. Little did they know, as they threw their nets out on a morning like any other, their lives were about to change forever.

> Jesus said to them, *"Follow Me, and I will make you fishers of men"*
> —Matthew 4:19

When I read how Jesus told Peter and Andrew He would make them fishers of men, I realized it was not through any efforts of their own that this would happen, but by their willingness to leave their nets behind, allowing Jesus to have His way in their lives.

Just as Jesus told Peter and Andrew He would make them fishers of men, He tells us we are His workmanship. As Jesus called Peter and Andrew, He calls us today.

> For we are His workmanship, created in Christ Jesus for good works; which God prepared beforehand that we should walk in them.
> —Ephesians 2:10

> I beseech you therefore, brethren, by the mercies of God, that you present your bodies a living sacrifice, holy, acceptable to God, *which is* your reasonable service.—Romans 12:2

> And *whatever* you do in word or deed, *do* all in the name of the Lord Jesus, giving thanks to God the Father through Him.
> —Colossians 3:17

Let's be willing to leave our nets behind and allow Christ to have His way in our lives. As we seek Him in prayer, He will guide our path and direct our steps.

> Trust in the LORD with all your heart,
> And lean not on your own understanding;
> In all your ways acknowledge Him,
> And He shall direct your paths.
> —Proverbs 3:5-6

"Blessed are those who are persecuted for righteous sake, for theirs is the kingdom of heaven.
Blessed are you when they revile
and persecute you, and say all kinds of evil
against you falsely for My sake.
Rejoice and be exceedingly glad, for great
is your reward in heaven."

Matthew 5:10-12

There is purpose in persecution.
It tests our faith and draws us
closer to the Lord.
Will we defend our faith,
or decide the cost is too great?

Stand

Matthew 5:10-12

"Blessed are those who are persecuted for righteousness sake,
For theirs is the kingdom of heaven. Blessed are you when they revile and persecute you,
and say all kinds of evil against you falsely for My sake.
Rejoice and be exceedingly glad, for great is your reward in heaven."

As Jesus taught the multitudes, he shared the blessings that come to those who live out His teachings:

"Blessed are the poor in spirit, for theirs is the kingdom of heaven.
Blessed are those who mourn, for they shall be comforted.
Blessed are the meek, for they shall inherit the earth.
Blessed are those who hunger and thirst for righteousness,
for they shall be filled." —Matthew 5:3-7

However, as He continued, His teachings began to change. It was no longer about rewards, as a result of their obedience. The greatest reward would come when they were being persecuted *"for righteousness sake"*. These were such great rewards that they could rejoice and be exceedingly glad. Could it be we show our greatest faith when we are persecuted for Christ?

Persecution comes in many different ways. It is those who are martyred for their faith, willing to be put to death, we tend to consider "persecuted". However, when we are excluded because of our beliefs, if we are falsely accused, or our name is dishonored, is this also considered persecution? Jesus taught the multitudes:

"Blessed are those who are persecuted for righteousness sake,
For theirs is the kingdom of heaven.
Blessed are you when they revile and persecute you,
and say all kinds of evil against you falsely.
Rejoice and be exceedingly glad, for great is your reward in heaven."

There is purpose in persecution. It tests our faith and draws us closer to the Lord. Will we defend our faith or decide the cost is too great? During persecution, we make our choice. May we stand strong in our faith, knowing the One whom we defend goes with us—we are not alone.

When you pass through the waters, I *will* be with you.
And through the rivers they shall not overflow you.
When you walk through the fire, you shall not be burned,
Nor shall the flame scorch you.—Isaiah 43:2

Who Do You Say I Am?

Matthew 16:15

He said to them,
"But who do you say that I am?"

Jesus had gathered with His disciples in the region of Caesarea Philippi. As they spoke among themselves, Jesus asked the disciples,

"Who do men say that I, the Son of Man, am?—Matthew 16:13

The disciples told Jesus that many thought Him to be John the Baptist, Elijah, Jeremiah, or one of the prophets. Jesus then asked them the question He asks each of us, *"But who do you say that I am?"*

Have you ever thought what you would tell someone if they asked you that question?

The Son of God
The Son of Man
Lord and Savior
Prince of Peace
Lamb of God
Steadfast Love
Redeemer
Messiah
Comforter
Shepherd
Teacher
Friend
Avenger
Justifier
Mediator
King of King and Lord of Lords!

In Christ I find my purpose for living, hope for all my tomorrows, and joy within only He can give. Jesus is my life.

Simon Peter answered and said,
"You are the Christ, the Son of the living God."
— Matthew 16:16

Who do you say He is?

*"But when you pray, go into your room,
and when you have shut the door,
pray to your Father who is in the secret place;
and your Father who sees in secret will
reward you openly."*

Matthew 6:6

"A heart humbled before My Father takes me to His secret place."

The Secret Place

Matthew 6:6

*"But when you pray, go into your room,
and when you have shut your door,
pray to your Father who is in the secret place;
and your Father who sees in secret will reward you openly."*

As I read in this Scripture, "pray to your Father who is in the secret place", I wondered, where is the "secret place"? If my heavenly Father is there, I want to be there with Him.

This brought me to one of my favorite Psalms, one I have above my desk:

"He who dwells in the secret place of the Most High
shall abide under the shadow of the Almighty.
I will say of the LORD, *He* is my refuge and my fortress;
My God, in Him I will trust."—Psalm 91:1-2

Then I read how the secret place of the Most High is for all who fear Him,

The secret of the LORD is with those who fear Him,
And He will show them His covenant.—Psalm 25:14

When we humble ourselves before the Most High, coming to Him in obedience, we are meeting Him in the secret place.

"If My people who are called by My Name will humble themselves,
and pray and seek My face, and turn from their wicked ways, then I
will hear from heaven, and will forgive their sin and heal their land.
—2 Chronicles 7:14

Then I understood, my Father is waiting for me to meet Him with a willingness to share my heart. He isn't looking for pretense, solutions, or explanations. He is looking for a humble heart seeking His direction, insight, and counsel. A heart humbled before my Father takes me to His secret place—"Oh, Lord that it might be."

"God resists the proud, but gives grace to the humble."
Therefore humble yourselves under the mighty hand of God,
that He may exalt you in due time.—1 Peter 5:5b-6

Then you shall call, and the LORD will answer;
You shall cry, and He shall say, "Here I *am.*"—Isaiah 58:9

"For if you forgive men their trespasses
your heavenly Father will also forgive you.
But if you do not forgive men their trespasses,
neither will your Father forgive your trespasses."

Matthew 6:14-15

As we pray for those who have
hurt us, we find our bitterness
replaced with compassion, and
our mourning turned into joy.

Forgiveness

Matthew 6:14-15

"For if you forgive men their trespasses, your heavenly Father will also forgive you.
But if you do not forgive men their trespasses,
neither will your Father forgive your trespasses."

How hard is it to forgive those who have spoken falsely against you? I have to admit, this is hard for me. It takes a long time to get past the hurt I feel.

How important is it to know your heavenly Father forgives you of your trespasses? I'm sure we would all agree it is life changing. Without forgiveness from our Father we would feel lost, like sheep without their shepherd.

I read a story of a little girl whose teacher was extremely mean to her. When the little girl listened to her daddy reading about how Jesus forgave those who crucified Him, crying out,

"Father forgive them for they do not know what they do."—Luke 23:34

...the little girl decided to pray the same prayer for her teacher. The harshness against her didn't stop, but in the midst of the cruel treatment, the little girl found comfort in knowing she was doing what Jesus would have done.

Jesus told the disciples how to respond in such a situation:

"'But I say to you, love your enemies, bless those who curse you,
do good to those who hate you, and pray for those who spitefully
use you and persecute you.—Matthew 5:44

As we pray for those who have hurt us, we find our bitterness replaced with compassion and our mourning turned into joy. Obedience to the Word of God is always for our good.

May our heart be tender toward lessons the Lord has for us as we remain submissive to Him.

"Search me, O God, and know my heart;
Try me, and know my anxieties;
And see if *there is any* wicked way in me
And lead me in the way everlasting.—Psalm 139:23-24

Hurting people hurt people, may God's love fill us to forgive those in desperate need of His love.

"*Do not lay up for yourselves treasures on earth,*
But lay up for yourselves treasures in heaven.
For where your treasure is,
there your heart will be also."

Matthew 6:19-21

It is so easy to accumulate
riches on earth.
We find such pleasure in
buying worldly treasures.

Treasures

Matthew 6:19-21

"Do not lay up for yourselves treasures on earth,
where moth and rust destroy and where thieves break in and steal;
But lay up for yourselves treasures in heaven,
where neither moth nor rust destroys and where thieves do not break in and steal.
For where your treasure is there your heart will be also."

It is so easy to accumulate riches on earth. We find such pleasure in buying worldly treasures in pursuit of happiness.

"Do not lay up treasures on earth," Jesus tells the multitudes as they gather around, *"But lay up for yourselves treasures in heaven."*

> Happy is the man who finds wisdom,
> And the man who gains understanding;
> For her proceeds are better than the profits of silver,
> And her gain than fine gold.—Proverbs 3:13-14
>
> For the LORD gives wisdom;
> From His mouth come knowledge and understanding
> —Proverbs 2:6
>
> For thus says the High and Lofty One who inhabits eternity,
> Whose name is Holy: "I dwell in the high and holy place,
> With him who has a contrite and humble spirit".—Isaiah 57:15
>
> You also be patient. Establish your hearts,
> for the coming of the Lord is at hand.—James 5:8

Wisdom
  Knowledge
    Understanding
      Patience
        A contrite and humble spirit

Do we spend as much time seeking these spiritual treasures as we do accumulating treasures of this world?

"For where your treasure is your heart will be also."—Matthew 6:21

May our treasures be found in Him.

*"But seek first the kingdom of God
and His righteousness,
and all these things shall be added to you."*

Matthew 6:33

In seeking God,
we seek the kingdom of God
and His righteousness.

The Kingdom of God

Matthew 6:33

But seek first the kingdom of God and His righteousness,
and all these things shall be added to you.

Jesus explained to the multitude they need not worry about what they would wear, what they would eat, or what they would drink. He compared their lives to how He takes care of the birds of the air and the lilies of the field.

> *"Look at the birds of the air, for they neither sow nor reap nor gather into the barns; yet your heavenly Father feeds them. Are you not of more value than they?"*—Matthew 6:26

But, He told them, *seek the Kingdom of God and His righteousness.*

As He taught the multitudes across the hills of Galilee, He teaches us;

Seek the LORD and His strength;
Seek His face evermore!—Psalm 105:4

Seek the LORD while He may be found,
Call upon Him while He is near.—Isaiah 55:6

For everyone who asks receives, and he who seeks finds,
and to him who knocks it will be opened.—Luke 11:10

When we spend time in the Word of God we are seeking the Kingdom of God. When we kneel in prayer, asking the Lord to meet us there, we are seeking the Kingdom of God. When we cry out to Him in desperation; pleading for an answer to our heartache, we are seeking the Kingdom of God. The Kingdom of God is anywhere God is, and He is as close as our greatest concern, broken heart, overflowing joy, and times of victory. He is closer then our very breath. In seeking God, we seek the kingdom of God and His righteousness.

Surely in the LORD I have righteousness and strength.
—Isaiah 45:24

And their righteousness is from Me,"says the Lord.
—Isaiah 54:17

O GOD, You *are* my God; Early I will seek You
—Psalm 63:1

*"Therefore do not worry about tomorrow,
for tomorrow will worry about its own things.
Sufficient for the day is its own trouble."*

Matthew 6:34

Is it possible to not worry
about tomorrow?
It is if we know *who* holds
all our tomorrows.

Why Worry

~~~

Matthew 6:34

*"Therefore do not worry about tomorrow,
for tomorrow will worry about its own things.
Sufficient for the day is its own trouble."*

It has been said worrying is like rocking in a rocking chair—you don't get anywhere, but it gives you something to do. We worry about our finances, children, and aging parents. If that isn't enough, we borrow trouble from tomorrow. "What if my husband loses his job?—we will lose our house and have to move. Oh my, it's going to be terrible." Oh, what needless pain we bear.

Jesus tells us to not worry about tomorrow. Nevertheless, He knows our frame and how this is easier said than done. At times like this, He doesn't leave us without hope, but teaches what we are to do:

> Be anxious for nothing, but in everything by prayer and supplication, with thanksgiving, let your requests be made known to God; and the peace of God that passes all understanding will keep your hearts and minds in Christ Jesus.—Philippians 4:6-7

> Casting all your care upon Him, for He cares for you.—1 Peter 5:7

When we bend our knee in humility, thanking Him for hearing our prayer and commit our concern to Him, He replaces our worry with His peace.

Is it possible to *not* worry about tomorrow? It is if we know *who* holds all our tomorrows. Let's not play tug-a-war, but take Him at His word, and make the trade—our *worry* for *His peace*. He will calm our fears and carry our burdens.

> "Oh, what peace we often forfeit
> "Oh, what needless pain we bear,
> All because we do not carry everything to Him in prayer."
> —Joseph M. Scriven

> You will keep *him* in perfect peace,
> *Whose* mind *is* stayed *on You,*
> Because he trust in You.
> —Isaiah 26:3

"Therefore, whatever you want men to do to you, do also to them."

Matthew 7:12

Christ showed us ultimate grace when as sinners He called us to Himself.

Grace

Matthew 7:12

"Therefore, whatever you want men to do to you, do also to them."

Jesus stood on the mount teaching the multitudes. Preparing to finish speaking He addressed one last subject:

> *"For with what judgment you judge, you will be judged; and with the measure you use, it will be measured back to you."*—Matthew 7:2

How easy it is for us to look at others and find fault. Jesus warned strongly against such an attitude;

> *"And why do you look at the speck in your brother's eye,*
> *but do not consider the plank in your own eye?*
> *"Or how can you say to your brother,*
> *"Let me remove the speck from your eye";*
> *and look a plank is in your own eye?*
> *"Hypocrite! First remove the plank from your own eye, and then you*
> *will see clearly to remove the speck from your brother's eye."*—Matthew 7:3-5

He is warning that when we find insignificant fault with others, our judging causes us to overlook the faults in our own lives.

We want to be treated with respect, as a person with value. When we are hurting, kindness and compassion by others means so much. When our ideas or opinions differ from others, what we want is for them to give us opportunity to explain why we think or feel the way we do.

Is this how we treat others? Do we treat them with respect, with the value their lives deserve? Are we kind and compassionate? When their opinions or ideas differ from ours, do we give them an opportunity to explain?

Christ showed us ultimate grace when as sinners he called us to Himself. In exchange for judgment, may we be willing to give others the grace that has so freely been given to us.

> *"Judge not, that you be not judged."*
> —Matthew 7:1

> *"And just as you want men to do to you, you also do to them likewise."*
> —Luke 6:31

"Not everyone who says to Me, Lord, Lord,
shall enter the kingdom of heaven,
but he who does the will of
My Father in heaven."

Matthew 7:21

In prayer we praise Him for
who He is, lay our burdens at
His feet, seek direction for our
lives, and fall more in love
with our Savior.

His Will

Matthew 7:21

Not everyone who says to Me, Lord, Lord,
shall enter the kingdom of heaven,
but he who does the will of My Father in heaven.

As I pondered this passage, I thought of the many hours Jesus spent in prayer with His Father.

"Most assuredly, I say to you, the Son can do nothing of Himself,
but what He sees the Father do; for whatever He does, the Son does
in like manner."— John 5:20

Just as Jesus sought the will of His Father, when we pray, we do the same...

The effective, fervent prayer of a righteous man avails much.
—James 5:16

as God did not leave Jesus alone while on earth...

"And He who sent Me is with Me. The Father has not left
Me alone, for I always do those things that please Him."
—John 8: 29

He has not left us alone:

"But the Helper, the Holy Spirit, whom the Father will send
in My name, He will teach you all things, and bring to your
remembrance all things that I said to you".—John 14:26

Fear not, for I *am* with you;
Be not dismayed, for I *am* your God.
I will strengthen you, yes I will help you,
  I will uphold you with My righteous right hand.—Isaiah 41:10

In prayer, we praise Him for who He is, lay our burdens at His feet, seek direction for our lives, and fall more in love with our Savior.

Samuel heard the Lord speak and cried out;
"Speak, for Your servant hears."—1 Samuel 3:10

As we bow in His presence, may we be as Samuel, waiting to hear the voice of our Lord, that we, too, may do His will.

"I delight to do Your will, O my God,
And your law *is* within my heart."—Psalm 40:8

But He said to them, "Why are you fearful,
O you of little faith?"
Then He arose and rebuked the winds
and the sea, and there was a great calm.

Matthew 8:26

As He gently carries us
to the other side,
we find our trust has grown,
our love for Him increased.

A Great Calm

Matthew 8:26

But He said to them, *"Why are you fearful, O you of little faith?"*
Then He arose and rebuked the winds and the sea,
and there was a great calm.

Jesus and His disciples were crossing the sea when a great tempest arose, covering the boat with it's waves. Afraid they would perish, the disciples cried out:

"Lord, save us! We are perishing!" —Matthew 8:25

Then we read:

But He was asleep. —Matthew 8:24

How often have we felt like the disciples? A great storm comes into our lives and our first thought is, "Jesus save me!" And where is Jesus? *Sleeping.*

The disciples crossed the sea in obedience to Jesus. Yet, when the winds came and the waves threatened to take them under…Jesus was asleep. How could this be? We, too, can feel this way. We study His Word, fellowship with believers, and pray for direction in our lives. Nevertheless, like a violent storm on the seas of Galilee, a tragedy hits and our whole world comes crashing in. At times like this, we, too, can feel Jesus is asleep.

Regardless of how we are feeling, if we listen closely we will hear our Savior say,

"Why are you fearful, O you of little faith?" —Matthew 8:26

Nothing catches God by surprise. He is fully aware of whatever it is we are going through. More importantly, He alone has the answer to save us from the storm. As we pour our heart out to Him, He puts purpose in our pain. As He gently carries us to the other side, we find our trust has grown, our love for Him increased.

Let's take Him at His Word and in times of distress cry out, "Lord save me!" And as we cry out, may we trust He is not asleep, but with only a word will calm our raging storm.

Then they cry out to the LORD in their trouble,
And He brings them out of their distresses.
He calms the storm, so that its waves are still.
—Psalm 107:28-29

So the men marveled saying,
"Who can this be,
that even the winds and the sea obey Him?"

Matthew 8:27

When was the last time you
felt like the disciples, filled
with such wonderment you
could hardly catch your breath?

Who Can This Be?

Matthew 8:27

So the men marveled saying,
"Who can this be, that even the winds and the sea obey Him?"

Filled with fear, the seas billowing round about, the disciples cried out, "Lord, save us! We are perishing!" As the roaring waters calmed to His command, the disciples stood speechless, eyes wide with disbelief, clinging to one another in awe. Too shaken to speak, they whispered, "Who can this be?"

When was the last time you felt like the disciples, filled with such wonderment that you could hardly catch your breath? Was it when you came to know Christ as your Savior?—You asked Him to forgive you of your sins, inviting Him into your life, and in that moment everything changed.

> Therefore, if anyone *is* in Christ, *he* is a new creation;
> old things have passed away; behold all things have
> become new. —2 Corinthian 5:17

Possibly it was when you watched Him turn your pain into purpose, giving your life new direction. Perhaps it was when He turned your ashes into beauty and your mourning into dancing.

> You have turned for me my mourning into dancing.
> You have put off my sackcloth and clothed me with
> gladness. —Psalm 30:11

Maybe it was when a prodigal child, so far away you were sure he would never come home, returned to your embrace. Possibly it was when you watched Jesus call your love one home and with a peace impossible to explain, you knew He had done what was best.

Who can this be? He is the One to whom we commit all our tomorrows, release all our dreams, and on bended knee cry,

> "For You *are* my praise!"—Jeremiah 17:14

If you have lost the amazement of our heavenly Father, cry out to Him, "Bring back the new again!" and as He does, live again in the "awe" of our Savior. He is the same today and forever.

For she said to herself,
"If only I may touch His garment,
I shall be made well."

Matthew 9:21

As she reached out to touch
the hem of His garment,
He reached out to her in love.

If Only

Matthew 9:21

For she said to herself,
"If only I may touch His garment,
I shall be made well."

After calming the raging seas, Jesus crossed over and came to His own city. Immediately the people brought the sick to Him for healing.

This is where we meet a woman, having a flow of blood for twelve years, pushing her way through the crowd toward Jesus to touch the hem of His garment…

"If only I may touch His garment, I shall be made well."

"If only," two small words with so much meaning. What do we have in our lives that we think to ourselves, 'If only?' If only I could pay my bills without such struggle, if only my children were walking with the Lord, if only I knew my health would improve. The "if onlys" are as varied as there are hard places in our lives.

Let's see what Jesus told the woman:

But Jesus turned around and when He saw her said,

"Be of good cheer, daughter; your faith has made you well."
And the woman was made well from that hour.
—Matthew 9:22

Do you see that Jesus called the woman *daughter?* What a reflection of endearment. As she reached out to touch the hem of His garment, He reached out to her in love. Because of her faith she exchanged her "if only" for the touch of the Master's hand.

What if, like the woman with the issue of blood, we took our "if only" and reached out in faith to touch the hem of His garment? What if we exchanged our "if only" for the touch of the Master's hand? Can you think of anything more promising than having Jesus turn around, and seeing you reaching for His garment, speak these words,

"Be of good cheer, daughter, your faith has made you well."
—Matthew 9:22

He said to them,
"Make room, for the girl is not dead,
but sleeping."
And they ridiculed Him.

Matthew 9:24

Regardless of the ridicule,
we will bring glory to God
as our heart remains
faithful to Him.

Ridiculed

Matthew 9:24

He said to them,
"Make room, for the girl is not dead, but sleeping."
And they ridiculed Him.

When Jesus came into the ruler's house and saw the flute players and noisy crowd wailing, He said to them, *"Make room, for the girl is not dead, but sleeping."* And they ridiculed Him. But, when the crowd was put outside, He went in and took her by the hand, and the girl arose. And the report of this went out to all the land. —Matthew 9:23-26

Their daughter had died, leaving them overwhelmed with heartache. Then Jesus arrived and everything changed. As Jesus took her hand, she rose from her sleeping bed. *"The girl is not dead, but sleeping,"* Jesus told the crowd. Did He know something they didn't know or was He talking nonsense? They didn't care. They simply ridiculed Him.

This did not stop Jesus from doing what He had come to do.

> But when the crowd was put outside, He went in and
> took her by the hand, and the girl arose. And the report
> of this went out to all the land.　　　—Matthew 9:25-26

He had come to bring God glory and that was exactly what He was going to do. The result? The report of this went out to all the land.

What do we do when we feel a calling on our life, yet others ridicule us? Do we stay at task or cower under the pressure?

> "For the eyes of the LORD run to and fro throughout
> the whole earth, to show Himself strong on behalf of *those*
> whose heart is loyal to Him."　　　—2 Chron. 16:9

We are called to bring God glory in spite of how we are treated. May we be the one the Lord finds loyal, as His eyes run to and fro throughout the whole earth. Regardless of the ridicule, we will bring glory to God as our heart remains faithful to Him...

> And the report of this went out to all the land.
> 　　　　　　　　　　　　　—Matthew 9:26

And he who does not take up his cross
and follow after Me is not worth of Me.

Matthew 10:38

The next time we feel we
are sacrificing too much
by taking up our cross,
let's consider what we have
lost, and rejoice in the life
we have found instead.

Take Up Your Cross

Matthew 10:38

And he who does not take up his cross
and follow after Me is not worthy of Me.

What does it mean to take up your cross? I always thought it meant to take up your hardship, your burden, and follow Christ. This confused me because I know the Word of God tells us to give our burdens to the Lord.

Cast all your care on Him, for He cares for you.
—1 Peter 5:7

Then I read what Jesus told His disciples:

"If anyone desires to come after Me, let him deny himself, and take up his
cross, and follow Me.   —Matthew 16:25

Reading this, I realized taking up our cross means being willing to lay aside our fleshly desires for the sake of Christ. A cross is a place of crucifixion, a place to be put to death. This is what we are asked to do as we lay down our worldly ways.

As I considered the carnal behaviors I must deny myself, as I take up my cross, I thought of what the Word of God tells me—I must lay down; pride, jealousy, bitterness, fleshly lusts, greed. However, by letting these go and allowing Christ to have His way in my life, in their place I am given; love, joy, peace, patience, kindness, goodness, faithfulness, gentleness, and self-control. God promises so much more than I could ever find for myself.

"He who finds his life will lose it, and he who loses his life for
My sake will find it.   —Matthew 10:39

The next time we feel we are sacrificing too much by taking up our cross, let's consider what we have lost, and rejoice in the life we have found instead.

If we live in the Spirit, let us also walk in the Spirit.
—Galatians 5:25

But without faith *it is* impossible to please *Him,* for he who comes to God must believe that He is, and *that* He is a rewarder of those who diligently seek Him. —Hebrews 11:6

"And blessed is he who is not offended because of Me."

Matthew 11:6

Blessed are we when we are not offended by what comes into our lives, but stay strong in our faith.

Blessed Is He

Matthew 11:6

"And blessed is he who is not offended because of Me."

John the Baptist sat in prison while Jesus was free to journey from city to city. Knowing he had been obedient to his calling as he preached,

"Repent, for the Kingdom of God is at hand"—Matthew 3:2

John felt forgotten by his Lord. Not understanding how this could be, John sent two disciples to find Christ:

"And when John had heard in prison about the works of Christ, he sent two of his disciples and said to Him, "Are You the Coming One, or do we look for another?"   —Matthew 11:2-3

Have you ever come to the place in your life when even what you know to be truth begins to confuse you? You know Jesus has the answer and His promises are true; nevertheless, when life doesn't make sense, you begin to question the very basis for your faith. "Is Christ really the One? Does He really have answers to my questions, my heartache?"

Let's see what Christ told the two disciples to tell John, and what He tells us today:

Jesus answered and said to them, *Go and tell John the things which you hear and see: 'The blind see and the lame walk; the lepers are cleansed and the deaf hear; the dead are raised up and the poor have the gospel preached to them. And blessed is he who is not offended because of Me."*   —Matthew 11:5-6

Jesus assured John he would be blessed if he would not become offended because of His ways, but simply trust Him. He tells us the same. Blessed are we, when we are not offended by what comes into our lives, yet stay strong in our faith. As we trust Jesus, we will find that as we allow Him to work in our lives, what we thought we could never endure, He has used to draw us closer to Himself. He is our Savior and He loves us. May we trust Him.

For my thoughts *are* not your thoughts,
Nor *are* your ways My ways," says the LORD.
For as the heavens are higher than the earth,
So are My ways higher than your ways,
And My thoughts than your thoughts.   —Isaiah 55:8

You Are Mine

Isaiah 43:2-3

When you pass through the waters, *I will be* with you;
And through the rivers, they shall not overflow you.
When you walk through the fire, you shall not be burned,
Nor shall the flame scorch you. For *I am* the LORD your God,
The Holy One of Israel, your Savior.

How many times have we gone through trials that were threatening to over-come our very existence? We thought we were strong, our faith solid, then, like an out of control tornado, the heartache of a lifetime comes roaring through our life. Perhaps it is an unexpected telephone call, a pink slip ending a career, a child refusing to listen to our guidance, a life threatening disease attacking our body. Whatever it may be, trials can send us into depths of despair we didn't think possible.

Do you see the word "through" in these Scriptures? When you pass *through* the waters, *through* the rivers, *through* the fire. Nowhere does it say we will be overcome, but instead it assures us we will go *through* the trials of life. Why?

> For *I am* the LORD your God,
> The Holy One of Israel, your Savior.   —Isaiah 43:3

The Holy One of Israel, our Savior, will! carry us *through* the waters, *through* the rivers, and *through* the fire.

> Fear not, for *I am* your God.
> I will strengthen you,
> Yes, I will help you,
> I will uphold you with My righteous right hand.
>   —Isaiah 41:10

The next time trials seem to be winning, let's remember to *whom* we belong and hold on tight to the hand of our Savior. He alone will carry us *through*.

> Be strong and of good courage, do not fear nor be afraid
> of them; for the LORD your God, He *is* the One who goes
> with you. He will not leave you nor forsake you.
>   —Deuteronomy 31:6

"I desire mercy and not sacrifice."

Matthew 12:7

Christ desires a relationship
with His children,
not a religion.

Mercy

Matthew 12:7

"I desire mercy and not sacrifice."

As Jesus and His disciples walked through grain fields on the Sabbath, becoming hungry, the disciples began removing heads of grain to eat. Immediately, the Pharisees started spewing accusations toward the disciples of doing what is not lawful.

Jesus saw this as an opportunity to help the Pharisees understand that without mercy the many sacrifices they believed were bringing them closer to God were of no avail.

Christ desires a relationship with His children—not a religion. He is looking for those willing to obey because of their love for Him, not because it is a requirement. The Pharisees followed a religion far from the heart of Christ.

Christ showed ultimate mercy when He died on the cross for our sins.

> But God, who is rich in mercy, because of His great love with
> which He loved us, even when we were dead in trespasses, made
> us alive together with Christ (by grace you have been saved), and
> made *us* sit together in the heavenly *places* in Christ Jesus.
> —Ephesians 2:4-6

> Do not withhold Your tender mercies from me, O LORD;
> Let Your loving kindness and Your truth continually preserve me.
> —Psalm 40:11

As Christ showed us mercy on the cross, He desires that we, too, show mercy to others. He teaches to forgive others as we have been forgiven (Matt. 6:12), not think of ourselves more highly than we ought (Romans 12:3), judge not so that we would be not judged (Matt. 7:1), and as He spoke through the prophet Micah:

> He has shown you, O man, what is good;
> And what does the LORD require of you
> But to do justly,
> To love mercy,
> And to walk humbly with your God?
> —Micah 6:6-8

A bruised reed He will not break
And a smoking flax He will not quench.

Matthew 12:20

When we come to a place of
hopelessness, with divine
gentleness, Jesus promises
to restore us to wholeness
once again.

A Bruised Reed

Matthew 12:20

*A bruised reed He will not break
And a smoking flax He will not quench.*

When we come to a place of hopelessness, with divine gentleness, Jesus promises to restore us to wholeness once again. In the same way, when we are discouraged, when we're feeling that God is not coming to our rescue as quickly as we need, He promises that He will not allow us to succumb to faithlessness; but with divine compassion, will ignite the Spirit within us.

At times like these, we need to remember the words of Solomon:

"He has made all things beautiful in its time."
— Ecclesiastes 3:11

And the words of Paul to the Romans:

"And we know that all things work together
for good to those who love God,
to those who are called according
to *His* purpose." —Romans 8:28

The Lord will never leave us nor forsake us (Deuteronomy 31:6). In our place of desperation He promises,

He gives power to the weak,
And *to those who have no* might He increases strength.
Even the youths shall faint and be weary,
And the young men shall utterly fall,
But those who wait on the LORD
Shall renew *their* strength;
They shall mount up with wings like eagles,
They shall run and not be weary,
They shall walk and not faint. —Isaiah 40:29-31

As we wait on the Lord, we will find the strength we need:

In quietness and confidence shall be your strength.
—Isaiah 30:15

The name of the Lord is a strong tower;
The righteous run to it and are safe. —Proverbs 18:10

For by your words you will be justified,
and by your words you will be condemned.

Matthew 12:37

If we are to follow the
example of Jesus we will
choose our words carefully,
speaking words of love and
encouragement to others.

Words

Matthew 12:37

For by your words you will be justified,
and by your words you will be condemned.

Isn't it amazing how words from another person can affect our entire day? We have all had hurtful words spoken to us, words that continue to sting long after they are spoken. We have also had kind words spoken, words that lift our spirit, carrying us through the day with confidence and vigor.

As I look at the example set by Jesus, I think of the times I have been reading the Bible and found the encouragement I longed for. It is here that I have found comfort in the midst of heartache, hope in the midst of despair, and direction in making a decision.

The Word of God has much to say about the tongue:

> If anyone among you thinks he is religious, and does not bridle his tongue, but deceives his own heart, this one's religion is useless.
> —James 1:26

> Even so the tongue is a little member and boasts great things. See how great a forest a little fire kindles! And the tongue *is* a fire, a word of iniquity. The tongue is so set among our members that it defiles the whole body, and sets on fire the course of nature; and it is set on fire by hell.
> —James 3:5-6

As Christ taught the multitudes He said to them:

> *"Hear and understand: Not what goes into the mouth defiles a man;*
> *but what comes out of the mouth, this defiles a man".*—Matthew 15:11

> *'But those things which proceed out of the mouth come*
> *from the heart, and they defile a man".* —Matthew 15:18

If we are to follow the example of Jesus we will choose our words carefully, speaking words of love and encouragement to others.

> Let no corrupt word proceed out of your mouth, but what is good for necessary edification, that it may impart grace to the hearers.
> —Ephesians 4

> *He who would love life and see good days,*
> *Let him refrain his tongue from evil and his lips from deceit.*
> —1 Peter 3:10

"He who has ears to hear, let him hear!"

Matthew 13:9

Let's make the decision to sit
at the feet of Jesus with a
heart to obey, allowing Him
to teach us His ways.
He promises to meet us there.

Let Him Hear

Matthew 13:9

"He who has ears to hear, let him hear!"

Teaching before the multitudes, Jesus taught concerning the sower and the seed:

> "Some fell by the wayside and were devoured, some fell on stony places where they had no depth some fell among the thorns and were choked, some fell on good ground and yielded a crop *"He who has hears to hear let him hear!!"*

Becoming confused, the disciples questioned Jesus:

> And the disciples came and said to Him,
> "Why do You speak in parables?"—Matthew 13:10

Have you ever felt like you try to study the Bible but don't understand what you are reading? Take heart my friend. Jesus knew there would be times we would feel this way. He also promised those who continued searching and praying for discernment would grow in their faith and understanding.

> If you seek her as silver,
> And search for as *for* hidden treasures;
> Then you will understand the fear of the Lord,
> And find the knowledge of God.
> For the LORD gives knowledge and understanding.
> —Proverbs 2:4-6

We are not alone as we study. Jesus promised He would send a Helper to instruct us in all things:

> *"But the Helper, the Holy Spirit, whom the Father will send in My name, He will teach you all things, and bring to your remembrance all things that I said to you."*—John 14:26

Let's make the decision to sit at the feet of Jesus with a heart to obey, allowing Him to teach us His ways. He promises to meet us there.

> Then you will call upon Me and go and pray to Me,
> and I will listen to you.
> And you will seek Me and find *Me*, when you search for
> Me with all your heart. —Jeremiah 29:1

But immediately Jesus spoke to them, saying,
"Be of good cheer! It is I; do not be afraid."

Matthew 14:27

Jesus has come to me,
not walking on the water,
but by a word spoken,
a smile given, a note received,
or devotional I've read—
giving me hope for one more day.

Do Not Be Afraid

Matthew 14:27

But immediately Jesus spoke to them, saying,
"Be of good cheer! It is I; do not be afraid."

Before going to the mountains to pray, Jesus instructed the disciples to get into a boat and go to the other side of the sea. Because Jesus stayed on the mountain longer than they had expected, the disciples found themselves alone and being tossed about by furious winds. Jesus, seeing they were in distress, came walking across the waters,

> Now in the fourth watch of night Jesus went to them, walking on the sea. And when the disciples saw Him walking on the sea, they were troubled, saying, "It is a ghost!" And they cried out for fear. But immediately Jesus spoke to them, saying, "Be of good cheer! It is I; do not be afraid!"   —Matthew 14:25-27

As I thought of what was happening to the disciples, afraid for their lives, and then seeing someone walking on the water toward them, I understood *why* they cried out in fear. I would too!

Then I read Jesus' reply,

> "Be of good cheer! It is I; do not be afraid."

This made me think of the times I have been afraid. Times I didn't know where to turn…what to do. I realized Jesus has come to me in those moments, not walking on the water, but by a word spoken, a smile given, a note received, or a devotional I've read—giving me hope for one more day. He has led me, not to the other side of the sea, but to the other side of my heart-ache, confusion, or fear. And as He said to the disciples, He has said to me,

> "Be of good cheer! It is I; do not be afraid."

> For God has not given us a spirit of fear,
> but of power and of love and of a sound mind.
>   —2 Timothy 1:6

> For I, the LORD your God, will hold your right hand,
> Saying to you, "Fear not, I will help you."   —Isaiah 41:13

But when he saw the wind *was* boisterous,
he was afraid; and beginning to sink he cried out,
saying, "Lord save me!"

Matthew 14:30

Not until he looked at the raging waters did he lose his focus and fall.

Refocus

Matthew 14:30

But when he saw the wind *was* boisterous,
he was afraid; and beginning to sink he cried out,
saying, "Lord, save me!"

In the midst of a violent storm, Jesus came walking on the water to the disciples. Realizing it was Jesus, Peter cried out to Him:

"Lord if it is You, command me to come to You on the water."
So He said, *"Come."* And when Peter had come down
out of the boat, he walked on the water to go to Jesus.
—Matthew 14: 28-29

Imagine how Peter must have felt. Without solid ground beneath his feet, waves billowing all about, he was walking on the water to Jesus. Not until he looked at the raging waters did he lose his focus and fall.

How many times have we done the same? We feel we are sinking, our world caving in around us. Having no idea what to do, we cry out to Jesus for help. And at that moment, we hear Him say, just as He did to Peter, *"Come"*.

"Come to Me, all you *who labor and are heavy laden,*
and I will give you rest."   —Matthew 11:28

All is fine while we keep our eyes on Jesus. He surrounds us with His love, and calms our fears. As long as we keep our eyes on Him, we have the peace only He can give.

You will keep *him* in perfect peace,
Whose mind is stayed *on You,*
Because he trusts in You.   —Isaiah 26:3

But like Peter, when we take our eyes off Jesus we begin to once again succumb to hopelessness. It is then we need to refocus, look once again to the only One who can carry us to the other side of the storm. As we do, He will reach out and save us, setting our feet on solid ground.

For in time of trouble
He shall hide me in His pavilion;
In the secret place of His tabernacle
He shall hide me;
He shall set me high upon a rock   —Psalm 27:5

Come Around the Corner

Jeremiah 33:3

"Call to Me, and I will answer you,
and show you great and mighty things,
which you do not know."

When life comes crashing in around us, it is easy to lose hope and feel life is over. Unfortunately, often the life we knew before the devastation happened is over. Nevertheless, with God all things are possible. In times such as this, His desire is not for us to give into despair, but call on Him, that we might see great and mighty things which we did not know.

My Mom found herself in this place after the death of Dad—a marriage of 54 years. While she was talking with her brother, he said to her, "Just come around the corner." In other words, be willing to ask the Lord, "What do you have for me now Lord?"

When Joni Eareckson Tada dove into shallow water and broke her neck 45 years ago, becoming a quadriplegic, she definitely felt her life was over. For the rest of her life she would be confined to a wheelchair, unable to use her arms or legs. What good was life? Why go on living? In her despair, Joni came around the corner. She allowed the Lord to show her great and mighty things He had for her now that her life had changed so drastically. Today, she has a worldwide ministry helping others who also live confined to a wheelchair. What Joni has done for others, the encouragement, summer camps, and ministry she has given, is matchless to none. Ask those she has helped and they will tell you: "Because of Joni's love for the Lord, and her willingness to follow His leading, my life has been changed forever."

So often we find ministries begin because of a tragedy or heartache. Those involved don't give up, but come around the corner. They allow the Lord to use them for His honor and glory. This is where raising money for research often begins, books written offering hope are birthed, and those hurting come to know the Lord. When we call out to the Lord, He will take what looked like the end, and turn it into a beautiful beginning.

When you find yourself at the end of what you knew, come around the corner. You will find the Lord waiting for you there, wanting to show you great and mighty things you did not know. He loves you and has a plan for your life.

These people draw near to Me with their mouth,
And honor Me with their lips,
But their heart is far from Me.

Matthew 15:8

Do I honor the Lord with my lips, yet doubt He will do what He says He will do?

Honor

Matthew 15:8

These people draw near to Me with their mouth,
And honor Me with their lips,
But their heart is far from Me.

The Scribes and Pharisees began criticizing the disciples for not following the laws of their religion. This enraged Jesus. It was clear they held their traditions of greater value than the conditions of a person's heart.

As I read this, I couldn't help but consider the condition of my heart. Do I honor the Lord with my lips, yet doubt He will do what He says He will do?

When I read in His Word...

> "Cast your burden on the LORD,
>   And He shall sustain you;
>   He shall never permit the righteous to be moved."
> —Psalm 55:22

> "Call to Me, and I will answer you and show you great
>   and mighty things, which you do not know."
> —Jeremiah 33:3

...I wondered, do I surrender my heartaches, my burdens, to the LORD? Do I call on the Lord, trusting He will show me His ways?

Then I thought of the cry of David:

> One *thing* I have desired of the LORD,
> That will I seek:
> That I may dwell in the house of the LORD
> All the days of my life,
> To behold the beauty of the LORD,
> And to inquire in His temple.   —Psalm 27:4

At that moment, my heart's cry became to continue to tell others about the love and faithfulness of God, but more importantly to give Him the honor He deserves. I know this will only come as I put my hope in Him, trusting Him with all my heart.

> Search me, O God, and know my heart;
> Try me, and know my anxieties;
> And see if *there is any* wicked way in me,
> And lead me in the way everlasting.   —Psalm 139:23-24

Do you not yet understand or remember
the five loaves of the five thousand
and how many baskets you took up?

Matthew 16:9

Once I acknowledge to whom
I am praying,
and His faithfulness,
my problems come into
prospective and I realize
I have nothing to fear.

Remember

Matthew 16:9

*Do you not yet understand or remember the five loaves
of the five thousand and how many baskets you took up?*

Jesus was talking with His disciples concerning the Pharisees and Sadducees:

> *"Take heed and beware of the leaven of the
> Pharisees and the Sadducees."* —Matthew 16:6

Not understanding what He was saying, the disciples thought Jesus was concerned about them not bringing bread on their journey. Because Jesus knew their thoughts, He chided them with the reminder of what He had done for them in the past.

How often have I come to a place of confusion, fear, or desperation, and instead of remembering all the Lord has done for me, and walking in His faithfulness to never leave me nor forsake me?

> For He Himself has said,
> *"I will never leave you nor forsake you."* —Hebrews 13:5

I begin walking in worry and doubt, like a sheep without a Shepherd. When I find myself in this place I need to:

A - Acknowledge Who Christ is—Praise Him for His attributes
C - Confess my lack of trust
T - Thank Him for all He has done for me in the past
S - Bring my supplications, my requests, before Him,
    and trust He will take care of me.

Once I acknowledge to whom I am praying, and His faithfulness, my problems come into prospective and I realize I have nothing to fear.

> *"I am the good shepherd. The good shepherd gives His life for the sheep."*
> —1 John 10:11

> For God has not given us a spirit of fear,
> but of power and of love and of a sound mind. —2 Timothy 1:7

> In quietness and confidence shall be your strength. —Isaiah 30:15

But He turned and said to Peter,
"Get behind Me, Satan!
You are an offense to Me,
for you are not mindful of the things of God,
but the things of men."

Matthew 16:23

When life is hard we discover
how strong our faith really is,
and how willing we are to cast
our burdens on Him.

Offense

Matthew 16:23

But He turned and said to Peter,
"Get behind Me, Satan! You are an offense to Me,
for you are not mindful of the things of God, but the things of men."

Jesus began explaining to the disciples that He must go to Jerusalem, suffer at the hand of the scribes and chief priests and be crucified. Peter, being devastated at the news, began chiding Jesus, telling Him this couldn't possibly happen. Hearing this, Jesus, turning to Peter, began rebuking him, saying to him, *"You are an offense to Me."*

As I read these words I thought, "Am I an offense to God?" As hard as it was, I had to admit when I allow the cares of this world to consume my thoughts, instead of trusting in the Word of God, I, too, am being an offense to Jesus.

"Cast all your burdens on Him, for He cares for you."

—1 Peter 5: 7

"Trust in the Lord with all your heart,
lean not on your own understanding;
In all your ways acknowledge Him,
And He shall direct your paths."   —Proverbs 3:5

It is easy to praise the Lord when all is well in our world. However, when life is hard we discover how strong our faith really is, and how willing we are to cast our burdens on Him. In times such as these, may we be willing to walk in faith knowing He cares for us.

When you pass through the waters, I *will* be with you;
And through the rivers, they shall not overflow you.
When you walk through the fire, you shall not be burned.
Nor shall the flame scorch you.   —Isaiah 43:2

And as we walk in what we know is Truth, may we proclaim:

"It is well,
It is well with my soul!"

"You will keep *Him* in perfect peace
Whose mind is set *on You,"*   —Isaiah 26:3

Therefore whoever humbles himself as this child is the greatest in the kingdom of heaven.

Matthew 18:4

Christ longs for us to humble
ourselves as little children,
and regardless of what comes
into our life, hold tight
to our Daddy's hand.

As a Child

Matthew 18:4

*Therefore whoever humbles himself as this little child
is the greatest in the kingdom of heaven.*

Jesus was gathered with the disciples when they presented Him with the question,

"Who then is greatest in the kingdom of heaven?"
—Matthew 18:1

Without hesitation, Jesus called a little child to Himself and placing him on His knee, said to them,

*Assuredly, I say to you, unless you are converted and become as little children,
you will by no means enter the kingdom of heaven.*   —Matthew 18:3

What does it mean to humble ones self as a little child? When I think of this question, I think of my husband as a little boy on a beautiful summer day, sitting on the back stoop of his house, tying his shoes and saying to himself, "I have the whole day to play!" Not a care in the world, not a worry in sight, all he could think about was being on his bike, having a fun-filled day. Wouldn't it be wonderful if we could live in that place forever?

As we become older, the cares of this world, the worries of finances, health, and the future, begin consuming our lives. Before we know it, instead of having the whole day to play, we feel we have the weight of the world on our shoulders. Our heavenly Father came that we may have peace in the midst of these times,

*"In the world you will have tribulation,
But be of good cheer,
I have overcome the world."*   —John 16:33

Christ longs for us to humble ourselves as little children, and regardless of what comes into our life, hold tight to our Daddy's hand. He is always with us, and as we lean on Him, will carry us through whatever it is we are facing.

"I will never leave you nor forsake you"   —Hebrews 13:5

For thus says the Lord God,
The Holy One of Israel:
In quietness and confidence
Shall be your strength."   —Isaiah 30:15

And his master was angry,
and delivered him to the torturers
until he should pay all that was due to him.
"So My heavenly Father also will do to you
if each of you, from his heart, does not forgive
his brother his trespasses."

Matthew 18:34-35

Just as the master delivered
the servant to the torturers
until he could pay all that was
due, we are sent to the dungeons
within our heart when
we don't sincerely forgive.

Forgiven

Matthew 18:34-35

And his master was angry, and delivered him to
the torturers until he should pay all that was due to him.
"So My heavenly Father also will do to you if each of you,
from his heart, does not forgive his brother his trespasses."

Peter came to Jesus and said, "Lord, how often shall my brother sin against me, and I forgive him? Up to seven times?"   —Matthew 18:21

Jesus said to him, *"I do not say to you, up to seven times, but up to seventy times seven."*
          —Matthew 18:22

Jesus then told a parable about a king wanting to settle accounts with his servants. When one of the servants, owing thousands of dollars, could not pay he fell down before him and begged to be released of his debt. Feeling compassion for the servant, the king forgave him.

Immediately after being forgiven, the servant found a fellow servant who owed him much less than he had owed the king and demanded he pay him back in full. When the fellow servant begged to be forgiven of his debt because he could not pay, the servant refused.

When I read this parable, it was clear how I could be that servant. After Christ has forgiven me of such great sin, why is it I feel justified in not forgiving a fellow brother or sister who has hurt me?

Jesus told his disciples not only must they forgive, but they must also forgive from their heart. Just as the master delivered the servant to the torturers until he should pay all that was due, we are sent to the dungeons within our heart when we don't sincerely forgive. We become bitter, building a barrier in our closeness with the Lord. Instead of joy, we feel only anguish.

As I bowed my head in prayer, my heart's cry became, "May I forgive as I have been forgiven! Where would I be without it?"

> If You, Lord, should mark iniquities,
>   O Lord, who could stand?
> But *there is* forgiveness with You
>   That You may be feared.   —Psalm 130:3-4

"O woman, great is your faith!
Let it be to you as you desire."
And her daughter was healed from that very hour.

Matthew 15:28

I knew it was time I began walking in what I knew to be true; there is no problem in my life too big for God.

Let It Be

Matthew 15:28

"O woman, great is your faith!
Let it be to you as you desire."
And her daughter was healed from that very hour.

Having a demon possessed daughter, a Canaan woman came to the Lord pleading for help;

> Then she came and worshiped Him saying,
> "Lord, help me!" —Matthew 15:25

As I read this, I noticed not only had she cried out, but also in the midst of her weeping, she had worshiped the Lord. I began pondering the times I have cried out to the Lord in desperation. Had I considered these as times of worship? I knew I had not. But then I realized, when we call on the Lord in despair, within, we are worshipping Him as we pray, "It is You I trust with this heartache, Lord! You alone have the answer!"

> God is Spirit: and they that worship Him
> must worship Him in spirit and in truth.
> —John 4:24

My next thought was, "How great is my faith? Is it as great as this mother? Do I believe He hears the cry of my heart? Will He speak to me as He spoke to her; *"O Woman, great is your faith! Let it be to you as your desire."* If not, what keeps me from having this kind of faith, unwavering in my trust and belief?

> He who doubts is like a wave of the sea
> driven and tossed by the wind.
> For let not that man suppose that he will
> receive anything from the Lord
> He is a double-minded man,
> unstable in all his ways. —James 1:6-8

I knew it was time I began walking in what I knew to be true; there is no problem in my life too big for God. As I bowed my head in humility for the times I have prayed doubting, I felt much like the father who cried out in tears,

> "Lord, I believe; help my unbelief!" —Mark 9:24

So Jesus stood still and called them, and said,
"What do you want Me to do for you?"

Matthew 20:32

Jesus longs for us to cry out
to Him in the desperate
places of our lives.

What Do You Want?

Matthew 20:32

So Jesus stood still and called them, and said,
"What do you want Me to do for you?"

Jesus and the disciples were leaving Jericho, surrounded by a great multitude. This is where we find two blind men sitting by the road crying out to Him, "Have mercy on us, O Lord, Son of David." In spite of the chatter all about, Jesus hears their desperate plea and stops to find the two men. Seeing them sitting alone, unable to find their way, with compassion, He calls to them, *"What do you want Me to do for you?"*

Jesus must have known what they wanted. Surely they were desperate to be healed of their blindness. So why did He ask? Could it be Jesus wanted them to speak their need, and in doing so proclaim their faith in Him?

The Scriptures continue with these words,

> So Jesus had compassion and touched their eyes.
> And immediately their eyes received sight,
> and they followed Him. —Matthew 20:34

As Jesus asked them what it was they wanted, He asks us the same. He longs for us to cry out to Him in the desperate places of our lives. And just as He stopped for the blind men, He will stop for us.

> In the day when I cried out, You answered me,
> And made me bold *with* strength in my soul. —Psalm 138:3

> This poor man cried out, and the LORD heard *him,*
> And saved him out of all his troubles. —Psalm 34:6

> From the end of the earth I will cry to You,
> When my heart is overwhelmed;
> Lead me to the rock that is higher than I. —Psalm 61:2

> Then you will call upon Me and go and pray to Me,
> And I will listen to you.
> And you will seek Me, and find *Me,*
> when you search for Me with all your heart.
>
> —Jeremiah 29:12-13

Words Matter

Psalm 19:14

Let the words of my mouth
and the meditation of my heart
Be acceptable in Your sight,
O LORD, my strength and my Redeemer.

"Pleasant words are like a honeycomb...sweetness to the soul and health to the bones. "   —Proverbs 16:24

I have this Scripture hanging on a wall in my home. It is a constant reminder that what comes out of my mouth matters. It matters to God, it matters to the hearer, and it should matter to me. As children of YAHWEH, we should want to live our lives in such a way others see Jesus by our actions and by our words.

Do all things without complaining and disputing, that you may become blameless and harmless, children of God without fault in the midst of a crooked and perverse generation, among whom you shine as lights in the world?   —Philippians 2:14-15

Let your speech always *be* with grace, seasoned with salt, that you may know how you ought to answer each one.   —Colossians 4:6

Death and life *are* in the power of the tongue,
And those who love it will eat its fruit.   —Proverbs 18:21

A soft answer turns away wrath,
But a harsh word stirs up anger.   —Proverbs 15:1

Let no corrupt word proceed out of your mouth,
but what is good for necessary edification,
that it may impart grace to the hearers.   —Ephesians 4:29

There are six *things* the LORD hates,
Yes seven *are* an abomination to Him;
A proud look; a lying tongue, hands that shed innocent blood,
A heart that devices wicked plans,
Feet that are swift in running to evil,
A false witness *who* speaks lies,
And one who sows discord among brethren.   —Proverbs 6:16-19

So Jesus stood still and called them, and said,
"What do you want Me to do for you?"
They said to Him, "Lord, that our eyes may be opened."
So Jesus had compassion and touched their eyes.
And immediately their eyes received sight,
and they followed Him.

Matthew 20:32-33

May we be willing to ask,
that we too, might see.

Sight

Matthew 20:32-33

So Jesus stood still and called them, and said,
"What do you want Me to do for you?"
They said to Him, "Lord, that our eyes may be opened."
So Jesus had compassion and touched their eyes.
And immediately their eyes received sight, and they followed Him.

Leaving Jericho, Jesus and the disciples came upon two blind men sitting by the side of the road. Having pity, Jesus called to them, *"What do you want Me to do for you?* The blind men cried out, "Lord, that our eyes may be opened."

These men were speaking of physical blindness, something many of us have never experienced. However, until we accept Christ as our Savior, we are all spiritually blind. The Bible makes no sense to us. Only by accepting Christ and receiving the Holy Spirit are our spiritual eyes opened.

> But the natural man does not receive the things of the Spirit
> of God, for they are foolish to him; nor can he know *them*
> because they are spiritually discerned.   —1 Corinthians 2:14

> *But the Helper, the Holy Spirit, whom the Father will send in My*
> *name, He will teach you all things, and bring to your remembrance*
> *all things that I said to you.*   —John 14:26

When Jesus asked the blind men, *"What do you want Me to do for you?"* and their reply was, "Lord, that our eyes may be opened," Jesus touched their eyes and immediately they could see.

In the same way, once we have dedicated our life to Christ as our Savior and pray, "Lord that my eyes may be opened," with compassion, Jesus will touch our spiritual eyes, giving us discernment that we might understand the Word of God. May we be willing to ask, that we, too, might see.

> *"If you ask anything in My name, I will do it."*   —John 14:14

> And this I pray, that your love may abound still more and more in
> knowledge and all discernment, that you may approve the things
> that are excellent, that you may be sincere and without offense till
> the day of Christ, being filled with the fruits of righteousness which
> *are* by Jesus Christ, to the glory and praise of God. —Philippians 1: 9-11

So the disciples went and did as
Jesus commanded them.

Matthew 21:6

We may never know how our
obedience has blessed someone's
life, or why we were sent, but
we can know that if He calls,
He will equip.

Obedience

Matthew 21:6

So the disciples went and did as
Jesus commanded them.

As Jesus and the disciples entered Jerusalem for the last time, Jesus knew what lie ahead. Although He would die a horrible death, He was obedient to His calling. As they entered the city, He sent two disciples, saying:

"Go into the village opposite you, and immediately you will find a
donkey tied, and a colt with her. Loose them and bring them to Me."
"And if anyone says anything to you, you shall say, 'The Lord has
need of them, and immediately he will send them."   —Matthew 21:2-3

The disciples must have wondered why Jesus needed a donkey and a colt. What was He going to do with them? Why would the animals' owner be willing to give his animals to complete strangers? There were so many questions without answers. Nevertheless, the disciples did as they were told.

This caused me to consider how quickly I obey the Lord's leading. Do I follow immediately, or do I contemplate His leading as a suggestion? What if it's out of my comfort zone? What if I'm not sure what I will face? Shouldn't I have answers before I obey His prompting? Not if I want to be obedient to my Savior. I must trust that where He sends me, He will go before. Likewise, I need not worry about what I will say or do, but trust He will speak for me.

Do not worry about how or what you shall speak.
For it will given to you in that hour what you should speak;
"for it is not you who speak, but the Spirit of your Father
speaks in you."   —Matthew 10:19-20

As I thought about this, I wondered how many blessings I have missed because I haven't obeyed the Lord. We may never know how our obedience has blessed someone's life, or why we were sent, but we can know that if He calls, He will equip. Christ doesn't call the qualified. He qualifies the called.

"You are My friends if you do whatever I command you."
—John 15:14

Has the Lord *as great* delight in burnt offerings and sacrifice,
As in obeying the voice of the Lord?
Behold, to obey is better than sacrifice.   —1 Samuel 15:22

"And whoever exalts himself will be humbled, and he who humbles himself will be exalted."

Matthew 23:12

What could be more successful then being exalted by the mighty hand of God?

Opposite Worlds

Matthew 23:12

"And whoever exalts himself will be humbled,
and he who humbles himself will be exalted. "

We live in a society where our profession, bank account, and neighborhood determine our status in life. The world believes big houses, expensive cars, and designer clothes qualify a person as having reached success. Daily we read magazines, watch TV, or listen to the radio about those who seem to have it all. This is opposite living from what Jesus taught His disciples;

"But he who is greatest among you shall be your servant."   —Matthew 23:11

The definition of "servant" in the Webster dictionary is, "someone who serves another." While the world believes those being served are the greatest, Jesus teaches the complete opposite.

As Christians, we bring God glory and honor as we live obedient to His teachings. As we follow Him, we find so much more satisfaction than the world could ever offer.

"For in Him we live and move and have our being"   —Acts 17:28

But now, O Lord, You *are* our Father;
We *are* the clay, and You our potter;
And we all *are* the work of Your hand.   —Isaiah 64:8

You were not redeemed with corruptible things,
like silver or gold, but with the precious blood of
Christ as of a lamb without blemish and without spot. —1 Peter 1:18:19

Beloved, now we are children of God; and it has not yet been
revealed what we shall be, but we know that when He is revealed,
we shall be like Him, for we shall see Him as He is.   —1 John 3:2

As we live our life opposite of the worlds ways, the Lord promises, in a way that only He can, He will exalt us in due time. What could be more successful than being exalted by the mighty Hand of God?

Therefore humble yourself under the mighty hand of God,
that He may exalt you in due time.   —1 Peter 5:6

First cleanse the inside of the cup and dish,
that the outside of them may be clean also.

Matthew 23:26

Only as we live our lives
from the inside out,
with our thoughts and actions
pleasing to Christ, will we draw
others to Jesus.

From the Inside Out

Matthew 23:26

First cleanse the inside of the cup and dish,
that the outside of them may be clean also.

When we are preparing for company, one of my favorite things to do is set a pretty table, one inviting to our guests. I want them to know we are glad they have come, that we have been getting ready for them.

What would happen, if as they sat down at the table they realized the dishes were not clean? How anxious do you think they would be to remain at the table?

This is a silly thought, one we know would never happen. Nevertheless, this is how we often treat our thought life. Christ tells us to cleanse the inside of the cup and dish; cleanse our mind and thoughts, that our words and actions may reflect a life obedient to Him.

> For though we walk in the flesh, we do not war according to the flesh. For the weapons of our warfare are not carnal but mighty in God for pulling down strongholds, casting down arguments and every high thing that exalts itself against the knowledge of God, bringing every thought into captivity to the obedience of Christ.
> —2 Corinthians 10:3-5

> Finally brethren, whatever things are true, whatever things *are* noble, whatever things *are* just, whatever things *are* pure, whatever things *are* lovely, whatever things *are* of good report, if *there is* any virtue and if there is anything praiseworthy-meditate on these things.
> —Philippians 4:8

How we appear to others can be so different than our attitude within. Only as we live our lives from the inside out, with thoughts and actions pleasing to Christ, will we draw others to Jesus. May we decide today to take every thought captive, every action obedient to Christ, that our light might shine, and others, too, will choose to know our Lord.

> *"Let your light so shine before men that they may see your good works*
> *and glorify you Father in heaven."*   —Matthew 5:16

Peter said to Him, "Even if I have to die
with You, I will not deny You!"
And so said all the disciples.

Matthew 26:35

Christ's blood was shed
for the remission of our sins.
Where would we be without it?

Remission of Sins

Matthew 26:35

Taking the bread and blessing it, He faced His disciples and said;
Peter said to Him, "Even if I have to die with You,
I will not deny You!" And so said all the disciples.

Celebrating Passover with the disciples, Jesus instituted the Lord's Supper and the new covenant.

"Take, eat, this is My body." Then taking the cup and giving it to the disciples He said, *"Drink from it, all of you. For this is My blood of the new covenant, which is shed for many for the remission of sins. But I say to you, I will not drink of this fruit of the vine from now on until that day when I drink it new with you in My Father's kingdom."* —Matthew 26:26-29

Finishing, He spoke words they could not believe;

"All of you will be made to stumble because of Me this night, for it is written:
"I will strike the Shepherd,
And the sheep of the flock will be scattered."
But after I have been raised, I will go before you to Galilee." —Matthew 26:31-32

Peter answering, said to Him, "Even if all are made to stumble because of You, I will never be made to stumble." —Matthew 26:33

Turning to Peter, Jesus answered,

"Assuredly, I say to you that this night before the rooster crows,
you will deny Me three times." —Matthew 26:34

How it must have grieved Peter to know Jesus would believe such a thing. But he did. Just as Jesus had said, before the rooster crowed, Peter had denied Christ three times.

Lest we become critical of Peter, believing we would never deny Christ, we best remember we, too, have been guilty of such sins. Do we defend Christ when others take His name in vain? Do we always give God the glory when blessings come our way? Do we put Christ first in every situation in our lives?

Christ's blood was shed for remission of sins. Where would we be without it?

If anyone sins, we have an Advocate with the Father
Jesus Christ the righteous. —1 John 2:1b

"Watch and pray, let you enter into temptation.
The spirit indeed is willing,
but the flesh is weak."

Matthew 26:41

May we decide this day
to watch and pray as we
seek the face of our Savior,
that we might live a life
pleasing to Him.

Stay Alert

Matthew 26:41

"Watch and pray, lest you enter into temptation.
The spirit indeed is willing, but the flesh is weak."

Coming to a place called Gethsemane, Jesus said to His disciples;

> *"Sit here while I go and pray over there."*   —Matthew 26:36

Returning later, He found them sleeping. Sadly He said,

> *"What? Could you not watch with Me one hour?"*
> *Watch and pray, lest you enter into temptation.*
> *The spirit indeed is willing, but the flesh is weak."*   —Matthew 26:40-41

How easy it is to fall asleep in our Christian walk. We begin believing, because we love Jesus, we will never waver. However, before we realize it, Satan has enticed us with lies contrary to our beliefs.

> Be sober, be vigilant; because your adversary the devil
> walks about like a roaring lion, seeking whom he may devour.
> —1 Peter 5:8

> Do not be conformed to this world, but be transformed by the
> renewing of your mind, that you may prove what *is* that good
> and acceptable and perfect will of God.   —Romans 12:2

We were never meant to walk life alone. Christ longs to direct our steps, giving us understanding for each new day.

> Direct my steps by your word,
> And let no iniquity have dominion over me.   —Psalm 119:133

> The steps of a *good* man are ordered by the LORD,
> And He delights in his way   —Psalm 37:23

Temptation comes so easily. May we decide this day to watch and pray, as we seek our Father, that we might live a life that is pleasing to Him.

> Seek the LORD while He may be found,
> Call upon Him while He is near.   —Isaiah 55:6

> Keep your heart with all diligence,
> For out of it *spring* the issues of life.   —Proverbs 4:23

Immediately the Spirit drove Him into
the wilderness. And He was there in the
wilderness forty days, tempted by Satan,
and was with the beasts;
and angels ministered to Him.

Mark 1:12-13

Christ promises to not only
make a way of escape in the
midst of temptation, but
also to bless us as we endure
the temptation.

The Wilderness

Mark 1:12-13

Immediately the Spirit drove Him into the wilderness.
And He was there in the wilderness forty days, tempted by Satan,
and was with the beasts; and angels ministered to Him.

John had just baptized Jesus, when the Spirit descended upon Him:

> Immediately, coming up from the water, He saw the heavens parting and
> the Spirit descending upon Him like a dove.   —Mark 1:10

Then we read: "Immediately, the Spirit drove Him into the wilderness." Why
would Jesus be driven into the wilderness to be tempted by Satan? As I pondered this, I wondered, "Could it be so He would understand the temptations
we face in our lives?"

> For we do not have a High Priest who cannot sympathize with our weak
> nesses, but was in all *points* tempted as *we are, yet* without sin. Let us there-
> fore come boldly to the throne of grace, that we may obtain mercy and
> find grace to help in time of need.   —Hebrews 4:15-16

The Scriptures continue with words of encouragement, "and angels ministered to Him." During time of great temptation Christ was not alone, but
ministered to by angels. In the same way, when we are tempted we are not
alone,

> No temptation has overtaken you except such as is common to man; but
> God is faithful, who will not allow you to be tempted beyond what you are
> able, but with the temptation will also make the way of escape, that you
> may be able to bear it.   —1Cor. 10:13

Christ promises to not only make a way of escape in the midst of our temptation, but also bless us as we endure the temptation.

> Blessed *is* the man who endures the temptation; for when he has
> been approved, he will receive the crown of life which the Lord
> has promised to those who love Him.   —James 1:12

Isn't it incredible how Jesus saves us from falling into temptation by making
a way of escape when we are tempted? Yet He also blesses us with a crown
of life for our obedience. We serve an amazing King!

"I AM WHO I AM"

Exodus 3:14

And God said to Moses, I AM WHO I AM."
"Thus you shall say to the children of Israel, "I AM has sent me to you."

Aren't you thankful God called Himself, I AM and not I Was, or I Will be?
The great I AM was in our past, HE IS in our present, and HE will be in our
future. From the Old Testament to the New Testament He was and is and
always will be "I AM"

He is our living bread:

Exodus 16:4   Then the Lord said to Moses, "Behold, I will rain bread
              from heaven down to you."

John 6:51   *"I am the living bread which came down from heaven. If anyone
              eats of this bread, he will live forever"*

He is the light of the world:

Psalm 27:1   The Lord *is* my light and my salvation. Whom shall I fear?

John 8:12   *"I AM the light of the world. He who follows Me shall not walk
              in darkness, but have the light of life".*

He is our Good Shepherd:

Psalm 23:1   The Lord is my shepherd; I shall not want.

John 10:11   *"I AM the good shepherd. The good shepherd gives His life for
              the sheep."*

He is our Life:

Deut. 30:19   Choose life that both you and your descendants may live.

John 11:25   *"I am the resurrection and the life. He who believes in Me,
              though he may die, he shall live."*

He is our Salvation:

Psalm 68:20   Our God *is* the God of Salvation

Acts 4:12   "Nor is there salvation in any other name under heaven
              Given among men by which we must be saved."

Psalm 18:46   The LORD lives! Blessed *be* my Rock!

"I am the Alpha and the Omega," says the Lord, *who is and was and who is to come,
the Almighty."*   —Revelation 1:11

When Jesus saw their faith,
He said to the paralytic,
"Son, your sins are forgiven you."

Mark 2:5

We need to live out our faith,
not simply share with others
what we believe.

Believe

Mark 2:5

When Jesus saw their faith, He said to the paralytic,
"Son, your sins are forgiven you."

Jesus had come to Capernaum to preach. Because of an overflowing crowd, there was no room for people to enter through the door.

When four men, bringing their paralytic friend to be healed, saw they could not go through the door, they uncovered the roof and let their friend down where Jesus stood. They believed if they could only get their friend to Jesus, he would be healed.

Reading this caused me to consider my faith. Do I simply talk about what I believe, sharing Scriptures with others, and yet, when coming to a place requiring action, cower under the influence of unbelief?

The four friends didn't stop and ask the crowd what they thought about uncovering the roof, so their friend could see Jesus. They didn't turn away because the situation looked impossible. Standing firm in their faith, they seized the moment and brought their friend to Jesus in the only way possible. When Jesus saw such faith as this, He responded to their need.

The world is watching to see if we walk the walk we talk. When the situation looks impossible, yet we stand on our faith, the world notices. When we smile in the midst of heartache, others see the difference our faith makes in our life. We need to live out our faith, not simply share with others what we believe.

Jesus saw the faith of the four men, as well as their friend on the mat. When we step out, our Father sees our faith and meets us at our need.

> Let him ask in faith, with no doubting, for he who doubts
> is like a wave of the sea driven and tossed by the wind.
> For let not that man suppose that he will receive anything
> From the Lord, he is a double-minded man, unstable
> in all his ways.   —James 1:6

> Jesus said to her, *"Did I not say to you that if you would believe you would see the glory of God?"*   —John 11:40

And He sat down, called the twelve,
and said to them,
"If anyone desires to be first,
he shall be last of all and servant of all. "

Mark 9:35

We live for an
audience of One.
In Christ alone
we find our worth.

Servant of All

Mark 9:35

And He sat down, called the twelve,
and said to them,
*"If anyone desires to be first, he shall be last
of all and servant of all."*

As the disciples walked along the road to Capernaum, they disputed among themselves as to who *would* be the greatest. This reminded me so much of us today. We all want to be the greatest, the most well known, popular, and successful. Why is it we feel our status in this world defines who we are?

When we accept Jesus Christ as our Personal Savior our values change. The world tells us to be proud of our accomplishments. Jesus instructs us to be humble, knowing our achievements come from Him alone.

> For I know that in me (that is, in my flesh) nothing good
> dwells; for to will is present with me, but *how* to perform
> what is good I do not find.   —Romans 7:18

> I can do all things though Christ who strengthens me.
>   —Philippians 4:13

As in every lesson, Christ gives us the ultimate example of humility. There has never been anyone like Jesus. He was, and still is, the greatest man who ever walked this earth. Yet, He humbled Himself and becoming of no reputation, died on the cross for our sins.

> And being found in appearance as a man, He humbled
> Himself and became obedient *to the point* of death, even
> the death of the cross.   —Philippians 2:8

If we are to be like Christ, we too, must be willing to live our lives for others, rather than for ourselves. We live for an audience of One. In Christ alone we find our worth.

> *Let* nothing *be done* through selfish ambition or conceit, but in
> lowliness of mind let each esteem others better than himself.
>   —Philippians 2:3

> Therefore humble yourselves under the mighty hand of God,
> that He may exalt you in due time.   —1 Peter 5:6

And some of the scribes were sitting there
and reasoning in their hearts.

Mark 2:6

Jesus isn't offended or angry
when we don't understand
the "whys" of life.

Reasoning

Mark 2:6

And some of the scribes were sitting there
and reasoning in their hearts.

After being let down through the roof on a mat and being placed at the feet of Jesus, with compassion Jesus said to the paralyzed man, *"Son, your sins are forgiven you."*   —Mark 2:5

The scribes sitting amongst the crowd, taking offense to His words, began reasoning among themselves, "Why does this *Man* speak blasphemies like this? Who can forgive sins but God alone?"   —Mark 2:7

Do we ever reason in our heart how something Jesus tells us is truth couldn't possibly be truth? When the Scriptures tell us,

> "And we know that all things work together for good to those
> who love God, to those who are called according to *His* purpose.
>   —Romans 8:29

and we are living with such despair we are sure we will never survive, do we reason in our heart how this couldn't possibly work together for good?

Jesus isn't offended or angry when we don't understand the "whys" of life. With empathy and love He promises He will never leave us, but give the strength and help we need to make it through the heartache.

> "Fear not, for I *am* with you.
> Be not dismayed, for I *am* your God
> I will strengthen you,
> Yes, I will help you.
> I will uphold you with My righteous right hand." —Isaiah 41:10

Could it be we need to stop reasoning and start trusting? We can take God at His word. His love is never ending.

> "For My thoughts are not your thoughts,
> Nor *are* your ways My ways," says the Lord.
> " For as the heavens are higher than the earth,
> So are My ways higher than your ways,
> And My thoughts than your thoughts." —Isaiah 55:8-9

> The steadfast love of the LORD never ceases;
> His mercies never come to an end.   —Lamentations 3:22 (ESV)

Immediately he arose, took up the bed,
and went out in the presence of them all,
so that all were amazed and glorified God, saying
"We never saw anything like this!"

Mark 2:12

Every time we choose to respond
in a way pleasing to God in lieu
of the way of the world,
we bring glory to God.

Glorify God

Mark 2:12

Immediately he arose, took up the bed,
and went out in the presence of them all,
so that all were amazed and glorified God, saying
"We never saw *anything* like this!"

Four men brought their paralyzed friend to Jesus to be healed. When Jesus told the friend,

"I say to you, arise, take up your bed, and go to your house." —Mark 2:11

and the man stood, everyone was amazed.

Just as the four men were obedient in bringing their friend to Jesus, the paralytic was obedient as he rose from his mat. In their obedience, they glorified God. There was no denying why he could walk. It had to be Jesus.

When we are obedient to Jesus, we, too, bring glory to God. When He tells us to turn the other cheek,

"But I tell you not to resist an evil person. But whoever slaps you on your right cheek, turn the other to him also."

—Matthew 5:39

and we turn the other cheek instead of fighting back, we bring glory to God. The world is watching to see what we will do. Because it is not how they would react, we show them Jesus.

When we choose forgiveness over bitterness, calmness over anger, kindness in place of hurtful words, our obedience brings glory to God.

Let all bitterness, wrath, anger, clamor, and evil
speaking be put away from you, with all malice.
And be kind to one another, tenderhearted, forgiving
one another, even as God in Christ forgave you.
—Ephesians 4:31-32

Every time we choose to respond in a way pleasing to God, in lieu of the way of the world, we bring glory to God. The world is watching. May we choose obedience to Him.

"Has the LORD *as great* delight in burnt offerings and sacrifices,
As in obeying the voice of the LORD?
Behold, to obey is better than sacrifice."   —1 Samuel 15:22

Psalm 91

After a fierce fight with cancer, the Lord called my dear friend home. During her service, the pastor shared how during her battle she personalized Psalm 91, making it her own. I invite you to do the same, and be blessed.

"For in Him we live and move and have our being." Acts 17:28

Because I (your name) dwell in the secret place of the Most High
I shall abide under the shadow of the Almighty.
I will say to the Lord, "You are my refuge and my fortress;
My God, in You I will trust."

Surely the Lord shall deliver me from the snare of the fowler
And from the perilous pestilence.
The Lord shall cover me with His feathers,
And under His wings I shall take refuge;
The Lord's truth *shall be my* shield and buckler.
I shall not be afraid of the terror by night.
Nor of the arrow *that* flies by day.
Nor of the pestilence *that* walks in darkness
Nor of the destruction *that* lays waste at noonday.

A thousand may fall at my side,
And ten thousand at my right hand;
But it shall not come near me.
Only with my eyes shall I look,
And see the reward of the wicked.

Because I (your name) have made the LORD, *who is* my refuge,
Even the Most High, my dwelling place,
No evil shall befall me,
Nor shall any plague come near my dwelling;
For the Lord shall give His angels charge over me;
To keep me in all my ways.
In *their* hands they shall bear me up,
Lest I dash my foot against a stone.
I shall tread upon the lion and the cobra,
The young lion and the serpent I shall trample underfoot.

"Because I (your name) have set my love upon the Lord,
therefore He will deliver me;
The Lord will set me on high because I have known His name.
I shall call upon the Lord and He will answer me.
The Lord *will* be with me in trouble;
He will deliver me and honor me.
With long life the Lord will satisfy me,
And show me His salvation."

Under the Shadow of His Wings

Psalm 91:4

He shall cover you with His feathers,
And under His wings you shall take refuge
His Truth *shall be your* shield and buckler.

During the Celebration of Life for my friend, the Pastor shared Scriptures she held close during her fight with cancer. Chances are you aren't faced with something as difficult as she was, but we all face trials, heartache, and uncertainty at sometime in our life. It is the strength we draw from the promises of our LORD that carry us through these times. I pray the following promises of God will bless you, as they have me.

"Ah, Lord GOD! Behold, You have made the heavens and the earth by Your great power and outstretched arm. There is nothing too hard for You."   —Jeremiah 32:17

Now to Him who is able to do exceedingly abundantly above all that we ask or think, according to the power that works in us, to Him *be* glory in the church by Christ Jesus to all generations, forever and ever. Amen
                                    —Ephesians 3:20-21

But those who wait on the LORD shall renew their strength;
They shall mount up with wings like eagles,
They shall run and not be weary,
They shall walk and not faint.   —Isaiah 40:31

Jesus said to him, "I am the way, the truth, and the life. No one comes to the Father except through Me."   —John 14:6

He shall cover you with His feathers,
And under His wings you shall take refuge.   —Psalm 91:4

Because she knew who held all her tomorrows, my friend found peace knowing He would deliver her, if not from the disease, then into His loving arms.

Because he has set his love upon Me,
Therefore I will deliver him, I will set him on high,
Because he has known My name.   —Psalm 91:14

When Jesus heard it, He said to them,
"Those who are well have no need of a physician,
but those who are sick.
I did not come to call the righteous,
but sinners, to repentance."

Mark 2:17

Without repentance we
are separated from God,
our fellowship with
Christ severed.

Repent

Mark 2:17

When Jesus heard it, He said to them,
"Those who are well have no need of a physician,
but those who are sick. I did not come to call the righteous,
but sinners, to repentance."

The Scribes and Pharisees were watching Jesus eat with the tax collectors and sinners. Becoming indignant over the kindness He showed them, they asked how He could eat with sinners such as these. As I read this, I couldn't help but ponder, "Am I like the Scribes and Pharisees? Do I judge others like they did, feeling their sins are greater than mine?"

The Word of God tells us we have all sinned:

For all have sinned and fall short of the glory of God
—Romans 3:23
...and only through repentance are our sins forgiven.

John came baptizing in the wilderness and preaching
a baptism of repentance for the remission of sins. —Mark 1:4

Without repentance we are separated from God, our fellowship with Christ, severed. Christ calls us to a surrendered heart that He may forgive our sins and cleanse us from all unrighteousness.

The sacrifices of God *are* a broken spirit,
A broken and contrite heart
These, O God, You will not despise.   —Psalm 51:17

Create in me a clean heart, O God,
And renew a steadfast spirit within me.
Do not cast me away from your presence,
And do not take your Holy Spirit from me.
Restore to me the joy of my salvation,
And uphold me *by your* generous Spirit.   —Psalm 51:10-12

May we humble ourselves before Almighty God that He may cleanse us from all unrighteousness and renew a right spirit within us.

He does not treat us as our sins deserve or repay us according
to our iniquities. For as high as the heavens are above the earth,
so great is His love for those who fear Him. —Psalm 103:11-12

"And no one puts new wine into old wineskins;
or else the new wine bursts the wineskins, the
wine is spilled, and the wineskins are ruined.
But new wine must be put into the wineskins."

Mark 2:22

We no longer live for ourselves,
but we live to glorify Christ.

New Wine

Mark 2:22

And no one puts new wine into old wineskins;
or else the new wine bursts the wineskins, the
wine is spilled, and the wineskins are ruined.
But new wine must be put into new wineskins.

While explaining to the Pharisees how the teachings of the Jewish law did not fit into the teachings of Christianity, Jesus used the parable of new wine being put into old wineskins.

As Christians, we have much to learn from this parable. When we accept Christ as our Personal Savior we become a new creature, old things are passed away.

> Therefore, if anyone is in Christ, *he is* a new creation;
> old things have passed away; behold, all things have become new.
> —2 Corinthians 5:17

We no longer depend on our own thoughts and ideas to shape our lives, but look to the Word of God.

> Behold, the former things have come to pass,
> And new things I declare;
> Before they spring forth I tell you of them.   —Isaiah 42:9

Likewise, we no longer live for ourselves, but we live to glorify Christ.

> And He died for all, that those who live should live
> no longer for themselves, but for Him who died for
> them and rose again.   —2 Corinthians 5:15

As we allow Christ to live through us, being crucified in the flesh and new in Him, we become as new wineskin, putting new wine into our life though Him.

> "I have been crucified with Christ; it is no longer I who
> live but Christ lives in me; and the *life* which I now live
> in the flesh I live by faith in the Son of God, who loved
> me and gave Himself for me."   —Galatians 2:20

> "Then I will give them one heart, and I will put a new spirit
> within them, and take the stony heart out of their flesh, and
> give them a heart of flesh.   —Ezekiel 11:19

Then He appointed twelve
that they might be with Him
and that He might send them out to preach.

Mark 3:14

The Word of God is as
relevant today as it was
when it was written over
two thousand years ago.

Friendship

Mark 3:14

Then He appointed twelve that they might
be with Him and that He might send them out to preach.

Jesus called the twelve disciples to be with Him as He taught. He longed for them to know Him as their friend. In the same way, He calls us His friend.

"No longer do I call you servants, for a servant does not know what his master is doing; but I have called you friends, for all things that I heard from My Father I have made known to you." —John 15:15

When our desire is to know Jesus as our friend, the more time we spend in His Word, the better we get to know Him. The Word of God is as relevant today as it was when it was written over two thousand years ago.

For the word of God *is* living and powerful, and sharper than any two-edged sword, piercing even to the division of soul and spirit, and joints and marrow, and is a discerner of the thoughts and intents of the heart.   —Hebrews 4:12

Abraham spent time with God and was known as His friend forever.

"Are you not our God, *who* drove out the inhabitants of this land…and gave it to the descendants of Abraham Your friend forever?"   —2 Chronicles 20:7

How well do you know Jesus? As you spend time in His Word, He promises to meet you there. As you give Him your time, He reveals truths you would have never known.

The friendship of the LORD *is* with those who fear Him,
And He will show them His Covenant.   —Psalm 25:14 ESV

"Call on Me, and I will answer you, and show you great and mighty things which you do not know."   —Jeremiah 33:3

May our desire be to get to know Him with such passion that like Abraham, we are called His friend forever. Jesus wants to be our friend. Is there any greater gift?

O GOD, You *are* my God;
Early will I seek You;
My soul thirsts for You   —Psalm 63:1

*"For whoever does the will of God
is My brother and sister and mother."*

Mark 3:35

"I have come to do
your will Lord.
What would You
have me do?"

Will of God

Mark 3:35

"For whoever does the will of God
is My brother and sister and mother."

Jesus was gathered with the multitudes when His mother and brothers came calling for Him;

> And He looked around in a circle at those who
> sat about Him and said,
> *"Here are My mother and my brothers!*
> *For whoever does the will of God is My brother*
> *and sister and mother."*   —Mark 3:34-35

As I read the words of Jesus, I pondered, "What is the will of God?"

> "I delight to do Your will, O my God,
> And your law is within my heart."   —Psalm 40:8

> He has shown you, O man, what *is* good;
> And what does the LORD require of you
> But to do justly, to love mercy,
> And to walk humbly with your God?   —Micah 6:8

Then I realized, to do justly, love mercy, and walk humbly with Him is the will of God. As I considered how I could possibly do this, I thought of how Jesus did not depend on His own will, but the will of His Father. It became clear, I would only do the will of God as I allowed the Spirit to lead.

> "*I can of Myself do nothing.*
> *As I hear, I judge, and My judgment is righteous,*
> *Because I do not seek My own will but the will of*
> *the Father who sent me."*   —John 5:30

> Teach me to do Your will,
> For You *are* my God;
> Your Spirit *is* good
> Lead me in the land of uprightness.   —Psalm 143:10

> *Your kingdom come, Your will be done*
> *On earth as it is in heaven.*   —Matthew 6:10

> "I have come to do Your will Lord.
> What would you have me do?"

But He said to them,
"Why are you so fearful?
How is it that you have no faith?"

Mark 4:40

It is impossible
to walk in faith,
when we are walking in fear.

Fearful

Mark 4:40

But He said to them, *"Why are you so fearful?*
How is it that you have no faith?"

What do you do when fear grips your heart, causing you to become anxious concerning what lies ahead? When the disciples became fearful, afraid they were going to drown in the raging waters, Jesus rebuked them with the question, *"How is it that you have no faith?"*

Have you ever considered that fear is the opposite of faith? It is impossible to walk in faith when we are walking in fear.

> Now faith is the substance of things hoped for,
> the evidence of things not seen.   —Hebrews 11:1

Instead of walking in the substance of things hoped for, we are walking in the substance of things we hope won't happen. We are walking in dread, even though we are told to walk in hope.

> For God has not given us a spirit of fear;
> but of power and of love and of a sound mind.
>   —2 Timothy 1:7

Fear does not come from God, but from the enemy of our soul. If the devil can keep us filled with fear, he has devoured our faith. He knows we can't walk in faith when we are paralyzed with fear.

> Be sober, be vigilant; because your adversary
> the devil walks about like a roaring lion, seeking
> whom he may devour.   —1 Peter 5:7

When fear comes knocking at the door of our heart we need to answer with faith, confident the Lord is with us.

> Behold, God *is* my salvation, I will trust and not be afraid;
> For YAH, the Lord, is my strength and song.
> He has also become my salvation."   —Isaiah 12:2

> I called on the Lord in distress;
> The LORD answered me and *set me* in a broad place.
> The Lord *is* on my side; I will not fear.   —Psalm 118:5-6

Jesus said to him, "*I am the way, the truth, and the life. No man comes to the Father except through Me.*"

John 14:6

Oh, to live with such love and gratitude for all Christ has done for us it brings us to tears.

Just As I Am

John 14:6

*Jesus said to him, "I am the way, the truth, and the life.
No one comes to the Father except through Me."*

As I stood in church this morning, singing the hymn, "Just As I Am," I witnessed something I have never seen before. A gentleman sitting in front of me sat weeping, his head in his hands. When asked what was wrong, he replied faintly, "I feel so bad that I was such an alcoholic for so many years." His remorse was so great he could not hold back the tears. The gratitude and love for Jesus this man demonstrated put me to shame. Have I ever been so sorry for my sins that I wept? I may have wept because of the pain it has caused my life, but have I wept because of what it meant to Jesus? Have I wept because it was my sins that hung Jesus on the cross?

> For all have sinned and fallen short of the glory of God;
> being justified freely by His grace through the redemption
> that is in Christ Jesus.   —Romans 3:23-24

Have you ever stopped to think where we would be if not for the saving grace of Jesus? Because of His willingness to go to the cross, no longer do we live under the shame of past sins, but we have been set free. We can walk as children of God, free from condemnation.

> *"Therefore if the Son makes you free, you shall be free indeed."*
>   —John 8:36

> *There* is therefore now no condemnation to those who are
> in Christ Jesus, who do not walk according to the flesh, but
> according to the Spirit.   —Romans 8:1

> The Spirit Himself bears witness with our spirit that we are
> children of God, and if children, then heirs—heirs of God
> and joint heirs with Christ.   —Romans 8:16-17a

Oh, to live with such love and gratitude for all Christ has done for us it brings us to tears. It was our sins that hung Him on the cross. And yet He loves us still. Where would we be without Him?

> *God so loved the world that He gave His only begotten Son,
> that whosoever believes in Him should not parish but have
> everlasting life.*   —John 3:16

And he departed and began to proclaim
in Decapolis all that Jesus had done for him;
and all marveled.

Mark 5:20

We all have a story to tell.

Proclaim

Mark 5:20

And he departed and began to proclaim in Decapolis
all that Jesus had done for him; and all marveled.

As Jesus came to Gadarenes, a man with unclean spirits, bound with shackles
and chains, ran to meet Him. Night and day he was in the tombs of the
mountains, crying out and cutting himself with stones.

When he saw Jesus from afar, he ran and worshiped Him.
—Mark 5:6

Imagine the scene. The man who had not been near another human being in
years, saw Jesus coming and instead of running away, ran to meet Him. How
did he know Jesus could help Him? Why did he worship Jesus?

How moved Jesus must have been by such devotion. Immediately Jesus
said to the man, *"Come out of the man, unclean spirit!"* —Mark 5:8

Sending the unclean spirits into a herd of swine feeding near the mountains,
the swine ran violently down into the sea. Immediately the demon possessed
man was healed, and began proclaiming all Jesus had done for him.

How often do we proclaim all Jesus has done for us? We all have a story to
tell. Before coming to Christ we were lost in our sins, separated from God.
Then Jesus brought us to Himself and everything changed.

"One thing I know: that though I was blind, now I see."
—John 9:25

Who is waiting to hear your story? Will you tell them today?

I have proclaimed the good news of righteousness
In the assembly; indeed I do not restrain my lips,
O LORD, You Yourself know.   —Psalm 40:9

For I am not ashamed of the gospel of Christ, for it is the
power of God to salvation for everyone who believes, for
the Jew first and also for the Greek.   —Romans 1:16

But the woman, fearing and trembling,
knowing what had happened to her,
came and fell down before Him
and told Him the whole truth.

Mark 5:33

He desires a heart humbled
before Him, reaching out
for His healing hand.

Truth

Mark 5:33

But the woman, fearing and trembling,
knowing what had happened to her,
came and fell down before Him
and told Him the whole truth.

Crossing over the sea, Jesus came to the multitudes. As a large crowd gathered, a certain woman plagued with an issue of blood strained to touch the hem of His garment.

> And Jesus, immediately knowing in Himself that power had gone out of Him, turned around in the crowd and said, "*Who touched My clothes?*" —Mark 5:30

The woman knew she must tell Jesus what her life had been like, all she had suffered. She also understood there was no time for pretense or denial. Jesus knew why she had come and she must be completely honest.

How many times have we come to Jesus, and afraid what He might think, justified our actions, or left part of it out completely. Jesus knows what we need from Him, why we have come.

Have you suffered and need His healing touch? Tell Jesus. Are you angry and need understanding? Tell Jesus. Are you filled with guilt and need forgiveness? Tell Jesus. Are you jealous and know it is wrong? Tell Jesus. Do you harbor bitterness in your heart and need to forgive? Tell Jesus. The women with the issue of blood fell at Jesus' feet and told Him the whole truth. That is exactly what He requires of us. He desires a heart humbled before Him, reaching out for His healing hand.

> For thus says the High and Lofty One
> Who inhabits the eternity, whose name *is* Holy:
> "I dwell in the high and holy *place*,
> With him *who* has a contrite and humble spirit,
> To revive the spirit of the humble,
> And to revive the heart of the contrite ones. —Isaiah 57:15

> The sacrifices of God *are* a broken spirit,
> A broken and a contrite heart—
> These, O God, You will not despise. —Psalm 51:17

And Jesus, when He came out, saw a multitude
and was moved with compassion for them,
because they were like sheep
not having a shepherd.

Mark 6:34

Do you know the Shepherd?
If you do, you know He will
never leave you,
nor forsake you.

My Shepherd

Mark 6:34

And Jesus, when He came out, saw a great multitude
and was moved with compassion for them, because
they were like sheep not having a shepherd.

Jesus encouraged the disciples to come away to a deserted place to rest and eat. Nevertheless, when the multitudes saw them departing they ran to meet them, wanting to be where Jesus was. Being moved with compassion, Jesus could not send them away, but began teaching. He wanted them to know how much He cared for them, assure them they were not alone.

"I am the good shepherd.
The good shepherd gives His life
For His sheep.   —John 10:11

I am the good shepherd;
And I know my sheep,
And am known by My own.   —John 10:14

Before inviting Christ into our hearts as our Lord and Savior, we are like the multitudes, lost without a Shepherd. And just as He taught them, He teaches us today, *"I love you and long to be your Shepherd."*

The LORD is my shepherd;
I shall not want.
He makes me to like down in green pastures;
He leads me beside the still waters.
He restores my soul;
He leads me in the paths of righteousness
For His name's sake.   —Psalm 23:1-3

Do you know the Shepherd? If you do, you know He will never leave you, nor forsake you. If you do not, will you humbly seek Him today, inviting Him into your heart? He will not turn you away, but promises to meet you there.

If you confess with your mouth the Lord Jesus
and believe in your heart that God has raised Him
from the dead, you will be saved.
For with the heart one believes unto righteousness,
And with the mouth confession is made unto salvation.
For *"whoever calls on the name of the Lord shall be saved.*
                        —Romans 10:9-10,13

So they all ate and were filled.

Mark 6:42

Little is much in the hands
of our Lord.

Little is Much

Mark 6:42

So they all ate and were filled.

As Jesus taught the multitudes, the disciples realized the hour was late and the thousands gathered would be hungry. Knowing food was scarce, they told Jesus to send them away.

> But He answered and said to them, *"You give them something to eat."* *"How many loaves do you have? Go and see."* And when they found out they said, "Five, and two fish." —Mark 6:37-38

> And when He had taken the five loaves and the two fish, He looked up to heaven, blessed and broke the loaves, and gave *them* to His disciples to set before them; and the two fish He divided among *them* all. —Mark 6:41

> Now those who had eaten the loaves were about five thousand men. —Mark 6:44

What most impressed me about this story is how Jesus didn't just turn little into much, but first looked up to heaven and blessed what He had.

How often do we feel we have too little to be of any help to anyone, or make a difference in any way? What would happen if we took that little, and instead of deeming it as inadequate, gave it to Jesus, and trusting, watched to see what He would do?

> Just a little time
> Just a little money
> Just a little knowledge
> Just a little experience
> Just a little compassion
> Just a little faith

It only took five loaves and two fish for Jesus to feed five thousand men. Just think what He could do with our "little" once we gave it to Him. Little is much in the hands of our Lord.

Give Him your "little," and see what He will do. You will be amazed.

And when they saw Him walking on the sea,
they supposed it was a ghost, and cried out;
for they all saw Him and were troubled. But immediately He talked with them and said to them,
"Be of good cheer! It is I; do not be afraid."

Mark 6:49-50

The Lord longs for us to
cry out to Him regardless
of what we are facing.

Be of Good Cheer

Mark 6:49-50

And when they saw Him walking on the sea,
they supposed it was a ghost, and cried out;
for they all saw Him and were troubled. But
immediately He talked with them and said to them,
"Be of good cheer! It is I; do not be afraid."

Departing to the mountains to pray, Jesus sent the disciples to the other side of the sea. As evening came He discovered them rowing fiercely against the great winds. Seeing their fear and despair, He came to them, walking on the water.

Imagine the scene: Twelve disciples straining against the boisterous seas, raging all about, when all of a sudden someone comes toward them walking on the water. Is it any wonder they cried out? We would too!

What do you do when you are afraid? Do you scream, becoming paralyzed? Perhaps you run, trying to escape. What would happen, if in that moment, your first thoughts were to call out to Jesus? Can you hear Him calmly saying, as He said to the disciples?

"Be of good cheer! It is I; do not be afraid."

The Lord longs for us to cry out to Him regardless of what we are facing.

> The LORD *is* my light and my salvation;
> Whom shall I fear?
> The LORD is the strength of my life;
> Of whom shall I be afraid?   —Psalm 27:1

In the midst of our fear, we can rest in Him, knowing He has come to our rescue.

> Fear not, for I am with you;
> Be not dismayed, for I am your God.
> I will strengthen you,
> Yes, I will help you.
> I will uphold you with My righteous right hand.   —Isaiah 41:10

> "Have I not commanded you? Be strong and of good courage;
> do not be afraid, nor be dismayed, for the LORD your God
> is with you wherever you go."   —Joshua 1:9

Whenever He entered, into villages, cities, or
the country, they laid the sick in the marketplaces,
and begged Him that they might just touch
the hem of his garment.
And as many as touch Him were made well.

If only we might touch the
hem of His garment.

The Hem of His Garment

Mark 6:56

Wherever He entered, into villages, cities, or the country,
they laid the sick in the marketplaces, and begged Him that
they might just touch the hem of His garment.
And as many as touched Him were made well.

Jesus and the disciples crossed the seas and came to the land of Gennesaret. As they came out of the boat, the people recognized Jesus and immediately began running to Him.

The touch of the Master's robe, that is all the people longed for. They didn't desire silver, gold, or great possessions, just to touch His garment. They knew if they could touch His hem, their lives would be made whole.

How desperate are we to run to Jesus? Do we believe He is enough?

> Trust in Him at all times, you people;
> Pour out your hearts before Him;
> God is a refuge for us. —Psalm 62:8

So often, instead of running to Jesus, we try on our own to find answers to our problems and heartaches. Just like the people knew if they could only touch His garment, Jesus longs for us to know the same. He alone knows what it is we need.

> The LORD also will be a refuge for the oppressed,
> A refuge in times of trouble.
> And those who know Your name
> will put their trust in You;
> For YOU, LORD, have not forsaken
> those who seek You. —Psalm 9: 9-10

> The LORD *is* good,
> A stronghold in the day of trouble;
> And He knows those who trust in Him. —Nahum 1:7

> Cast all your cares upon Him,
> for He cares for you. —1 Peter 5:7

If only we might touch the hem of His garment.

"And as many as touched Him were made well." —Mark 6:56

Now when they saw some of His disciples
eat bread, that is, with unwashed hands,
they found fault.

Mark 7:2

The next time we are
tempted to judge another,
let's share Jesus instead.

Who Are We?

Mark 7:2

Now when they saw some of His disciples
eat bread with defiled, that is,
with unwashed hands, they found fault.

The scribes and Pharisees, coming from Jerusalem to where Jesus was, saw His disciples eating bread with unwashed hands. Because it was the tradition of the Pharisees to wash their hands in a special way, holding the tradition of the elders, they immediately found fault with the disciples.

Unfortunately, we, too, can be as critical of others as the scribes and Pharisees. Too often, when others believe differently than we do, our first response is to criticize him or her. We become their judge and jury without knowing all the facts, or understanding what they believe.

It is important we remember we came to Christ desperate and lost, in need of a Savior,

> He also brought me up out of a horrible pit,
> Out of the miry clay,
> And set my feet upon a rock,
> *And* established my steps. —Psalm 40:2

not because we have done anything to earn our salvation.

> For by grace you have been saved through faith,
> and that not of yourselves, *it is* the gift of God,
> not of works, lest anyone should boast. —Ephesians 2:8

Christ warns against being judgmental toward others,

> *Judge not, that you be not judged.*
> *For with what judgment you judge,*
> *you will be judged;*
> *and with the measure you use,*
> *it will be measured back to you.* —Matthew 7:1-2

The next time we are tempted to judge another, let's share Jesus instead. Just as we needed a Savior before coming to Christ, they too, are in need of a Savior. May we never forget, "But for the grace of God, there go I," and share with them the same grace and mercy Christ has shown us.

> For all have sinned and fall short
> of the glory of God. —Romans 3:23

See, I have inscribed you
on the palms of *My hands;*
Your walls are continually before Me.

Isaiah 49:16

"Father, how much do you
love me?" I asked.
"This much!" He replied,
And He stretched out
His arms and died.

He Knows Your Name

Isaiah 49:16

See, I have inscribed you on the palms of *My hands;*
Your walls are continually before Me.

Life holds so many ups and downs. It seems all can be well one moment and with just a phone call, doctor's appointment, or unexpected financial crisis, our world comes crashing down around us. Jesus warned this would happen.

> *In this world you will have tribulation;*
> *but be of good cheer, I have overcome the world.* —John 16:33

When these times come we need to remember Jesus is beside us, more than able to comfort and care for us.

> God *is* our refuge and strength,
> A very present help in trouble. —Psalm 46:1

He knew us before we were born,

> For You formed my inward parts;
> You covered me in my mother's womb.
> I will praise You, for I am fearfully
> *and* wonderfully made; marvelous are Your works,
> And *that* my soul knows very well. —Psalm 139:13-14

And He promises He will always be with us.

> Can a woman forget her nursing child,
> And not have compassion on the son of her womb?
> Surely they may forget, yet I will not forget you. —Isaiah 49:15

> Even to *your* old age, I *am* He,
> And *even* to gray hairs, I will carry *you!*
> I have made, and I will bear;
> Even I will carry, and will deliver *you.* —Isaiah 46:4

What are you facing today that is too heavy for you to carry? Will you give it to your Father? He loves you with an everlasting love.

> "Father, how much do you love me?" I asked.
> *"This much!"* He replied,
> And He stretched out His arms and died.

If You, LORD, should mark iniquities,
O Lord, who could stand?
But *there is* forgiveness with You,
That you may be feared.

Psalm 130:3-4

"But."

It's amazing how one small
word can change everything.

But

Psalm 130:3-4

If You, LORD, should mark iniquities,
O Lord, who could stand?
But *there is* forgiveness with You,
That you may be feared.

As I read these Scriptures, the word "but" seemed to jump off the page. I thought about where I would be if not for the three letter word, "but." *But there is forgiveness* with the Lord. Instead of being sentenced to a life of rejection, shame, and guilt, I am forgiven, accepted into the family of God.

Many places in the Word of God the Lord instructs us to not do one thing, but do another;

Be anxious for nothing, *but* in everything by prayer and supplication, with thanksgiving, let your requests be made known to God; and the peace of God which surpasses all understanding will guard your hearts and minds through Christ Jesus.   —Phil 4:6-7

> If any of you lacks wisdom, let him ask of God, who gives to all liberally and without reproach, and it will be given to him. But let him ask in faith, with no doubting, for he who doubts is like a wave of the sea driven and tossed by the wind.   —James 1:5-6

> Therefore gird up the loins of your mind, be sober, and rest *your* hope fully upon the grace that is to be brought to you at the revelation of Jesus Christ; as obedient children, not conforming yourselves to the former lusts *as* in your ignorance; *but* as He who called you *is* holy, you also be holy in *your* conduct, because it is written, *"Be Holy, for I am holy."*
> —1 Peter 1:13-16

"But." It's amazing how one small word can change everything.

> "This book of the Law shall not depart from your mouth, *but* you shall meditate in it day and night, that you may observe to do according to all that is written in it. For then you will make your way prosperous, and then you will have good success.   —Joshua 1:8

> For God has not given us a spirit of fear, *but* of power and of love and of a sound mind.   —2 Timothy 1:7

Finally, my brethren,
be strong in the Lord
and in the power of His might.
Ephesians 6:10

When we are faced
with a trial,
we can be assured
this didn't catch
God by surprise.

Strong

Ephesians 6:10

Finally, my brethren, be strong in the Lord
and in the power of His might.

Having coffee with my friend, we were discussing the many trials she has dealt with during her lifetime. I commented how through it all she has exhibited such peace. With that she smiled and said, "It makes you strong. I have complete confidence I can rest in God."

This made me think about my life, trials I have endured. As I have faced different painful experiences in my life, I have come to know it is only through leaning on Jesus that I am able to bear what seems like the impossible. As hard as the trial may be, on the other side (yes, there is always the other side – Praise God!) – I realize, "I wouldn't want to go through the trial again, but wouldn't trade for the world what I have learned about the faithfulness of God because of it." Through the trial, the Lord draws me to Himself, and as only He can, places purpose in the pain.

When we are faced with a trial, we can be assured this didn't catch God by surprise. He was there before the affliction, and He will be there to walk through the heartache with us. We can walk in confidence as we rest in Him.

> "My brethren count it all joy when you fall into various trials, knowing that the testing of your faith produces patience, But let patience have *its* perfect work, that you may be perfect and complete, lacking nothing. —James 1:2-4

> The LORD is good, a stronghold in the day of trouble; and He knows those who trust in Him. —Nahum 1:7

> Blessed *is* the man who trusts in the LORD,
> And whose hope is the LORD. —Jeremiah 17:7

> Let us therefore come boldly to the throne of grace, that we may obtain mercy and find grace to help in time of need. —Hebrews 4:16

> "In quietness and confidence shall be your strength." —Isaiah 30:15

And they were astonished beyond measure,
saying, "He has done all things well.
He makes both the deaf to hear
and the mute to speak.

Mark 7:37

His ways were perfect
in the beginning—
they will be perfect to the end.

All Things Well

Mark 7:37

And they were astonished beyond measure, saying,
"He has done all things well. He makes both the
deaf to hear and the mute to speak."

As Jesus came to the Sea of Galilee, the people brought Him one who was deaf and slow in speech. Begging Jesus to heal him, they longed for Him to put His hand on their friend. The Scriptures continue;

> And looking up to heaven, He sighed, and said to him, *"Ephphatha,"* that is, *"Be opened."* Immediately his ears were opened, and the impediment of his tongue was loosed, and he spoke plainly.
> —Mark 7: 34-35

As Jesus healed their friend, the people were amazed. They couldn't believe He had answered their request. This made me wonder; did they bring him to Jesus with wishful thinking, expectations they didn't really think possible, or did they bring him to Jesus because they had heard of the many healings He had done?

When we pray, asking Jesus for a miracle, are we astonished when He answers? Those bringing their friend to Jesus proclaimed, "He has done all things well," because their friend was healed. What if Jesus hadn't healed him? Would they still be willing to say He does all things well?

Are we willing to put our total confidence in Jesus always doing all things well, even if it isn't as we hoped it would be? We can rest knowing Jesus always answers our prayers. Sometimes He answers with yes, giving us what we have prayed for. Sometimes He says no, because He knows it is not what is best. And sometimes He simply asks us to wait. Whatever the answer, we can trust the sovereignty of our Lord. Jesus never changes. His ways were perfect in the beginning; they will be perfect to the end.

Jesus Christ *is* the same yesterday, today, and forever.   —Hebrews 13:8

Casting all your care upon Him, for He cares for you.   —1 Peter 5:7

When we can't trace His hand, may we trust His heart.

Make Peace

James 3:18

Now the fruit of righteousness
is sown in peace
by those who make peace.

As I read this Scripture, I understood only as we sow peace will we display righteousness. What I didn't understand is how it's possible to make peace. How are we to respond in difficult situations so that we exhibit peace in the midst of turmoil?

Pursue peace with all *people*, and holiness, without which no one
will see the Lord.   —Hebrews 12:14

If it is possible, as much as depends on you, live peaceably with
all men.   —Romans 12:18

Therefore let us pursue the things *which make* for peace and the
things by which one may edify another.   —Romans 14:19

A soft word turns away wrath, but a harsh word stirs up anger.
                                                         —Proverbs 15:1
Let the Word of God dwell in you richly in all wisdom.
                                                         —Colossians 3:16

To make peace means to respond to difficult situations with a Christ like attitude.

Surely, I have calmed and quieted my soul. Like a weaned child with
his mother; like a weaned child *is* my soul within me.   —Psalm 131:2

In quietness and confidence shall be your strength.   —Isaiah 30:15

The work of righteousness will be peace. And the effect of
righteousness, quietness and assurance forever.   —Isaiah 32:17

Yes, it is possible for us to make peace. As we respond to one another in quietness of soul, knowing God will take care of the situation, we will make peace and display the fruit of righteousness. Oh Lord, may it be!

Let the words of my mouth and the meditation of my heart be
acceptable in Your sight, O Lord my strength and Redeemer.
                                                         —Psalm 19:14

"Therefore, whatever you want men to do to you, do also to them."

Matthew 7:12

Christ showed us ultimate
grace when as sinners
He called us to Himself.

Grace

Matthew 7:12

"Therefore, whatever you want men to do to you, do also to them."

Jesus stood on the mount teaching the multitudes. Preparing to finish speaking He addressed one last subject,

> *"For with what judgment you judge, you will be judged; and with the measure you use, it will be measured back to you."* —Matthew 7:2

How easy it is for us to look at others and find fault. Jesus warned strongly against such an attitude;

> *"And why do you look at the speck in your brother's eye,*
> *But do not consider the plank in your own eye?*
> *" Or how can you say to your brother, "Let me remove the speck from your eye"; and look a plank is in your own eye?*
> *"Hypocrite! First remove the plank from your own eye, and then you will see clearly to remove the speck from your brother's eye."* —Matthew 7:3-5

He is warning that while we find insignificant fault with others, the fact is we our judging causes us to have fault the size of a plank in our lives.

We want to be treated with respect, as a person with value. When we are hurting, kindness and compassion by others means so much. When our ideas or opinions differ from others', what we want is for them to give us opportunity to explain why we think or feel the way we do.

Is this how we treat others? Do we treat them with respect, with the value their lives deserve? Are we kind and compassionate? When their opinions or ideas differ from ours, do we give them an opportunity to explain?

Christ showed us ultimate grace when as sinners he called us to Himself. In exchange for judgment, may we be willing to give others the grace that has so freely been given to us.

> *"Judge not, that you be not judged."* —Matthew 7:1

> *"And just as you want men to do to you, you also do to them likewise."* —Luke 6:31

But He sighed deeply in His spirit, and said,
"Why does this generation seek a sign?
Assuredly, I say to you, no sign shall be given
to this generation."

Mark 8:12

May we be willing to rest
instead of test our Lord,
confident of who He is.

Rest in Him

Mark 8:12

But He sighed deeply in His spirit, and said,
*"Why does this generation seek a sign? Assuredly, I say to you,
no sign shall be given to this generation."*

After feeding four thousand with just seven loaves of bread and a few small fish, Jesus and the disciples left the multitudes to go to Dalmanautha. Upon arriving at their destination, the Pharisees came out and began disputing with Jesus, testing Him and seeking a sign from heaven.

Jesus had done miracle after miracle, yet the Pharisees continued to ask for a sign of who He was. Do we do the same? When we are facing a heartache, trial, or an impossible situation, do we test God? Do we question whether He will be there for us? We know Jesus has always been there in the past, but is this time going to be different?

Jesus longs for us to rest in Him, regardless of what we are facing. He yearns for us to walk in such faith that we know regardless of the outcome, our Abba Father is taking care of us. May we be willing to rest instead of test our Lord, confident of who He is.

Throughout Scripture He implores us to rest in Him, our portion forever.

My soul finds rest in God alone;
my salvation comes from Him.   —Psalm 62:1(NIV)

He will not allow your foot to be moved;
He who keeps you will not slumber.   —Psalm 121:3

Therefore do not cast away your confidence, which has
great reward.   —Hebrews 10:35

My flesh and my heart fail;
But God *is* the strength of my heart and my portion forever.
                                                                    —Psalm 73:26

You will keep *him* in perfect peace *whose* mind *is* stayed *on You*,
Because he trusts in You.   —Isaiah 26:3

I have set the LORD continually before me;
Because *He is* at my right hand, I will not be shaken.
                                                                    —Psalm 16:8

"For whoever desires to save his life
will lose it,
But whoever loses his life
for My sake and the gospel's will save it."

Mark 8:35

When we live our life for Christ,
it matters little where
He calls us.
What matters is we are in
the will of our Father.

The Exchanged Life

Mark 8:35

For whoever desires to save his life will lose it,
But whoever loses his life for My sake and the gospel's will save it.

Jesus taught the disciples that if they were to be His true followers, they must be willing to die to their worldly desires. No longer should they live for a life of luxury, nor a place of prominence. They must be willing to follow Christ wherever He might lead, regardless of the life He had for them.

We live in a world where we are told, "the sky is the limit," "plan your work and work your plan," "if it is to be, it is up to me," and "if you can dream it you can do it." What are we to think when Jesus tells us we must lose our life, letting go of our own dreams and desires? How, we wonder, will we amount to anything or make a difference in this world if we die to our own ambitions?

Jesus went on to tell the crowd gathered about;

> *For what will it profit a man if he gains the whole world, and*
> *loses his own soul? Or what will a man give in exchange for his soul?*
> —Mark 8:36-37

As followers of Christ, our greatest desire should be to live for Him. How many times have we heard others say, or possibly said ourselves, "If I only knew what I am supposed to do for Jesus." When Jesus tells us to lose our life for His sake, it is because He has a plan for our life. When we surrender our life, He will lead us into a life of fulfillment beyond what we could have thought possible. He alone knows the true desire of our heart. When we live our life for Christ, it matters little where He calls us. What matters is we are in the will of our Father.

> But now, O LORD,
> You *are* our Father;
> We *are* the clay, and You our potter;
> And all we *are* the work of You hand. —Isaiah 64:8

> Take me,
> Mold me
> Use Me,
> Fill me,
> I give my life to the Potter's Hand.
>
> —*The Potter's Hand* by Hillsong

But they did not understand this saying,
and were afraid to ask Him.

Mark 9:32

The Lord wants us to ask.
And in our asking,
trust His answer.

Trust

Mark 9:32

But they did not understand this saying,
and were afraid to ask Him.

Jesus and the disciples were passing through Galilee when He said to them,

'The Son of Man is being betrayed into the hands of men, and they will kill Him. And after He is killed, He will rise the third day."
—Mark 9:31

The Scriptures tell us the disciples didn't understand what Jesus was telling them, but were afraid to ask what He meant. How could they understand? To think Jesus would be crucified on a cross and rise the third day would be more than any of us could comprehend.

Have you ever been faced with circumstances you didn't understand, but were afraid to come to Jesus for guidance or understanding for fear of what He might tell you?

As I thought about why they would be afraid to ask Jesus what He meant, I thought about times I haven't wanted to ask Jesus, fearing He would give me an answer I didn't want to hear. When my husband wanted to downsize and sell our home where we had raised our five children—I was devastated. I had no desire to sell our home, filled with so many wonderful memories. As much as I knew my husband was right, I wanted my way more than I wanted to do what was right. I begged the Lord to change my husband's mind. Nevertheless, our home sold in six weeks. As I sat crying before the Lord, asking why He would allow this to happen, He assured me as I trusted Him, I would understand. That wasn't the answer I wanted to hear. We are on the other side now. The Lord has healed my broken heart and given me more than I could have imagined. God can be trusted regardless of His answers.

Had the disciples asked Jesus to explain, I wonder if His dying on the cross would have been less painful, as He explained what He meant when He said He would rise the third day. The Lord wants us to ask. And in our asking, trust His answer.

"Call to Me, and I will answer you, and show you great and mighty things, which you do not know." —Jeremiah 33:3

"Get behind me, Satan!
For you are not mindful of the things of God,
but the things of men."

Mark 8:33

May we rest, knowing
He is in control.

Get behind Me Satan

Mark 8:33

"Get behind Me, Satan!
For you are not mindful of the things of God,
but the things of men."

As Jesus and the disciples walked along the road, Jesus began explaining to them how He was about to suffer many things, and that the scribes and chief priests would reject Him, turning Him over to the Jews to be killed, but that after three days He would rise again.

Unable to accept the words of Jesus, Peter began reprimanding Him. Turning around and looking at the disciples, Jesus rebuked Peter.

He rebuked Peter, saying,

> *"Get behind Me, Satan! For you are not mindful of the things of God,*
> *but the things of men."* —Mark 8:33

Because Peter could not accept what Jesus was saying, his immediate reaction was to question Him. As I read this, I thought about how often we respond in the same way. When our world is falling apart, we look at the situation through our own carnal eyes. Just as Peter was determined to take control of the situation, we react in the same way.

> For to be carnally minded *is* death,
> but to be spiritually minded *is* life and peace. —Romans 8:6

If Peter had considered how Jesus had always been there for him, and how much He loved him, he would have been able to rest instead of react. When we face impossible situations, we need to remember the same.

We see the situation through our carnal eyes and what we know today, Christ sees all our tomorrows. He knows what is best for our lives today and forever. This makes all the difference. May we rest, knowing He is in control.

> "For My thoughts *are* not your thoughts,
> *Nor are* your ways My ways," says the Lord.
> For as the heavens are higher than the earth,
> So are My ways higher than your ways,
> And My thoughts than your thoughts. —Isaiah 55:8-9

"Whoever receives one of these little children in My name receives Me; and whoever receives Me, receives not Me but Him who sent Me."

Mark 9:37

Walking with Christ becomes more amazing with each new day. May we live our lives in a way worthy of His love.

God In You

Mark 9:37

*"Whoever receives one of these little children in
My name receives Me; and whoever receives Me,
receives not Me but Him who sent Me."*

After a wonderful weekend of teaching at the Billy Graham Training Center,
a precious staff member approached me:

"Do you know God loves you as much as He loves His own Son?" she
asked.

What," I protested. "How could that be?"

"It's true," she continued, "read John 17:23."

I hurried to my room and opened my Bible.

*"I in them, and You in Me; that they may be made perfect in one,
and that the world may know that You have sent Me, and have
loved them as You have loved Me."* —John 17:23

She was right! God does love me as much as He loves Jesus. As a parent, I
love my children with a different love than my love for others. They are precious to me in a way no others could ever be. I always thought that was how
it was with God. I have never doubted His love, I knew He loved me with a
never ending love. However, I thought it was a love much like I have for
others. Not so. As Jesus bowed in prayer before His Father, He spoke words
hard to fathom:

"You have sent Me, and have loved them as You have loved me."

As I read the Words in Mark 9:37:

"Whoever receives Me, receives not Me but Him who sent Me."

...it confirmed what I knew, but had not considered. When we accept Christ
as our Personal Savior, we accept God the Father as well as Jesus His Son.
We become one in *Them:*

*"That they all may be one as You, Father, are in Me, and I in You; that they
also may be one in Us, that the world may believe that You sent Me.
"And the glory which You gave Me I have given them, that they may be one
just as We are one."* —John 17:21-22

Walking with Christ becomes more amazing each and every day. May we
live our lives in a way worthy of His love.

"For whoever gives you a cup of water to drink
in My name,
because you belong to Christ, assuredly
I say to you, he will be no means
lose his reward."

Mark 9:41

What if we lived each day
with one desire;
to show the love of
Jesus to others?

In My Name

Mark 9:41

"For whoever gives you a cup of water to drink
in My name,
because you belong to Christ, assuredly,
I say to you, he will by no means lose his reward."

As I read this portion of Scripture, the words "in My name," jumped off the page. My first thought was, "How often do I bless others with kindness to show them the love of Jesus? What is my motive for being helpful?" As I contemplated this, I realized I had never thought of my actions as being a blessing in the name of Jesus. I simply thought I was just being a blessing. What a privilege we have been given to be an example of the love of Christ with our actions, attitude, and lifestyle.

Let your light so shine before men, that they may see your good works
and glorify your Father in Heaven. —Matthew 5:16

We have been given the opportunity to live our life through the love of Christ, be His hands and feet:

How beautiful upon the mountains
Are the feet of him who brings good news,
Who proclaims peace,
Who brings glad tidings of good things,
Who says to Zion,
"Your God reigns!" —Isaiah 52:7

My husband came to the Lord because he witnessed in the life of a friend peace in the midst of heartache. A peace my husband did not know. When he asked him how he could be so calm when it appeared his world was falling apart, his friend knelt by the couch with my husband and introduced him to Jesus.

We live in a world of hurting people. Without Christ they live with little peace and a life of uncertainty. What if we lived each day with one desire; to show the love of Jesus to others? Giving those whose life we touch a cup of water "in His name," just may cause him or her to ask, as my husband asked his friend, "What is it you have?" And we, too, may have the opportunity to kneel by our couch and introduce him or her to Jesus. Could there be a greater honor?

"Salt is good, but if the salt loses its flavor, how will you season it? Have salt in yourselves, and have peace with one another."

Mark 9:50

Only by living a Christ centered life will we bring flavor to a crooked and perverse generation, and change the world for His glory.

Salt in Yourselves

Mark 9:50

"Salt is good, but if the salt loses its flavor,
how will you season it?
Have salt in yourselves, and have peace
with one another."

As Jesus taught the disciples, explaining to them once again of His death and resurrection, He needed them to understand the importance of living as the salt of the earth. It would be the difference in changing the world for His glory, or blending into a world filled with despair.

"You are the light of the world.
A city that is set on a hill cannot be hidden." —Matthew 5:14

As believers, we have a responsibility to live our lives differently than the world. As salt brings out flavor in food, and as light removes the darkness, we are to live our lives as Jesus lived.

Do all things without complaining and disputing, that you
may become blameless and harmless, children of God without
fault in the midst of a crooked and perverse generation, among
whom you shine as lights in the world. —Philippians 2:14-15

If it is possible, as much as depends on you, live peaceably with
all men. —Romans 12:18

Do not be overcome by evil, but overcome evil with good.
—Romans 12:21

The world notices when our response to difficult situations is to show the love of Jesus rather than react in a way they would expect. Only by living a Christ centered life will we bring flavor to a crooked and perverse generation, and change the world for His glory.

But sanctify the Lord God in your hearts, and always *be* ready
to *give* a defense to everyone who asks you a reason for the hope
that is in you, with meekness and fear —1 Peter 3:15

Let your light so shine before men, that they may see your good works
and glorify your Father in heaven. —Matthew 5:16

Why are you cast down, O my soul?
And why are you disquieted within me?
Hope in God, for I shall yet praise Him
For the help of His countenance.

Psalm 42:5

What does it say?

What does it mean?

What does it mean to me

personally?

Hope in God

Psalm 42:5

Why are you cast down, O my soul?
And *why* are you disquieted within me?
Hope in God, for I shall yet praise Him
For the help of His countenance.

This devotional is personal—I accidently deleted thirteen devotionals. When I discovered what I had done my heart sank, my enthusiasm waned, and my soul was totally cast down. As much as I knew I needed to pick myself up and begin again, I couldn't get past what I had done.

As I read this Scripture in my daily devotional, I knew it was not by accident it was there. I needed to ask the three questions:

1. What does it say?
2. What does it mean?
3. What does it mean to me personally?

This Scripture asks why David is cast down, his soul disquieted within him. It then tells him what to do; hope in God, praise Him for His help.

I knew why I was discouraged, cast down—my devotionals were gone. However, I then realized what I was to do about it. I was to put my hope in God, instead of the defeat I felt in trying to rewrite the lost devotionals. And I was to praise God for the help He would give me as I wrote anew.

The lesson I learned was that writing these devotionals isn't about getting them written, but the lessons I am learning as I write. I was looking toward the finished product, while God wanted me to cherish the time spent with Him. What a blessing to know God desires my time spent at His feet.

If you are discouraged, afraid, confused, or fearful, ask the Lord to give you a Scripture. Ask the three questions as you sit at His feet, and allow Him to speak to you as only He can. You will truly be blessed.

> Though the fig tree may not blossom, nor fruit be on the vines;
> Though the labor of the olive may fail, and the fields yield no food;
> Though the flock my be cut off from the fold, and there shall be no
> herd in stalls —Yet I will rejoice in the LORD, I will joy in the God of
> my salvation.
>
> —Habakkuk 3:17-18

*"Assuredly, I say to you,
whoever does not receive the kingdom of God
as a little child will by no means enter in."*

Mark 10:15

If the Bible told me
Jesus loves me,
then I believed
Jesus loves me.

The Bible Tells Me So

Mark 10:15

"Assuredly, I say to you,
whoever does not receive the kingdom of God
as a little child will by no means enter in."

Where were you the first time you heard this song?

> Jesus loves me this I know
> For the Bible tells me so
> Little ones to Him belong
> We are weak, but He is strong
>
> Yes, Jesus loves me
> Yes, Jesus loves me
> Yes, Jesus loves me
> The Bible tells me so.   —William Batchelder Bradbury

I was in my first Sunday School Class, surrounded by other little people, sitting in our miniature chairs facing the teacher. I still remember the arm movements, and when we sang "strong" all the little boys flexing what they thought looked like muscles. As we sang "Jesus Loves Me," it never entered my mind not to believe those words. If the Bible told me Jesus loves me, then I believed Jesus loves me.

As adults, Jesus wants us to live with this same child like faith. He knows as the responsibilities of adulthood come upon us we find weakness in our own abilities, limitations we never thought possible, and demands beyond what we ever imagined. However, in the midst of these places He wants us to remember; He is stronger than our greatest weakness.

> He gives power to the weak,
> And to *those who have* no might He increases strength.
>   —Isaiah 40:29

When we are faced with loneliness, despair, or fear of what lies ahead, His desire is that we remember to whom we belong.

> Do not be afraid nor dismayed because of this great multitude,
> for the battle *is* not yours, but God's. —2 Chronicles 20:15

"Jesus loves me this I know, for the Bible tells me so." May these words be as real to us today as they were the first time we sang them.

And the Passover of the Jews was near,
and many went from the country
up to Jerusalem before the Passover,
to purify themselves.
John 11:55

There is nothing more
important than being
clean before my Lord.

Purify Yourself

John 11:55

And the Passover of the Jews was near,
and many went from the country
up to Jerusalem before the Passover,
to purify themselves.

The Feast of the Passover was drawing near and following the commands of the Jewish faith, they must be purified before attending.

Although we no longer go through a purification process before coming to the Lord, in the same way the Jews purified themselves by the washing of their hands, we are to come with a humble and surrendered spirit. When we allow the Holy Spirit to look into our innermost parts, revealing to us the errors of our ways, and with a repentant heart ask for forgiveness, we are asking Him to purify us.

"Search me, O God, and know my heart;
Try me, and know my anxieties;
And see if *there is any* wicked way in me,
And lead me in the way everlasting."   —Psalm 139:23

As I pondered this Scripture I asked myself, "How willing am I to invite the Lord into the secret places of my heart, the places where I hold forgiveness from another person? Am I willing to admit jealousy because of another person's position or prosperity? How willing am I to surrender my heart to Christ, willing to let Him search me, see if there be any wicked way in me?" These were hard questions to consider, but ones I knew must be asked if I was to live a life totally surrendered and purified before the Lord.

Just as purification was a process of cleansing in the Old Testament, as we surrender our hearts to Christ, we are purified through Him.

With a desire to be clean before the Lord, I bowed my head in humility, and cried out to Him, "Search me, O God, and know my heart that I may live totally surrendered, purified before You!" There is nothing more important than being clean before my Lord.

The sacrifices of God *are* a broken spirit,
A broken and surrendered heart
These, O God, You will not despise.   —Psalm 51:17

Casting all your care upon Him,
for He cares for You.

1 Peter 5:7

"I do not play tug-a-war."

Tug-a-War

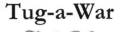

1 Peter 5:7

Casting all your care upon Him,
for He cares for you.

As I was pondering this Scripture, the word "all" stood out among the rest. The Lord is telling us to cast not just some of our care, but all our care upon Him. He wants the care we feel we can handle, the care that seems impossible, and the care that tears at our heartstrings, threatening to rob us of our peace.

I will never forget going through a particularly hard time in my life. After crying until I was exhausted, I finally fell asleep. In a dream I saw the Lord walking up to me with a big white box. As He held the box out to me, He gently said, *"Cyndy, put everything that has to do with this situation in the box."* I remember putting harsh words spoken and shattered relationships into the box. Then I put the lid on the box and handed it back to Him. As Jesus took the box from me, He took the lid off, and with compassion said to me, *"I said put all that has to do with the situation in the box. You have only put some."* He wanted total commitment; I put myself in the box. As He took the box back He looked at me and spoke these words;

> *"This is the situation. If you will let me have it, I promise to take care of this heartache for you. But, I do not play tug-a-war. If you reach for the box I will let go and let you have it. Just know, if you take it back, there is nothing I can do. Either you will have the box, or I will. If you want me to fix it, give me the box."*

Then I woke up. Nothing had changed. The heartache was as real as it had been before falling asleep. But, I knew what I must do. I must give it all to Jesus. From that point on I hung onto His words, *"I do not play tug-a-war,"* as I kept giving the heartache back to Him. True to His promise, and in His perfect way, He brought peace in the midst of turmoil, and joy unspeakable back into my life.

Only as we are willing to put everything in the box and hand it all to Jesus will we find the peace we so desperately need. How important it is to remember; Jesus knows how to take care of our needs, we only think we know how. As we hand our heartache to Him, He will take what looks impossible to us, and use it for our good and for His glory.

O LORD of hosts, blessed is the man who trusts in You! —Psalm 84:12

Jesus said, *"Take away the stone."*
Martha, the sister of him who was dead,
said to Him,
"Lord, by this time there is a stench,
for he has been dead four days."
Jesus said to her,
*"Did I not say to you that if you would believe
you will see the glory of God?"*

John 11:39-40

Could it be, as we roll away

out stone, we too,

will see the glory of God?

Without Doubt

John 11:39-40

Jesus said, *"Take away the stone."*
Martha, the sister of him who was dead, said to Him,
"Lord, by this time there is a stench, for he has been dead four days."
Jesus said to her,
"Did I not say to you that if you would believe you will see the glory of God?"

Four days before Jesus came to the home of Mary and Martha, their brother Lazarus had died. When Jesus told Martha to take away the stone, she immediately began explaining to Jesus why this couldn't possibly be the right thing to do.

Does this sound familiar? Do we, as His children, question what it is He asks us to do? Like Martha, do we explain to Him why what He is asking us to do couldn't possibly be the answer?

He tells us to bless those who persecute us; we resent them.
He tells us to commit our works to Him, let Him establish our thoughts;
    we try to figure life out on my own.
He tells us to cast our burdens on Him; we carry them around with us,
    allowing them to weigh heavy on our heart.
He tells us to be anxious for nothing; we worry.

God's promises for our obedience are endless, providing what we long for; peace, direction, hope, and a calmness in our soul. Could this be what Jesus meant when He said,

> *"The thief does not come except to steal, and to kill, and to destroy. I have come that they may have life, and that they may have it more abundantly."*
> —John 10:10

Have we allowed the enemy of our soul to steal, kill, and destroy all Jesus died on the cross to give us? When our response to His leading is to explain to Him why His ways couldn't possibly be the answer, either by our actions or our response to Him, are we missing out on the abundant life?

Martha rolled away the stone, and as Jesus promised, they saw the glory of God as Lazarus was raised from the dead. Could it be, as we roll away our stone, we too, will see the glory of God? Let's be willing to trust the Lord and roll away our stone. He has so much for us.

"I have come that they may have life, and that they may have it more abundantly."

Be still, and know that I am God;

Psalm 46:10

May we not just be still,
but just be,
that Christ may live.

Just Be

Psalm 46:10

Be still, and know that I *am* God;

My girlfriend left a message on my voicemail sharing she had listened to a sermon about how we are to be still, but not just be still, but just be. I knew this message was for me.

God doesn't need us to always be doing. He longs for us to be still, sit at His feet, be a Mary instead of a Martha. As Mary sat at Jesus' feet, captivated by all He was teaching, Martha hurried about with much to do. When she asked Jesus to tell Mary to help her, Jesus gently rebuked her.

> *"Martha, Martha, you are worried and troubled about many things.*
> *But one thing is needed, and Mary has chosen that good part, which*
> *will not be taken away from her."* —Luke 10:41-42

Every time I read this portion of Scripture I can hear Jesus saying to me, *"Cyndy, Cyndy, you are always so busy with things you think are important. Won't you come sit and let me share with you what is really important? I have so much to teach you."* When I try to think of what I feel is so important that I should allow it to take away time with Christ, I can't think of anything. It is the God of the universe who desires for me to sit with Him. What could be more important than that?

I heard a Christian speaker define "abiding" as sitting at the feet of Jesus with a heart to obey. We have an invitation to sit at the feet of Jesus, get to know Him as our loving Father, grow in our dependence on Him, and give Him more of ourselves with each passing day. How foolish for us to always be doing. "Be still and know that I am God." May we not just be still, but just be, that Christ may live.

> *"Abide in Me, and I in you. As the branch cannot bear fruit of itself,*
> *unless it abides in the vine, neither can you, unless you abide in Me."*
> —John 15:4

> *When You said,* "Seek My face."
> My heart said to You,
> "Your face, LORD, I will seek." —Psalm 27:8

> For to me, to live *is* Christ, and to die *is* gain. —Philippians 1:21

And the disciples were astonished at His words.
But Jesus answered again and said to them,
"Children, how hard it is for those
who trust in riches
to enter the kingdom of God!!"

Mark 10:24

We are children of the
King of Kings
and Lord of Lords.
Do we live that way?

His Children

Mark 10:24

And the disciples were astonished at His words.
But Jesus answered again and said to them,
*"Children, how hard it is for those who trust in riches
to enter the kingdom of God!"*

As I read this Scripture, what caught my attention was Jesus referring to His disciples as His children.

I thought of my children, the love I have for them, my constant concern for their safety and well being. Regardless of where they may be, my heart is always with them. How humbling to know the love I have for my children fades in comparison to the love my Heavenly Father has for me.

I thought of what I desire from my children. First of all, I desire love and respect. I want my children to feel free to call me regardless of what they are facing, knowing I will help them in anyway I can.

Knowing I am My Father's child, I pondered, "Do I give My Father the love and respect I desire from my children? Do I live as a daughter who knows He is always there for me?"

I thought of how much I miss my children when I don't hear from them as often as I would like. This made me wonder, "Does My Father miss me when I think I'm too busy for Him?" I'm sure He does.

My greatest longing is that my children will fall in love with Jesus and live in obedience to Him. Again I asked myself, "Am I that child to My Father? Do I live in obedience to His teachings?"

As children of Our Father, we have a responsibility to be the children He desires for us to be. We are children of the King of King and Lord of Lords. Do we live that way? Love, respect, obedience, and devotion, is this what my Father finds in me? "Oh, Lord, that it would be."

> The Spirit Himself bears witness with our spirit
> that we are children of God.   —Romans 8:16

> But as many as received Him, to them He gave the right
> to become children of God, to those who believe in
> His name.   —John 1:12

"Peace I leave with you, My peace I give you;
not as the world gives do I give to you.
Let not your heart be troubled,
neither let it be afraid."

John 14:27

With each step you take,
each heartache you face,
when you cannot walk,
He will carry you.

My Peace

John 14:27

"Peace I leave with you, My peace I give you;
not as the world gives do I give to you.
Let not your heart be troubled, neither let it be afraid."

Jesus and the disciples had gathered in the Upper Room before the crucifixion of Christ. Having finished supper, Jesus stood, and pouring water into a basin, began washing the feet of the disciples. It was in this setting Jesus began explaining to His disciples what was about to happen. He wanted them to understand this would not be the end, but only the beginning.

"Peace I leave with You, My peace I give you; not as the world gives do I give you," He spoke to His disciples. Regardless of the unrest all about, in Him they could have peace.

So often we base our peace on what is happening in our lives. A family member becomes ill and we lose our peace. In its place we become fearful of what lies ahead. A financial crisis comes crashing into our life and our peace is immediately replaced with worry of how we will pay our bills. We struggle with a rebellious child and begin asking why.

Just as Jesus told His disciples in the midst of their despair, He tells us, *"My peace I give you, not as the world gives do I give to you"*. Because His peace is based on who He is, not on our circumstances, we can rest in Him, regardless of what is happening in our lives.

"Let not your heart be troubled, neither let it be afraid." How? By resting in the only One who has the answer for what lies ahead. You are not alone today, you will not be alone tomorrow. With each step you take, each heartache you face, when you cannot walk, He will carry you.

> You will keep Him in perfect peace,
> *Whose* mind is stayed *on You,*
> Because he trusts in You.
> Trust in the LORD forever
> For in YAH, the LORD, is everlasting strength. —Isaiah 26:3-4

> The LORD will give strength to His people;
> The LORD will bless His people with peace. —Psalm 29:11

Your ears shall hear a word
behind you, saying,
"This *is* the way, walk in it,"
Whenever you turn to the right hand
Or whenever you turn to the left.

Isaiah 30:21

When we feel lost,
may we follow His map.
We can trust the Lord to
lead us in the way
we should go.

Holy Navigation

Isaiah 30:21

Your ears shall hear a word
behind you, saying,
"This *is* the way, walk in it."
Whenever you turn to the right hand
Or whenever you turn to the left.

Sitting in church Sunday morning, I was listening to the young people tell about their youth summer camping trip. They were told to leave their cell phones and all other electronics home; this was going to be a week of discovering God in their lives. When asked about their favorite day, many spoke of the day of solitude when they were left in a place of isolation with only a Bible and a notepad. During this time they were told to spend time in God's Word.

The lessons they learned were invaluable. One teenager shared how God showed him the Bible is like a map when taking a trip. If we will continue to follow the map, although we may not see where it is leading, we will eventually get to our destination.

As we travel this road called life, we all face times of uncertainty. Everything can be going along as we planned, we feel in complete control, and then in an instant, with an unexpected phone call, diagnosis, or broken relationship, we feel we have lost our way.

When we are lost, regardless of the reason, we have the assurance, as we cry out to the Lord, He will once again set our feet upon the Rock.

> For in the time of trouble
> He shall hide me in His pavilion;
> In the secret place of His tabernacle
> He shall hide me;
> He shall set me high upon a rock. —Psalm 27:5

> *I would have lost heart,* unless I had believed
> That I would see the goodness of the LORD
> In the land of the living. —Psalm 27:13

When we feel lost, may we follow His map. We can trust the Lord to lead us in the way we should go.

> Your ears shall hear a word behind you saying,
> "This is the way, walk in it." —Isaiah 30:21

*For to me, to live *is* Christ,*
and to die is gain.

Philippians 1:21

Paul knew letting Christ
have His way in his life,
allowing Him to *be* his life,
was finding true freedom.

Alive In Christ

Philippians 1:21

For to me, to live *is* Christ,
and to die is gain.

Paul was in prison, a place from which most people would desperately want to escape. Not so for Paul. He saw this as an opportunity to praise His Lord, share Christ with others.

> But I want you to know, brethren, that the things
> *which happened* to me have actually turned out for
> the furtherance of the gospel, so that it has become
> evident to the whole palace guard, and to all the rest,
> that my chains are in Christ.   —Philippians 1:12-13

Why wasn't Paul consumed with fervor to prove his innocence, make others see he didn't belong in prison? Paul had determined long before he was sent to prison his life belonged to Christ. He made the decision Christ wouldn't just be a part of his life, someone he prayed to in addition to all his other daily activities, but he would breath, eat, and sleep Christ. He would seek His face for every decision he would make, go only where Christ would lead, and do only what he felt Christ was encouraging him to do.

How easy is it to worship Jesus, pray for direction in our lives, and wisdom in our decisions, but then actually die to self and allow Him to have His complete way with our lives? What if we can't go where we use to go, do what we want to do?

Let's look at Paul's response to such an attitude. "For to me, to live *is* Christ, and to die is gain." Paul knew letting Christ have His way in his life, allowing Him to *be* his life, was finding true freedom. Paul was no longer responsible for where his life would take him, what he would eat, or where he would sleep. Whether to live or die, Paul knew in living for Christ, it would be gain.

"To die is gain." May we be willing to die to ourselves today, and live in Christ alone. Only then will we find true freedom.

"If anyone desires to come after Me, let him deny himself, and take up his cross daily, and follow Me."   —Luke 9:23

*"Call to Me, and I will answer you,
and show you great and mighty things,
which you do not know. "*

Jeremiah 33:3

How easy it is to lay
everything at His feet,
and with no effort on our
part, expect Him to take
care of our concern.

A Little Talk with Jesus

Jeremiah 33:3

"Call to Me, and I will answer you,
and show you great and mighty things,
which you do not know."

As I listened to testimonies on our local Christian radio station, a certain lady shared when she didn't know what to do she would go into her prayer closet (which was really the boiler room at work) and "have a little talk with Jesus." That made me smile. I had never thought of coming before the Lord as "having a little talk with Jesus." The truths Jesus showed her during their "little talks" changed her thinking and blessed her life.

Perhaps we all need to heed her advice. What if when we didn't know what to do, we were having a bad day, or dealing with feelings we knew weren't pleasing to the Lord, we would "have a little talk with Jesus?"

We know Jesus tells us to come to Him with everything,

> Be anxious for nothing, but in everything by prayer
> and supplication, with thanksgiving, let your requests
> be made to God; and the peace of God, which passes all
> understanding, will guard your hearts and minds through
> Christ Jesus.   —Philippians 4:6-7

But, do we stay in our prayer closet long enough to hear His voice? How easy it is to lay everything at His feet, and with no effort on our part, expect Him to take care of our concern. This dear lady told how she confessed to the Lord she knew her feelings toward a certain situation weren't pleasing to the Lord, but she didn't know how to change her thinking, nor her feelings. As she "talked with Jesus" He brought to her remembrance the exact Scripture she needed to turn her thinking around and in doing so change her feelings. She didn't just talk to Jesus, but took time to listen.

"I went into my prayer closet and had a little talk with Jesus." That is sound advice for us all. Regardless of where your prayer closet may be, you can be sure, as you go in to "have a little talk with Jesus," He will meet you there.

> Draw near to God and He will draw near to you.
>   —James 4:8

Finally, brethen, whatever things *are* true,
whatever things *are* noble, whatever things *are*
just, whatever things *are* pure, whatever things
are of good report, if *there is* any virtue and
if *there is* anything praiseworthy,
meditate on these things.

Philippians 4:8

As we meditate on the
Word of God,
allowing Christ to draw us
to Himself, we will find His
peace replacing our desperation.

Choose Life

Philippians 4:8

Finally, brethren, whatever things *are* true,
whatever things *are* noble, whatever things *are* just,
whatever things *are* pure, whatever things *are* of good report,
if *there is* any virtue and if *there is* anything praiseworthy-
mediate on these things.

How often do you think about what you are thinking about? How easy it is to let our mind wander into thoughts of discouragement and defeat.

There is a battle going on in our minds. Satan is a master of speaking lies in opposition to the Word of God. If he can keep us discouraged he has us where he wants us, and we are no longer trusting God.

When we are discouraged, we must remember our Father is a father of hope, encouragement, and instruction. At times like this we need to place our focus on the many promises of God, not on the lies of Satan. As we meditate on the Word of God, allowing Christ to draw us to Himself, we will find His peace replacing our desperation.

As we meditate on the Word of God, it is important to not only read the Word, but take it in, digest it into the very core of our being.

> Your words were found, and I ate them,
> And Your Word was to me the joy of rejoicing of my heart;
> For I am called by Your name.　　　—Jeremiah 15:16

Only then will we find true victory.

> "I call heaven and earth as witnesses today against you,
> *that* I have set before you life and death, blessing and
> cursing; therefore choose life, that both you and your
> descendants may live; "that you may love the LORD
> your God, that you may obey His voice, and that you
> may cling to Him, for He is your life and the length
> of your days."　　　　—Deuteronomy 30:19-20

Think about what you are thinking about. Choose life and live!

*"For the Son of Man has come
to save that which was lost."*

Matthew 18:11

Before coming to Christ
we were lost, destined for an
eternity separated from God.

In Need of a Savior

Matthew 18:11

"For the Son of Man has come to save that which was lost."

Sitting with a group of ladies during Bible Study, the subject of compromise became the topic of discussion. "Is there a place for compromise in the church today? Do we need to follow the Words of Jesus and be obedient to His leading in every aspect of our lives?"

Through the Word of God, the Lord instructs His children how to live. There is no place for compromise. He knows nothing good comes from disobedience, but only leads to heartache and painful consequences.

One precious lady said, "I look back at my life before Christ and some of the things I did and think to myself, "What was I thinking!" Have you been there? I surely have. I think back to my life of trying to find happiness in all the wrong places and cringe at some of my choices.

Before coming to Christ we were lost, destined for an eternity separated from God. We based all our decisions, actions, motives, and reasoning on who we were; sinners, lost and all alone, in need of a Savior.

> We did what was right in our own eyes.
> We felt we were the captain of our own ship.
> Success was defined according to the wealth we
> acquired, fame we achieved, or place we lived.

Why are we surprised when the world accepts wrong behavior as being right, compromising with a clear conscience? They are only doing what we did when we were in their place. They, too, are sinners in need of a Savior.

The next time we want to turn in disgust, judge others for their actions, or exclude them from our lives, let's remember "but for the grace of God there go I," and tell them about Jesus instead. Just like us, they need a Savior.

> For all have sinned and fall short of the glory of God.
> —Romans 3:23

> The Lord is not slack concerning *His* promise, as some count
> slackness, but is longsuffering toward us, not willing that any
> should perish but that all should come to repentance.
> —2 Peter 3:9

Through Him we have received grace
and apostleship for obedience to the faith
among all nations for His name.

Romans 1:5

We are to be light to the lost,
hope to the hopeless,
and help to the weary.

Salvation with a Purpose

Romans 1:5

Through Him we have received grace
and apostleship for obedience to the faith
among all nations for His name.

Paul, in preparation for his first visit to Rome, wrote to the Roman church proclaiming his faith in Jesus Christ. It was in this letter he pronounced his responsibility as an apostle, and what it meant to a lost and hurting world.

When we accept Christ as our Savior, we are accepted into His family, becoming apostles of Jesus Christ, and being called to obedience.

> "And now, Israel, what does the Lord your God require
> of you, but to fear the LORD your God, to walk in all His
> ways and to love Him, to serve the LORD your God with
> all your heart and with all your soul, *and* to keep the command-
> ments of the LORD and His statutes which I command you
> today for your good."   —Deuteronomy 10:12-13

We become a light in the darkness,

> *"You are the light of the world. A city that is*
> *set on a hill cannot be hidden."*   —Matthew 5:14

> *"Let your light so shine before men, that they may*
> *see your good works and glorify your Father in*
> *heaven."*   —Matthew 5:16

And our lives are made new in Him.

> Therefore, if anyone *is* in Christ, *he is* a new creation;
> old things are passed away; behold, all things have
> become new.   —2 Corinthians 5:17

There is purpose in our salvation. We are called to a higher calling through obedience to God. We are to be light to the lost, hope to the hopeless, and help to the weary. May we, like Paul, live in obedience as apostles of Jesus Christ.

> *"Assuredly I say to you, inasmuch as you did it to the least*
> *of these My brethren, you did it to Me."*   —Matthew 25:40

He has shown you, O man
what is good;
And what does the Lord require of you
But to do justly, to love mercy,
And to walk humbly with your God?

Micah 6:8

Could there be a greater
privilege than to walk humbly
with our God,
allowing Him to have
His way in our lives?

Walk Humbly with Your God

Micah 6:8

He has shown you, O man
what is good;
And what does the Lord require of you
But to do justly, to love mercy,
And to walk humbly with your God?

In the book of Micah, God pleads with Israel to put aside unkindness, injustice, and idolatry, and walk humbly with their God.

As I studied this Scripture, I realized the Lord was imploring Israel to do what Christ has done for us. When Christ bore our sins on the cross that we might become one with Him, we were freely justified by His grace.

> For all have sinned and fall short of the glory of God,
> being justified freely by His grace through redemption
> that is in Christ Jesus.   —Romans 3:23-24

God was telling Israel; be willing to not give others what they deserve, but show mercy. This, also, is what Christ has done for us.

> The LORD is longsuffering and abundant in mercy,
> forgiving iniquity and transgression.   —Numbers 14:18a

As God instructed Israel to walk humbly with their God, Christ asks the same of us. Could there be a greater privilege than to walk humbly with our God, allowing Him to have His way in our lives?

> Therefore humble yourselves under the mighty hand
> of God, that He may exalt you in due time.   —1 Peter 5:6

The next time we wonder what we can give back to the Lord for all He has given us, let's remember what He tells us is good, and do justly, love mercy, and with love and gratitude, walk humbly with our God.

> Therefore, as *the* elect of God, holy and beloved,
> put on tender mercies, kindness, humility, meekness,
> longsuffering; bearing with one another, and forgiving
> one another, if anyone has a complaint against another;
> even as Christ forgave you, so you also *must do*.
>   —Colossians 3:12-13

Paul, a bondservant of Jesus Christ,
called *to be* an apostle,
separated to the gospel of God
which He promised before through the prophets
in the Holy Scriptures.

Romans 1:1-2

Just as God spoke to Paul
through the prophets
in the Holy Scriptures,
He speaks to us today through
the Word of God.

The Promises of God

Romans 1:1-2

Paul, a bondservant of Jesus Christ,
called *to be* an apostle, separated to the gospel of God
which He promised before through the prophets in the Holy Scriptures.

In introducing himself as a bondservant of Jesus Christ, Paul stated this was promised through the prophets in the Holy Scriptures.

As I took this Scripture apart asking the three questions;

What does it say?
What does it mean?
What does it mean to me personally?

I was reminded: just as God spoke to Paul through the prophets in the Holy Scriptures, He speaks to us today through the Word of God. When I asked myself, "What does this mean to me personally?" I discovered three truths concerning my personal responsibility.

First, I must study the Word of God. Only by knowing His promises will I be able to stand on His Word.

Study to shew thyself approved unto God, a workman that
needeth not be ashamed, rightly dividing the word of truth.
—2 Timothy 2:15 KJV

Once I know God's promises, I must walk in faith, without doubting.

Let us hold fast the confession of *our* hope without wavering,
for He who promised *is* faithful.   —Hebrews 10:23

And I must crucify my flesh that Christ might live through me.

"I have been crucified with Christ; it is no longer I who live,
but Christ lives in me; and the *life* which I now live in the
flesh I live by faith in the Son of God who loved me and
gave Himself for me."   —Galatians 2:20

My greatest desire is to be a bondservant of Jesus Christ, that my life might be separated to the gospel of God. I long for my desires, decisions, and the path I walk to be set before me by Christ alone. Only then will I live pleasing in His sight, and make a difference to a lost and dying world.

"You are the light of the world. A city that is set on a hill cannot be hidden."
—Matthew 5:14

I Know the Plans

Jeremiah 29:11

" For I know the plans I have for you,"
declares the LORD, "plans to prosper you
and not to harm you,
plans to give you hope and a future." (NIV)

How often do you consider the plans the LORD has for you? Are there plans our Father has for all His children; plans that promise hope for all our tomorrows? As we reflect on the Word of God, I believe the answer to that question is a definite yes.

Consider the following Scriptures;

> Trust in the LORD with all your heart,
> And lean not on your own understanding;
> In all your ways acknowledge Him,
> And He shall direct your paths. —Proverbs 3:5-6

> Then Jesus said to him, *"You shall love the LORD your God with all your heart, with all your soul, and with all your mind.* —Matthew 22:37

> "Call to Me, and I will answer you, and show you great and mighty things, which you do not know." —Jeremiah 33:3

> *"Go therefore, and make disciples of all the nations, baptizing them in the name of the Father and of the Son and of the Holy Spirit."* —Matthew 28:19

> Let everything that has breath Praise the LORD.
>
> —Psalm 150:6

Trust in the LORD,
Acknowledge Him in all your ways,
Love the Lord with all your heart, soul, and mind
Turn to Him in prayer,
Share the LORD with others,
Praise the LORD!

As we live our life pleasing to the LORD, not only will we live with hope and a future, but we will receive the plans He has for us, plans overflowing with blessings and grace.

Through Him we have received grace
and apostleship for the obedience to the faith
among all nations for His name,
among whom you also are
called of Jesus Christ.

Romans 1:5-6

There is no room for lying
of any kind
in the Kingdom of God.

Obedience to the Faith

Romans 1:5-6

Through Him we have received grace and apostleship
for obedience to the faith among all nations
for His name, among whom you also
are called of Jesus Christ.

In addressing the Romans, Paul made it clear to the followers of Christ, they had received grace and apostleship for obedience to the faith. No longer were they to live as they deemed sufficient, but were to walk in submission to Christ.

We, too, have a responsibility for all Christ has done for us.

> For not the hearers of the law *are* just in the sight of
> God, but the doers of the law will be justified.   —Romans 2:13

Just as we are to love what the Lord loves, we should hate what He hates.

> These six *things* the LORD hates,
> Yes, seven *are* an abomination to Him:
> A proud look,
> A lying tongue,
> Hands that shed innocent blood,
> A heart that devises wicked plans,
> Feet that are swift in running to evil
> A false witness *who* speaks lies,
> And one who sows discord among brethren.   —Proverbs 6:16-19

When the LORD says He hates lying, He is talking of even white lies and exaggeration. There is no room for lying of any kind in the Kingdom of God. When He speaks of one who sows discord among the brethren, we all know nothing destroys harmony among the brethren faster than gossip. Gossip divides and destroys, hurts and humiliates, and the LORD hates it. And when He includes a heart that devices wicked plans, we are reminded to put on the mind of Christ, that we might live as He lived.

> For *"who has known the mind of the LORD that he may
> instruct Him?"* But we have the mind of Christ.   —1 Corinthians 2:16

As we seek to live in obedience to Christ, may we remember His Word and live.

> Keep my commands and live,
> And my law as the apple of your eye.   —Proverbs 7:2

For since the beginning of the world
Men have not heard nor perceived by the ear,
Nor has the eye seen any God besides You,
Who acts for the one who waits for Him.

Isaiah 64:4

In a world where acceptance
depends so much on
performance and status,
God accepts us just as we are.

The Love of God

Isaiah 64:4

For since the beginning of the world
Men have not heard nor perceived by the ear,
Nor has the eye seen any God besides You,
Who acts for the one who waits for Him.

Who can grasp the love and faithfulness of God? Who but God gives;

Unspeakable grace
Indescribable mercy
Unconditional forgiveness
Forever faithfulness
Never ending love

In a world where acceptance depends so much on performance and status, God accepts us just as we are. Before we knew Him as Savior, Christ made a way for our sins to be forgiven that we might live eternally with Him.

But God demonstrates His own love toward us, in that
while we were still sinners, Christ died for us.
Much more then, having now been justified by
His blood, we shall be saved from wrath through Him.

—Romans 5: 8-9

Through Christ we find rest for our souls and peace that passes all understanding. He is all we need.

He is air for our lungs,
Strength for our bodies
Food for our table
Shelter from the cold
A drink of cold water on a hot summer day

Who can fathom the love of God? There is no one like Him, nor will there ever be. May we Praise His Name forever as we live for Him!

I WILL bless the Lord at all times;
His praise *shall* continually *be* in my mouth.   —Psalm 34:1

And my tongue shall speak of Your righteousness
And of Your praise all the day long.   —Psalm 35:28

Great *is* the LORD, and greatly to be praised;
And His greatness *is* unsearchable.   —Psalm 145:3

*First, I thank my God through Jesus Christ
for all of you, that your faith is spoken of
throughout the whole world.*

Romans 1:8

Love reaps love, joy reaps joy,
faith reaps faith, and a life
that glorifies Christ,
reaps glory for our Savior.

My Corner of the World

Romans 1:8

First, I thank my God through Jesus Christ
for you all, that your faith is spoken of
throughout the whole world.

In writing to the Romans, Paul affirms their faith by praising them for their spiritual reputation. It was evident they loved the Lord Jesus and lived their lives with great faith. They were not ashamed of the gospel of Christ, but willingly shared their faith with others.

While reading this I began to wonder; what is my spiritual reputation? Do others know I love Jesus? Are lives changed because I share the gospel of Christ? Do others want to know Jesus because they see the difference He makes in my life?

In teaching the disciples, Jesus spoke these words;

> *"You are the light of the world. A city that is set on a hill cannot be hidden.*
> *Nor do they light a lamp and put it under a basket, but on a lampstand,*
> *and it gives light to all who are in the house.*
> *Let your light so shine before men, that they may see your good works and*
> *glorify your Father in heaven."* —Matthew 5:14-16

Christ was instructing them to live in such a way that others would see a difference in their lives. They were to be the light in a world filled with sin and darkness. Love reaps love, joy reaps joy, faith reaps faith, and a life that glorifies Christ, reaps glory for our Savior.

We all have a corner of the world where our lives can make a difference for Christ. May we choose this day to tell others about Him and all He means to us, that our light might shine for Jesus.

> For I am not ashamed of the gospel of Christ, for it is the
> power of God to salvation for everyone who believes, for
> the Jew first and also for the Greek. —Romans 1:16

> For I proclaim the name of the LORD:
> Ascribe greatness to our God. —Deuteronomy 32:3

> Declare His glory among the nations,
> His wonders among all peoples. —Psalm 96:3

Now as *Jesus* passed by,
He saw a man who was blind from birth.

John 9:1

He has come to sing songs of
deliverance over you.
Let Him sing!

Let Him Sing

John 9:1

Now as *Jesus* passed by,
He saw a man who was blind from birth.

Leaving the ridicule and rebellion of the Jews, Jesus left the temple and walked through the crowd of angry people. The Scriptures tell us as Jesus passed by, He saw a man who was blind from birth crying out for help.

Envision the setting with me for a moment... Jesus had just been accused of having a demon. The Jews were so defiant against Him they wanted him stoned. Knowing they did not understand, Jesus left the temple, and in the midst of such chaos, saw a blind man crying out for help.

I visualize this man sitting by the side of the road praying someone would notice him. I can't help but wonder; was the blind man apprehensive, possibly scared of what would happen as he realized someone had seen him? He had waited so long for this moment. Did he trust Jesus?

Do you suppose the voice of Jesus speaking to the man, and the touch of His hand on the blind man's eyes, sent a peace through him that could not be explained? Do you wonder if at that moment, the blind man knew Jesus had come to his rescue and he was healed?

What sorrow, despair, confusion, or hopelessness has you sitting by the side of the road, desperately needing the touch of the Master's hand? Do you know Jesus sees you sitting there and has come to your rescue?

> The *righteous* cry out, and the LORD hears,
> And delivers them out of all their troubles. —Psalm 34:17

> You *are* my hiding place;
> You shall preserve me from trouble;
> You shall surround me with songs of deliverance.
> Selah —Psalm 32:7

Will you trust Him, and allowing Him to lead, follow as He meets you at your need? He will make what looked impossible, possible. No longer must you sit by the road waiting to be noticed. He has come to sing songs of deliverance over you. Let Him sing!

And He aid to him, "*Go, wash
in the pool of Siloam.*"
So he went and washed, and came back seeing.

John 9:7

Jesus is looking for our obedience.

So He Went

John 9:7

And He said to him, *"Go, wash in the pool of Siloam."*
So he went and washed, and came back seeing.

Seeing a blind man by the side of the road, Jesus knew what He must do;

> He spat on the ground and made clay with the saliva;
> and He anointed the eyes of the blind man with clay.
> And He said to him, "Go, wash in the pool of Siloam"
> —John 9:6-7

I'm not surprised Jesus knew exactly what to do. I'm not surprised Jesus took immediate action, anointing the blind man's eyes with clay mixed with saliva. What does surprise me is the blind man did exactly what Jesus told him to do.

How many of us would believe clay mixed with saliva and applied to the blind eye would make a person see? Wouldn't we scoff at such an idea, contending this couldn't possibly be the answer to healing our blindness? The blind man didn't argue, complain, or doubt Jesus. He simply did what he was told to do. What was the result of such obedience? His sight was restored.

There is much to learn from the example set by the blind man. Because of his immediate obedience to Jesus, it is clear he trusted Him unconditionally. He didn't have to understand why or how, or question if Jesus knew what He was doing. He simply did as he was told.

What do we do when we don't understand what it is Jesus is asking us to do? Do we try reasoning with Him, explaining to Jesus why His way couldn't possibly be the answer? Do we talk to our friends, asking their opinion? Maybe we decide to pray about it a bit longer, hoping Jesus will change His mind, giving us a different answer.

Jesus is looking for our obedience. The blind man was obedient and he was healed. It would behoove us to follow his example. Just as it was with the blind man, it is by our immediate obedience to Jesus we demonstrate our complete trust in Him. So he went...may we do the same.

> If you are willing and obedient,
> You shall eat the good of the land   —Isaiah 1:19

Jesus heard that they had cast him out;
and when He had found Him, He said to him,
"Do you believe in the Son of God?"

John 9:35

Because we trust Him,
we know
what Jesus tells us is true.

Cast Out

John 9:35

Jesus heard that they had cast him out;
and when He had found him, He said to him,
"Do you believe in the Son of God?"

Being healed by Jesus, the Jews brought the blind man to the Pharisees to explain to them how he had been healed. When the blind man told them how Jesus had put clay on his eyes the Pharisees were outraged, casting him out of the synagogue. Hearing he had been cast out, Jesus came to him.

Have you ever been cast out, rejected, falsely accused of something you did not do? It is devastating. You feel so alone. May it be a comfort to know, even if the whole world turns against you, Jesus will never leave you nor forsake you. He will find you in the midst of your despair and devastation.

> For He Himself has said,
> *"I will never leave you nor forsake you."*
> So we may boldly say;
> *"The Lord is my helper;*
> *I will not fear.*
> *What can man do to me?"*   —Hebrews 13:5b-6

Jesus asked the man He had healed, *"Do you believe in the Son of God?"* When we are cast out, He asks us the same. Because we believe in Jesus, we can trust Him. Because we trust Him, we know what Jesus tells us is true. Though the whole world rejects us and we have been cast out from among those we thought we knew, Jesus is there. We can hang on tight to His hand as He leads us through the heartache to the other side of healing.

> The LORD *is* my light and my salvation;
> Whom shall I fear?
> The LORD is the strength of my life;
> Of whom shall I be afraid?   —Psalm 27:1

> "Have I not commanded you?
>   Be strong and of good courage;
>   do not be afraid, nor dismayed,
>   For the LORD your God *is* with you wherever you go."
>   —Joshua 1:9

"We know that God spoke to Moses;
as for this fellow,
we do not know where He is from."

John 9:29

It is easier to learn a new truth
than to unlearn what we
thought was truth.

New Truth

John 9:29

"We know that God spoke to Moses;
as for this *fellow,* we do not know where He is from."

As the Pharisees came against the blind man with all intentions of excommunicating him, they presented him once again with the same question;

"What did He do to you? How did He open your eyes?"
—John 9:26

In desperation, the man who had been healed of his blindness answered,

> "I told you already, and you did not listen. Why do you want to hear *it* again? Do you also want to become His disciples?"
> —John 9:27

Becoming outraged they reviled against him saying,
"You are His disciple, but we are Moses' disciple."
—John 9:28

The Pharisees refused to listen to what the man was telling them. Their only agenda was to destroy Jesus because He was a threat to what they believed to be truth. Before we condemn the Pharisees for their arrogance and refusal to listen, let's consider their response. The Pharisees knew their religion, what was required, what it represented and how it affected their lives. Jesus comes on the scene proclaiming He is God incarnate, God in the flesh. Because this was completely foreign to them, threatening what they had always believed, they refused to consider this could possibly be true. Their minds were made up before hearing all the facts.

How quickly we do the same? We do not disagree with how to receive salvation through Christ, but what about the different ways Christians worship? Do we assume because their choice of music or format of service is not like ours, they must be wrong? Do we come to a conclusion before knowing the facts? Why is it so hard to accept our way might not be the only way? Could it be it threatens what we have always thought was truth? It is easier to learn a new truth then to unlearn what we thought was truth. To admit we might be wrong puts us on the defense. The next time we judge before knowing the facts, let's remember the Pharisees and listen instead. It could change our life.

> There is one Lawgiver, who is able to save and to destroy.
> Who are you to judge another?   —James 4:12

Therefore, when Jesus saw her weeping,
and the Jews who came with her weeping,
He groaned in the spirit and was troubled.

John 11:33

Your Father is as close as your
deepest prayer, falling tears,
and broken heart.

Jesus Wept

John 11:33

Therefore, when Jesus saw her weeping,
and the Jews who came with her weeping,
He groaned in the spirit and was troubled.

Jesus had been called to the home of Mary and Martha where their brother
Lazarus had grown ill to the point of death. Although Jesus knew He would
raise Lazarus from the dead, to see Mary in such agony caused Him to weep.

Do you know when you weep, your heart broken beyond what you can bear,
Jesus weeps with you, collecting your tears in His bottle?

> You number my wanderings;
> Put my tears into Your bottle;
> *Are they* not in Your book? —Psalm 56:8

We cannot escape the comfort of our Lord:
> Blessed *be* the God and Father of our Lord Jesus Christ,
> the Father of mercies and God of all comfort,
> who comforts us in all our tribulation…
> —2 Corinthians 1:3-4

Nor can we escape His prayers over us:
> Therefore He is also able to save to the uttermost
> those who come to God through Him, since He
> always lives to make intercession for them. —Hebrews 7:25

May you find comfort in knowing your Lord is with you to sustain you in
times of despair. You need never feel alone. Your Father is as close as your
deepest prayer, falling tears, and broken heart. As you cry out to Him, He
will bring you to a place of peace once again.

> You will keep *him* in perfect peace,
> *Whose* mind *is* stayed *on You,*
> Because he trusts in You.
> Trust in the LORD forever,
> For in YAH, the LORD, *is*
> everlasting strength. —Isaiah 26:3-4

> Let us hold fast the confession of *our* hope without wavering,
> for He who promised *is* faithful. —Hebrews 10:23

"I in them, and You in Me;
that they may be made perfect in one,
and that the world may know that You have sent Me,
and have loved them as You have loved Me."

John 17:23

At that moment, dying to
myself was no longer
something I must do,
but an undeniable privilege.

One in Christ

John 17:23

"I in them, and You in Me;
that they may be made perfect in one,
and that the world may know that You have sent Me,
and have loved them as You have loved Me."

As I was returning to my motel room after a wonderful day of teaching by Anne Graham Lotz, a dear worker name Ellen approached me and said,

"My Father wanted me to tell you that He loves you
as much as He loves His own Son."

How could that possibly be? How could God love me as much as He loves His Son, Jesus? Seeing doubt written over my face, Ellen added, "It's true. Look up John 17:23."

I quickly ran to my room to check my Bible. She was right! Jesus, while praying to the Father, prayed that the world would know that the Father loves us as much as He loves His own Son.

As I tried to comprehend the love God has for me, I was reminded once again that only through Christ would I be one with Him:

For I know that in me (that is, in my flesh) nothing good
dwells; for to will is present with me, but *how* to perform
what is good I do not find.   —Romans 7:18

And how essential it is that I am willing to die to my selfish ways,

And if Christ *is* in you, the body is dead because of sin,
but the Spirit *is* life because of righteousness.
But if the Spirit of Him who raised Jesus from the dead
dwells in you, He who raised Christ from the dead will
also give life to your mortal bodies through His Spirit
who dwells in you.   —Romans 8:10-11

At that moment dying to myself was no longer something I must do, but an undeniable privilege. To allow the Spirit to have His way with my life became my greatest desire. I am His daughter, how could I want anything less?

For to me, to live is Christ, and to die is gain.   —Philippians 1:22

BEHOLD, what manner of love
the Father has bestowed upon us,
that we should be called children of God!

1 John 3:1

If not for the love of God
for His children,
we would be lost in our sins,
separated from Him
for all eternity.

What Manner of Love

1 John 3:1

BEHOLD, what manner of love
the Father has bestowed upon us,
that we should be called children of God!

Why would God send His Only Begotten Son to be beaten, scorned, and hung on a cross for people who sinned against Him, ridiculing Him? BE-HOLD, what manner of love is this?

This is a love completely beyond my comprehension. There is in me protectiveness for my children that causes the hair on my neck to stand at attention should anyone try to harm them. To think of sending my child to face all that Christ endured while He walked on this earth, knowing the end would bring such sorrow, would cause me to embrace my child and run as fast as I could in the other direction!

How often do we stop and thank the Father for the pain and agony He endured? Clearly we think of Jesus dying on the cross for our sins, the pain He took upon Himself in order that our sins may be forgiven. But, do we think of His Father; the pain He endured as He watched His Son?

When I am separated from my adult children because of distance, I miss their presence; there is an absence in my day. How would I cope knowing they were about to face heartache beyond comprehension, be beaten and hung on a cross, to die for people who hated and despised them?

If not for the love of God for His children, we would be lost in our sins, separated from Him for all eternity. May we praise God for the sacrifice He paid on our behalf and live our lives wholly for Him.

"How Deep the Father's Love for Us"   by Stuart Townend

"How deep the Father's love for us
How vast beyond all measure
That He should give His only Son
And make a wretch His treasure
How great the pain of searing loss
The Father turns His face away
As wounds which mar the chosen One
Bring many sons to glory."

I will say of the LORD,
"He is my refuge and my fortress;
My God, in Him I will trust."

Psalm 91:2

We rest knowing
who He says He is, He is,
and what He says He will do,
He will do.

My God

Psalm 91:2

I will say of the LORD,
"*He is* my refuge and my fortress;
My God, in Him I will trust."

As I read this Psalm from Moses, considering each word for the first time, I realized "*He is*" is in italics. Moses was speaking in the present tense, not in the past, nor in the future. He was saying, "Today God is my refuge and fortress." Do you suppose the reason Moses had such great faith was because he knew; "My God is with me now, this very moment?"

When life becomes hard and we need solace from turmoil and heartache, do we allow our Father to be our comfort? Do we believe Him when He tells us we need not worry? Do we rest in our Abba's arms? As a child totally worn out climbs up in his mother's lap, and laying his head on her chest falls fast asleep, our Father longs for us to come to Him.

> And because you are sons, God has sent forth the Spirit of
> His Son into your hearts, crying out, "Abba, Father!"
> —Galatians 4:6

Moses spoke with confidence of who his God is. He recognized his God is his shelter, his stronghold every single moment of every single day. He knew he could run to his Abba Father when he needed protection and safety. When we live with such confidence, we live with unwavering assurance we have a Father who is our shelter from the storms of life. We rest knowing who He says He is, He is, and what He says He will do, He will do. And just as Moses, we know our Father is with us right now, this very moment!!

> "Be still and know that I AM GOD"   —Psalm 46:10

> For you did not receive the spirit of bondage again to fear,
> but you received the Spirit of adoption by whom we cry out,
> "Abba Father."   —Romans 8:15

> Trust in Him at all times, you people;
> Pour out your heart before Him;
> God *is* a refuge for us.   Selah   —Psalm 62:8

"And this *will* be the sign to you:
You will find a Babe wrapped
in swaddling cloths,
lying in a manger."

Luke 2:12

From the cradle to the cross,
from the cross to
Christ our Savior.
This is Christmas.

Without the Cradle

Luke 2:12

"And this *will* be the sign to you:
You will find a Babe wrapped in swaddling cloths,
lying in a manger."

Have you ever considered that without the cradle, Christ would never have faced the cross? And without the cross, we would be facing a future of eternal separation with no promise of heaven?

There is so much more to Christmas than a Babe wrapped in swaddling cloths, lying in a manger. In the previous verses Luke tells of shepherds watching their flock by night.

> And behold an angel of the Lord stood before them, and the glory of the Lord shone around them, and they were greatly afraid. Then the angel said to them, "Do not be afraid, for behold, I bring you good tidings of great joy which will be to all people. "For there is born to you this day in the city of David a Savior, who is Christ the Lord."   —Luke 2:9-11

When Christ came to earth as a Babe wrapped in swaddling cloths, there was purpose in His coming. He came as our Savior, to make us clean before the Father. Through Christ alone we have a promise of life eternal.

> The next day John saw Jesus coming toward him, and said "Behold! The Lamb of God who takes away the sin of the world!"
> —John 1:29

As I focus on Christmas, I will no longer think only of a sweet little baby wrapped in swaddling cloths, lying in a manger. I will think of my Savior, and how He came for me, willing to take my punishment on the cross that I may have life eternal through Him.

From the cradle to the cross, from the cross to Christ our Savior. *This* is Christmas.

> *Therefore the Lord Himself will give you a sign: Behold, the virgin shall conceive and bear a Son, and shall call His name Immanuel."*   —Isaiah 7:14

> "For there is born to you this day in the city of David a Savior, who is Christ the Lord."   —Luke 2:11

For I am not ashamed of the gospel of Christ,
For it is the power of God to salvation
for everyone who believes,
for the Jew first and also for the Greek.

Romans 1:16

If not for us, who will
bring the gospel to the lost
and broken people?

Not Ashamed

Romans 1:16

For I am not ashamed of the gospel of Christ,
For it is the power of God to salvation
for everyone who believes,
for the Jew first and also for the Greek.

In the epistle of Paul to the Romans, Paul's desire was they understand the gospel is for the confirmation of all men through faith in Jesus Christ.

> For the grace of God that brings salvation
> has appeared to all men. —Titus 2:11

> "Nor is there salvation in any other, for there is no
> other name under heaven given among men by
> which we must be saved." —Acts 4:12

Paul made it clear without the power of God and love for His children, there would be no means to salvation. God alone raised Christ from the grave, that through Him we might have new life.

> Therefore we were buried with Him through baptism
> into death, just as Christ was raised from the dead by
> the glory of the Father, even so we also should walk
> in newness of life. —Romans 6:4

Just as Paul declared he was not ashamed of the gospel of Christ, neither should we be reluctant to share with others all Christ has done for us.

> "The Spirit of the Lord GOD *is* upon Me,
> Because the LORD has anointed Me
> To preach good tidings to the poor;
> He has sent Me to heal the brokenhearted,
> To proclaim liberty to the captives
> And the opening of the prison to *those who are* bound."
> —Isaiah 61:1

The world needs the good news of Jesus Christ. If not us, who will bring the gospel to the lost and broken people? May we be willing to tell others of the gospel of Jesus Christ that their lives may be changed, and they, too, might be set free!

When Jesus heard it, He said to them,
"*Those who are well have no need of a physician,
but those who are sick. I did not come to call the
righteous, but sinners to repentance.*"

Mark 2:17

No one is worthy to be saved.
That's the point of the gospel.

Repentance

Mark 2:17

When Jesus heard it, He said to them,
"Those who are well have no need of a physician,
but those who are sick. I did not come to call the righteous,
but sinners to repentance."

As Jesus passed by Levi, He said to him, *"Follow Me."* Immediately Levi rose and followed Him. Later on, as Jesus and Levi dined in his home, other tax collectors and sinners joined them at the table.

"Now it happened, as He was dining in *Levi's* house, that many
tax collectors and sinners also sat together with Jesus and His
disciples; for there were many, and they followed Him."   —Mark 2:15

When the scribes and Pharisees saw Jesus eating with the tax collectors and sinners they became outraged. How could Jesus eat with such people?

As I pondered this Scripture, I thought about how amazing it was that those who seemed to be the greatest of sinners, being tax collectors, followed Jesus, while those who seemed to have their lives in order, as scribes and Pharisees, did nothing but judge and condemn.

Satan's greatest tool is pride. It began in the Garden of Eden when Adam and Eve believed they could be like God, and it continues today. We look down on others and determine they are so much more a sinner then we could ever be. If only we would live as Christ has shown us. No one is worthy to be saved. That's the point of the gospel.

For all have sinned and fall short of the glory of God.   —Romans 3:23

Jesus did not come to call the righteous, there are none. We all come to salvation at the same place; the foot of the cross. The next time we are tempted to judge another let's remember Levi and join him at the table instead.

But God demonstrates His own love toward us, in that while
sinners, Christ died for us.   — Romans 5:8

Christianity is one beggar telling another beggar where to find bread.
—D.T. Niles

"O woman, great is your faith!
Let it be to you as you desire."
And her daughter was healed
from that very hour.

Matthew 15:28

I knew it was time I began
walking in what I knew to be
true; there is no problem in
my life too big for God.

Let It Be

Matthew 15:28

"O woman, great is your faith!
Let it be to you as you desire."
And her daughter was healed from that very hour.

Having a demon possessed daughter, a Canaan woman came to the Lord pleading for help:

> Then she came and worshiped Him saying,
> "Lord, help me!"   —Matthew 15:25

As I read this, I noticed not only had she cried out, but also in the midst of her weeping, she had worshiped the Lord. I began pondering the times I have cried out to the Lord in desperation. Had I considered these as times of worship? I knew I had not. But then I realized, when we call on the Lord in despair, within we are worshipping Him as we pray, "It is You I trust with this heartache, Lord! You alone have the answer!"

> God is Spirit: and they that worship Him
> must worship Him in spirit and in truth.
>   —John 4:24

My next thought was, "How great is my faith? Is it as great as this mother? Do I believe He hears the cry of my heart? Will He speak to me as He spoke to her; *"O Woman, great is your faith! Let it be to you as your desire."* If not, what keeps me from having this kind of faith, unwavering in my trust and belief?

> He who doubts is like a wave of the sea
> driven and tossed by the wind.
> For let not that man suppose that he will
> receive anything from the Lord
> He is a double-minded man,
> unstable in all his ways.   —James 1:6-8

I knew it was time I began walking in what I knew to be true; there is no problem in my life too big for God. As I bowed my head in humility for the times I have prayed doubting, I felt much like the father who cried out in tears,

> "Lord, I believe; help my unbelief!"   —Mark 9:24

"For with God nothing will be impossible."

Luke 1:37

I want to live my life
with such abandonment,
I, too, know the
character of God.

Character of God

Luke 1:37
"For with God nothing will be impossible."

As Mary walked along a dusty road on an ordinary day, the angel Gabriel came to her, revealing she had found favor with the Lord, and that she would conceive and bring forth a Son. His name would be Jesus, Son of the Highest.

> "*The* Holy Spirit will come upon you, and the power of the Highest
> will overshadow you; therefore, also, that Holy One who is to
> be born will be called the son of God"   —Luke 1:35

Immediately upon revealing to Mary she would be giving birth to the Son of God, Gabriel told Mary her relative Elizabeth, though she had been barren, had also conceived a son.

The Scriptures tell us Mary hastened to the home of Elizabeth and upon greeting Mary, the babe within her leaped for joy, filling Elizabeth with the Holy Spirit. What encouragement Elizabeth must have been to Mary. What joy Mary must have brought to Elizabeth. I love to ponder Mary's visit. Elizabeth wasn't supposed to be with child because of her age; Mary wasn't supposed to be with child because she had never known a man. Yet, both were indeed with child. Both believed the impossible, walking in unfaltering faith. Why do you suppose they were both willing to accept the impossible? Could it be they had lived their lives with such trust in God before this happened, they understood the character of God? They knew they could trust His faithfulness.

> I will say of the LORD,
> '*He is* my refuge and fortress;
> My God, in Him I will trust."   —Psalm 91:2

I want to live my life with such abandonment that I, too, know the character of God. I want to walk so closely with God, regardless of what comes my way, I trust Him without doubting. I want my reply to be without hesitation; He is My God, in Him will I trust!

> But without faith *it is* impossible to please *Him,*
> for He who comes to God must believe that He is,
> and *that* He is a rewarder of those who diligently seek Him.
>   —Hebrews 11:6

Not that I speak in regard to need,
for I have learned
in whatever state I am,
to be content.

Philippians 4:11

When we feel we can't go on,
may we be like Paul
and remember
who holds our life in His hands.

I Have Learned

Philippians 4:11

Not that I speak in regard to need,
for I have learned in whatever state I am,
to be content.

As I read this Scripture, I was taken back by the fact Paul, who had been through more than we can fathom, did not live in the midst of his needs, but learned to live with contentment regardless of his circumstances.

> Three times I was beaten with rods; once I was stoned; three times I was shipwrecked; a night and a day I have been in the deep; in journeys often, in perils of water, in perils of robbers, in perils in the city, in perils in the wilderness, in perils in the sea, in perils among the brethren; in weariness and toil, in sleeplessness often, in hunger and thirst, in fasting often, in cold and nakedness----
> —2 Corinthians 11:25-27

How could Paul be content in the midst of such misery? Why wasn't he bitter, depressed, or scared of what the future might hold? I wonder if it was because he remembered *who* held him in the palms of *His hands.*

> See, I have inscribed you on the palms *of My hands;*
> Your walls *are* continually before Me.   —Isaiah 49:16

Possibly, it was because Paul no longer lived for himself. Instead, his life had become about living for Christ, and Christ alone.

> For to me, to live *is* Christ, and to die *is* gain.
> —Philippians 1:21

Paul tells us he learned to be content; it did not come natural to him. How easy it is for us to succumb to fear and desperation when our life seems to be falling apart. When we feel we can't go on, may we be like Paul and remember who holds our life in His hands. We, too, can learn to be content regardless of our circumstances. The same God who held Paul holds us. He won't let us go.

> The LORD *is* your keeper;
> The LORD is your shade at your right hand.
> The LORD shall preserve your going out and your coming in
> From this time forth, and even forevermore.
> —Psalm 121:5, 8

Then the serpent said to the woman
"You will not surely die."

Genesis 3:4

Satan will do everything he can
to convince us we will not die if
we choose his ways over the
Truth of God.

Truth of God

Genesis 3:4

Then the serpent said to the woman,
"You will not surely die."

Once the creation of the world was complete, God placed Adam in the Garden of Eden, blessing him with a woman named Eve.

> And the LORD God said, "*It is* not good that man should be alone;
> I will make him a helper comparable to him."   —Genesis 2:18

The Word of God tells us Eve was discussing with the serpent, the most cunning beast in the Garden, about how they were not allowed to eat of the tree of the knowledge of good and evil or they would die. What foolishness for Eve to spend time with the shrewdest, most cunning being in the garden. Of course he would want to convince Eve otherwise.

Eve believed the lies of the serpent and ate of the tree of knowledge, giving it to Adam to eat. Although God told Adam not to eat of the tree of knowledge before He created Eve, Adam chose to believe Eve over the Word of God, eating the forbidden fruit.

> Then the eyes of both of them were opened, and they knew
> that they *were* naked; and they sewed fig leaves together and
> made themselves coverings.   —Genesis 3:7

Just as Adam and Eve fell for the shrewdness of the serpent, we, too, can fall into the snares of Satan. Satan will do everything he can to convince us we will not die if we choose his ways over the Truth of God. Sin will take us farther then we want to go, cost us more then we want to pay, and keep us longer then we want to stay. Satan knows exactly what he is doing.

When we find ourselves entangled in the snares of Satan, tempted to believe his lies, our Father promises a way of escape. May we be so attentive to His leading that we don't fall for the cunning ways of Satan.

> No temptation has overtaken you except such as is common to man;
> but God *is* faithful, who will not allow you to be tempted beyond what
> you are able, but with the temptation will also make the way of escape,
> that you may be able to bear *it*.   —1 Corinthians 10:13

> "Be strong and of good courage, do not fear nor be afraid of them; for
> the Lord your God, He *is* the One who goes before you. He will not
> leave nor forsake you."   —Deuteronomy 31:6

He has filled *the* hungry with good things,
And *the* rich He has sent away empty.

Luke 1:53

Often our relationship with God
is not about who He is,
but merely what He can
do for us.
This should not be.

Are You Hungry?

Luke 1:53

He has filled *the* hungry with good things,
And *the* rich He has sent away empty.

This Scripture is from what is referred to as *The Song of Mary*. Mary had just learned from the angel, Gabriel, the Holy Spirit would come upon her and she would bear the long awaited Messiah. Hurrying to her relative, Elizabeth, Mary poured out her heart as she shared with Elizabeth all that had happened, and what was to come.

For God to choose Mary to carry His Son, and for her to accept the responsibility so willingly, we can only assume Mary loved the Lord and walked closely with Him. She was hungry to know all she could about her LORD. She longed for understanding of the Word of God, His ways, and His never-ending love. God rewarded her hunger and surrender to Him with more than she could comprehend.

How hungry are you for God? So often we want all God has to give. We long for peace, joy, love, and kindness. However, we don't want to hunger and thirst to receive it. We want Him to pour it on us simply because we are His children. Often our relationship with God is not about who He is, but merely what He can do for us. This should not be.

Hungering and thirsting for God is a heart issue. Does our heart ache to know Him more? Do we desire to know Him in such an intimate way He is what our life is about? Are we willing to take reproof from the Word of God, as well as the blessings? Mary hungered for all of God and the Lord blessed her faithfulness.

God died on the cross to give us new life in Him. May we hunger and thirst for all He has for us, and be willing to spend time in His Word, that we too might draw close to our Lord with a heart to obey.

> O GOD, You *are* my God;
> Early will I seek You;
> My flesh longs for You
> In a dry and thirsty land
> Where there is no water. —Psalm 63:1
>
> As a deer pants for the water
> So pants my soul for You, O God. —Psalm 42:1

He has made everything beautiful in its time.
Also He has put eternity in their hearts,
except that no one can find out the work that
God does from beginning to end.

Ecclesiastes 3:11

We can know, if He allowed it,
He will use it for our good
and for His glory.

Blessings from the Burdens

Ecclesiastes 3:11

He has made everything beautiful in its time.
Also He has put eternity in their hearts,
except that no one can find out the work
that God does from beginning to end.

We have all sustained times in life when the pain and heartache we are enduring is more than we feel we can bear. Why would a God who is so good and loving allow such sorrow to come into our lives?

In times like these, we have a Father who is closer than the air we breathe, more loving than we can fathom, compassionate beyond compare, and who promises to turn our ashes into beauty. We have a Savior who came to carry us when we cannot walk.

> The Spirit of the LORD GOD *is* upon Me,
> Because the LORD has anointed Me
> To preach good tidings to the poor;
> He has sent Me to heal the brokenhearted,
> To proclaim liberty to the captives,
> And the opening of the prison to *those who are* bound.   —Isaiah 61:1

When we focus on the Only One who can carry us through, we will see on the other side of the heartache He has used what Satan meant for ruin to bring us closer to Himself, mold us more into His likeness, and teach us more about His faithfulness and unwavering love than we could learn any other way. We will be able to say, "I don't want to go through it again, but I wouldn't trade for the world what the Lord has taught me because of it!" In times like these, we can know if He allowed it, He will use it for our good, and for His glory.

> He will sit as a refiner and a purifier of silver;
> And purge them as gold and silver,
> That they may offer to the LORD
> An offering in righteousness.   —Malachi 3:3

> Why are you cast down, O my soul?
> And *why* are you disquieted within me?
> Hope in God, for I shall yet praise Him
> *For* the help of His countenance.   —Psalm 42:5

Cause me to hear Your loving kindness
in the morning,
For in You do I trust;
Cause me to know the way
in which I should walk,
For I lift up my soul to You.

Psalm 143:8

What would our days be like
if every morning our first
thought was to commit all
that lies before us to the Lord?

Early Will I Seek Thee

Psalm 143:8

Cause me to hear Your loving kindness
in the morning,
For in You do I trust;
Cause me to know the way in which I should walk,
For I lift up my soul to You.

A Christian who shared how he prays this Psalm each morning, before getting out of bed, brought this Scripture to my attention. What a wonderful idea. What would our days be like if every morning our first thought was to commit all that lies before us to the Lord?

Perhaps the tension we were feeling, the anxiety we were experiencing, or confusion we felt, would seem less overwhelming if we let our Father have our day. David, a man after God's own heart, knew this to be true in His life. There is much we can learn as we glean from his written word.

Cause me to hear your loving kindness in the morning
My voice You shall hear in the morning, O LORD;
In the morning I will direct it to You,
And I will look up.   —Psalm 5:3

But to You I have cried out, O Lord,
And in the morning my prayer comes before You.   —Psalm 88:13

Trust in the Lord with all your heart,
And lean not on your own understanding;
In all your ways acknowledge Him;
And He shall direct your paths.   —Proverbs 3:5-6

Cause me to know the way in which I should walk,
The steps of a *good* man are ordered by the LORD,
And He delights in his way.   —Psalm 37:23

For I lift up my soul to You.
I WILL lift up my eyes to the hills-
From whence comes my help?
My help *comes* from the LORD,
Who made heaven and earth.   —Psalm 121:1-2

Thus says the LORD:
"Let not the wise *man* glory in his wisdom,
Let not the mighty *man* glory in his might,
Nor let the rich *man* glory in his riches;
But let him who glories glory in this,
That he understands and knows Me,
That I *am* the LORD, exercising loving kindness,
judgment, and righteousness in the earth.
For in these I delight," says the LORD.

Jeremiah 9:23-24

The LORD tells us to glory in
knowing Him as we build our
life on the rock of Jesus.
Only then will we know
true success.

Success God's Way

Jeremiah 9:23-24

Thus says the LORD:
"Let not the wise *man* glory in his wisdom,
Let not the mighty *man* glory in his might,
Nor let the rich *man* glory in his riches;
But let him who glories glory in this,
That he understands and knows Me,
That I *am* the LORD, exercising loving kindness,
judgment, and righteousness in the earth.
For in these I delight," says the LORD.

In a world where success is measured by our bank account, the size of our home, the kind of car we drive, and the position we hold, the Lord makes it clear this is not how He measures success.

> The fear of the LORD *is* the beginning of knowledge,
> *But* fools despise wisdom and instruction.   —Proverbs 1:7

The world's definition of success is based on Satan's value system. If he can convince us that we are of great value on our own and captain of our own ship, he has cunningly persuaded us to build our lives on what the Lord hates most; pride. We become prideful in our achievements, status, and intelligence, setting aside the truth that without the blessing of the LORD we would have none of this.

The LORD tells us to glory in knowing Him as we build our life on the rock of Jesus. Only then will we know true success.

> *Therefore, whoever hears these sayings of Mine, and does them, I will liken him to a wise man who built his house on the rock."*   —Matthew 7:24

The next time we are tempted to run after the ways of the world, building a life we diem to be successful, we would be wise to remember what is important to the LORD. We would, instead, build our life on the only One who cares about us with such love He sent His Only Son to die on the cross to save us from our sins. He alone is worthy of our praise, honor, and devotion.

> For the LORD *is* great and greatly to be praised;
> He *is* also to be feared above all gods.   —1 Chronicles 16:25

Or do you not know your body is the
temple of the Holy Spirit who is in you,
whom you have from God,
and you are not your own?

1 Corinthians 6:19

Why do we settle for
so much less
than the Lord promises
to give us?

Temple of Christ

1 Corinthians 6:19

Or do you not know your body is the
temple of the Holy Spirit who is in you,
whom you have from God, and you are not your own?

When we accept Christ as our personal Savior, asking Him to forgive us of our sins and inviting Him to live within us, He comes to indwell us through the Holy Spirit. Christ lives in us!

If we confess our sins, He is faithful and just to forgive us *our* sins and to cleanse us from all unrighteousness. —1 John 1:9

But he who is joined to the Lord is one spirit *with Him*.
—1 Corinthians 6:17

The Scriptures tell us no longer are we our own, but have become a new creation through Christ.

Therefore, if anyone *is* in Christ, *he is* a new creation; old things have passed away; behold, all things have become new. —2 Corinthians 5:17

Since this is true, why do we try so hard to figure everything out on our own, hanging on so tightly to our own desires, ambitions, and attitudes? Why don't we lay everything at the feet of Jesus, asking Him to direct our path and teach us His Truth? Why do we settle for so much less than the Lord promises to give us?

For *"who has known the mind of the LORD that he may instruct Him?"* But we have the mind of Christ. —1 Corinthians 2:16

But the Helper, the Holy Spirit, whom the Father will send in My name, He will teach you all things, and bring to your remembrance all things I have said to you. —John 14:26

Finally, brethen, whatever things *are* true,
whatever things *are* noble,
whatever things *are* just,
whatever things *are* pure,
whatever things *are* lovely,
whatever things *are* of good report,
if *there is* any virtue and if there is anything
praiseworthy, meditate on these things.

Philippians 4:8

Are you heavy laden by the
cares of this world?
Set your heart on Him.

Whatever Things Are True

Philippians 4:8

Finally, brethren, whatever things *are* true,
whatever things *are* noble, whatever things *are* just,
whatever things *are* pure, whatever things *are* lovely,
whatever things *are* of good report, if *there is* any virtue and if
there is anything praiseworthy meditate on these things.

In writing to the saints in Philippi, Paul continually implored them to be thankful for all God had done, assuring them God would complete the good work He had begun in them.

> Being confident of this very thing, that He who has begun a good work in you will complete *it* until the day of Jesus Christ.
> —Philippians 1:6

As I pondered this letter, I began reflecting on the promises of God and marveled at the assurances He gives His children throughout His Holy Word. How different our lives would be if we would think on these things?

Whatever things are true:

> The LORD *is* my strength and song,
> And He has become my salvation.   —Psalm 118:14

> You will keep *him* in perfect peace, *whose* mind is stayed *on You*, because he trusts in You.   —Isaiah 26:3

> Cast your burden on the LORD, and He shall sustain you; He shall never permit the righteous to be moved.   —Psalm 55:22

> *"In the world you will have tribulation; but be of good cheer, I have overcome the world."*   —John 16:33

> 'Ah, LORD GOD! Behold You have made the heavens and the earth by Your great power and outstretched arm. There is nothing too hard for You.   —Jeremiah 32:17

Are you heavy laden by the cares of this world? Set your heart on Him.

> The peace of God, that surpasses all understanding will guard your hearts and minds through Christ Jesus.   —Philippians 4:7

Finally, brethen, whatever things *are* true,
whatever things *are* noble,
whatever things *are* just,
whatever things *are* pure,
whatever things *are* lovely,
whatever things *are* of good report,
if *there is* any virtue and if *there is* anything
praiseworthy, meditate on these things.
Philippians 4:8

The Word of God
has much to say about
living a life of integrity.

Whatever Things Are Noble

Philippians 4:8

Finally, brethren, whatever things *are* true,
whatever things *are* noble, whatever things *are* just,
whatever things *are* pure, whatever things *are* lovely,
whatever things are of good report, if *there is* any virtue and if
there is anything praiseworthy, meditate on these things.

Looking up the word noble in the dictionary, I found the word to mean honorable, moral, decent, and upright. We are to be a people of upmost integrity, living our lives pleasing to the Lord.

The Word of God has much to say about living a life of integrity.

> *Let* nothing *be done* through selfish ambition or conceit,
> but in lowliness of mind let each esteem others better than himself.
> Let each of you look out not only for his own interests,
> but also for the interests of others.   —Philippians 2:3-4

> He has shown you, O man, what *is* good;
> And what does the LORD require of you
> But to do justly,
> To love mercy,
> And to walk humbly with your God?   —Micah 6:8

> For thus says the High and Lofty One
> Who inhabits eternity, whose name *is* Holy;
> "I dwell in the high and holy *place,*
> With him *who* has a contrite and humble spirit,
> To revive the spirit of the humble,
> And to revive the heart of the contrite ones.   —Isaiah 57:15

> Therefore humble yourselves under the mighty hand
> of God, that He may exalt you in due time.   —1 Peter 5:6

> And *whatever* you do in word or deed, *do* all in the name
> of the Lord Jesus, giving thanks to God the Father
> through Him.   —Colossians 3:17

May we be a people of highest integrity, walking humbly with our God.

And be kind to one another, tenderhearted,
forgiving one another,
even as God in Christ forgave you.

Ephesians 4:32

"To err is human, to
forgive, divine."

Alexander Pope

Forgive One Another

Ephesians 4:32

And be kind to one another, tenderhearted,
forgiving one another, even as God in Christ forgave you.

I once heard a pastor teach on forgiveness and why it is so hard to forgive those who have wronged us. He explained the reason is because we feel by forgiving them, we are saying we approve of their actions. We may not want revenge, but we certainly don't want them to feel what they did was ok!

The sad truth is, as long as we refuse to forgive our perpetrator, what we are really doing is allowing them to consume our emotions, thoughts, and many times our actions. We are even allowing them to affect our witness and closeness with the Lord. It isn't the perpetrator who suffers, but us.

> *"And whenever you stand praying, if you have anything against anyone,*
> *forgive him, that your Father in heaven may also forgive you your trespasses.*
> *But if you do not forgive, neither will your Father in heaven forgive you*
> *your trespasses."* —Mark 11:25-26

Jesus taught we are to forgive others even as God in Christ has forgiven us. What if Christ had refused to forgive us because it was our sins that nailed Him to the cross? Where would we be?

> In Him we have redemption through His blood,
> the forgiveness of sins, according to the riches
> of His grace. —Ephesians 1:7

Christ forgave us according to the riches of His grace. When we forgive the one who has hurt us, we will be forgiving as God forgave us.

> The Lord our God is merciful and forgiving, even though
> we have rebelled against Him. —Daniel 9:9 NIV

The next time we refuse to forgive our perpetrator, let's remember all we have been forgiven and choose to forgive as God has forgiven us instead.

> *"For if you forgive men their trespasses, your heavenly Father*
> *will also forgive you."* —Matthew 6:14

"To err is human, to forgive, divine." —Alexander Pope

Let us lay aside every weight,
and the sin which so easily ensnares us,
and let us run with endurance
the race set before us.
Hebrews 12:1

There are no magic formulas or
correct words that make it
possible to lay down our weight.

Lay It Down

Hebrews 12:1

Let us lay aside every weight,
and the sin which so easily ensnares us,
and let us run with endurance the race that is set before us.

There is much we could say about this Scripture. We could discuss sin, how it threatens to steal our peace, our testimony, discouraging us as we walk in the love and grace of our Savior, Jesus Christ. Or we could confer about what it means to run the race with endurance, with persistence and resolution. However, what piqued my interest was the laying aside of every weight.

When I think of a weight, I immediately think of something heavy, hard to carry. We all know what it is like to lay awake at night, overwhelmed with worry or grief, concerned about what the future holds for us, or a loved one. This is a weight, something heavy to carry as we face another day. We can have a difficult time accepting the forgiveness of Christ; continue to carry around the guilt and shame of our past. This is a weight. It tears us down and wears us out, our peace is gone, and the joy of the Lord escapes us as we try to rise above the nagging in our soul. What is it in your life that you feel you must carry around, refusing to lay it down at the feet of Jesus? Jesus says lay it down, give it to Him. He can carry whatever it is that keeps us from living the life He died on the cross to give us.

> *"Come to Me, all you who labor and are heavy laden, and I will give you rest. Take my yoke upon you and learn from Me, for I am gentle and lowly in heart, and you will find rest for your souls. For My yoke is easy, and My burden is light."* —Matthew 11:28-30

Jesus did not die on the cross so that we would continue to walk in defeat. He brought us to Himself, forgiving our past, willing to carry our burdens, so that we might live in freedom. There are no magic formulas or correct words that make it possible to lay down our weight. Laying down our weights only comes when we decide once and for all to be obedient to the Word of God, casting all our cares on Him.

> Cast your burden on the LORD,
> And He shall sustain you;
> He shall never permit the righteous to be moved.
> —Psalm 55:22

Therefore, humble yourselves under
the mighty hand of God,
that He may exalt you in due time.

1 Peter 5:6

The cost is great,
but the reward priceless!!

Humble Yourself

1 Peter 5:6

Therefore, humble yourselves under the mighty hand of God,
that He may exalt you in due time.

In a world telling us to be all we can be, the sky is the limit, and how great we are, it seems contrary to think we are to be humble.

Throughout Scripture, the Lord admonishes us to die to ourselves, allowing Christ to have His way in our lives. Never does it say we are to be a proud people, impressed with our achievements and status in life. This is the way of the world. As children of God we have been set apart, called to live a life of godliness.

> But know that the LORD has set apart for Himself
> him who is godly;
> The LORD will hear when I call to Him.   —Psalm 4:3

We must decide whom we will follow, the passion of the world, or the voice of the Lord. When we try to live for both our Father tells us we are lukewarm and He will spit us out of His mouth.

> " *I know your works, that you are neither cold nor hot.*
> *I could wish you were cold or hot,*
> " *So then, because you are lukewarm, and neither cold or hot.*
> *I will vomit you out of My mouth.* "   —Revelations 3:15-16

It's exhausting to try and live a Godly life and still live in the world. The world's ways are not pleasing to the Lord, and the Lord's ways are not amenable with the world. As a result, we feel torn between the two. We are miserable because we know we should take a stand as a child of God, and yet we are afraid the price will be too costly.

> *"If anyone desires to come after Me, let him deny himself and*
> *take up his cross, and follow Me.*
> *"For what profit is it to a man if he gains the whole world, and loses his*
> *own soul? Or what will a man give in exchange for his soul?*
> *"For the Son of Man will come in the glory of His Father with*
> *His angels, and then He will reward each according to his works."*
> —Matthew 16:24-27

> Choose for yourselves this day whom you will serve.
> But for me and my house, we will serve the Lord.
> —Joshua 24:15

The cost is great, but the reward priceless!!

And *whatever* you do in word or deed,
do all in the name of the Lord Jesus,
giving thanks to God the Father through Him.

Colossians 3:17

When we live our lives pleasing
to the Lord, we will care little
what the world may think.
Our heart's desire will be to
please the Lord alone.

Glory of God

Colossians 3:17
And *whatever* you do in word or deed,
do all in the name of the Lord Jesus,
giving thanks to God the Father through Him.

Ministering to the Colossians, Paul thanked them for their faith in Christ.

> We give thanks to the God and Father of our Lord Jesus
> Christ, praying always for you, since we heard of your faith
> in Jesus Christ and of your love for all the saints.
>
> —Colossians 1:3-4

As he continued, he exhorted them to be heavenly minded in all their affairs. We are admonished to live the same. Regardless of what we do in word or deed, we are to do it as unto the Lord and not to men. Whether an employer
employee
office manager, or
stay at home mom,
do all on to the Lord and for His glory.

How easy it is to allow society to dictate our worth. We look at others and determine what they are doing is of so more importance than are ways.

If we would live our lives for God and not for men, we would rejoice in knowing it is God who directs our path. We would remember His ways are not our ways. What is important to Him is often of little significance to the world. Likewise, what is significant to the world is of little importance to Him.

> O LORD, *You are* the portion of my inheritance and my cup;
> You maintain my lot. —Psalm 16:5

When we live our lives pleasing to the Lord, we will care little what the world may think. Our heart's desire will be to please the Lord alone.

> Knowing that from the Lord you will receive the reward
> of the inheritance; for you serve the Lord Christ. —Colossians 3:24

And whatever you do, do it heartily, as to the Lord and not to men.
—Colossians 3:23

"It is I, do not be afraid."

John 6:20

Just as they didn't reason,
but received Jesus,
I need to do the same.

Why Are You Afraid?

John 6:20

"It is I, do not be afraid."

Leaving the Sea of Galilee, the disciples rowed toward Capernaum. As the night grew dark the seas rose all about, threatening to overturn their boat into the raging waters. Just as they were losing hope, feeling as if this was the end, they saw someone walking on the water. "Who is coming toward our boat?" "Is it a ghost, an illusion, and how can they be walking on the water?" they proclaimed in fear.

"It is I, do not be afraid," they heard someone speak. Did they hear right? Was that really Jesus?

As I read this portion of Scripture I thought about the fears, apprehensions, and circumstances in my life that keep me awake at night, causing doubt and worry to consume my every thought. Just as the disciples tossing all about the raging seas, I become afraid of what the future may hold. My thoughts become filled with "what if's," creating problems in my mind that never come to pass. If I would only listen with a heart toward Christ instead of allowing fear to consume me, I would hear Him say, as He said to the disciples, *"It is I, do not be afraid."*

The Scriptures continue with the words,
"Then they willingly received Him into the boat."
—John 6:21

As I read these words, I considered how willing I would be to receive Jesus if He came walking to me on the water. Too often, when He tells me to not be afraid I try to reason with Him, explain to Him how He doesn't understand the many aspects of my situation, and how impossible it would be for it to work out with any sense of success. As I thought about my response, I knew it was time I learn from the disciples. Just as they didn't reason, but received Jesus, I need to do the same.

"Is anything too hard for God?"   —Genesis 18:14

"Ah, LORD GOD! Behold You have made the heavens and
the earth by Your great power and outstretched arm. There is
nothing too hard for You."   —Jeremiah 32:17

"It is I, do not be afraid."   —John 6:20

"He who believes in Me,
as the Scripture has said,
out of his heart will flow rivers of living water."

John 7:38

Allowing living waters to flow
from our heart will only be
possible as we empty ourselves,
allowing Christ
to live through us.

Living Water

John 7:38

"He who believes in Me, as the Scripture has said,
out of his heart will flow rivers of living water."

Attending the Jews Feast of Tabernacle, Jesus stood and cried out, saying,

"If anyone thirsts, let him come to Me and drink.
He who believes in Me, as the Scripture has said,
out of his heart will flow rivers of living water."   —John 7:37-38

What, you may ask, is Living Water? Living Water is the Word of God, alive and powerful, changing lives, and setting the captive free.

"For the word of God *is* living and powerful, and sharper
than any two-edged sword, piercing even to the division
of soul and spirit, and of joints and marrow, and is a discerner
of the thoughts and intents of the heart.   —Hebrews 4:12

As I read this, I couldn't help but wonder whether or not the Truths I have learned as I've studied the Word of God are evident in my life. How I desire for my life to be a reflection of Christ.

As Jesus met the Samaritan woman at the well, asking her for a drink, the woman said to Him,

"How is it that You, being a Jew, ask a drink from me, a
Samaritan woman?"

Jesus answered and said to her, *"If you knew the gift of God,*
and who it is who says to you, "Give Me a drink, you would have
asked Him, and He would have given you living water." —John 4: 9-10

Allowing living waters to flow from our heart will only be possible as we empty ourselves, allowing Christ to live through us. We must be in the Word of God, gleaning all it has for us, and applying it to our life. Only then will our heart and soul dwell with the heart of Christ.

Be diligent to present yourself approved to God,
a worker who does not need to be ashamed,
rightly dividing the word of truth.   —2 Timothy 2:15

All Scripture *is* given by inspiration of God,
and *is* profitable for doctrine, for reproof,
for correction, for instruction in righteousness. —2 Timothy 3:16

He answered and said,
"Whether He is a sinner *or not* I do not know.
One thing I know that though
I was blind now I see."

John 9:25

What do you say when
someone asks you how you
know you are going to heaven?

Now I See

John 9:25

He answered and said,
"Whether He is a sinner *or not* I do not know.
One thing I know that though I was blind
now I see."

Jesus had just healed the blind man by spatting on the ground, making clay with saliva, anointing his eyes with clay, and telling him to go wash in the pool of Siloam. Even though the man had been blind from birth and now could see, the Pharisees refused to believe Jesus was who He said He was.

Asking the blind man how he could now see, he told the Pharisees how Jesus had anointed his eyes and his sight had returned. Becoming furious with the truth, the Pharisees approached the blind man's parents. They, too, told the Pharisees their son had been blind from birth and now could see.

> "but by what means he now sees we do not know, or who opened his eyes we do not know. He is of age; ask Him. He will speak for himself."   —John 9:21-22

Becoming completely outraged, the Pharisees once again asked the blind man who healed him. In desperation, and offended by their continual unbelief, the blind man told them for the last time;

> "One thing I know that though I was blind now I see."   —John 9:25b

What do you say when someone asks you how you know you are going to heaven? Do you explain to them how you have repented of your sins and asked Jesus into your heart to be your Lord and Savior? And do they look at you in unbelief; as if you don't have a clue what you are talking about? Do they try and offend you with their cynical remarks? This is how the Pharisees treated the blind man. They didn't want to believe Jesus was God in the flesh. But He is!! And what the blind man spoke was true—for him—and for all believers. Once we were blind but now we see! Let's be willing to share this Truth with those who have yet to meet our Savior, regardless of their response. We once were blind, but now we see! Praise God!!

> *"I say to you that likewise there will be more joy in heaven over one sinner who repents than over ninety-nine just persons who need no repentance."*   —Luke 15:7

The joy of the Lord is your strength.

Nehemiah 8:10

Satan comes as a thief
in the night
to steal our peace,
rob our joy,
and convince us
we are not enough.

The Joy of the Lord

Nehemiah 8:10

The joy of the Lord is your strength.

In a world filled with self-assured strong people, it is easy for us to feel unsure of ourselves. We feel "less than" and thus, live our lives trying to prove to ourselves, and to others, we are enough.

As children of the Living God, we have no need to feel or live this way. In our weakness we find strength in the Lord.

> And He said to me, *"My grace is sufficient for you, for My strength is made perfect in weakness."* Therefore, most gladly I will boast in my infirmities, that the power of Christ may rest upon me.　　　—2 Corinthians 12:9

When we live in the joy of the Lord and all He has done for us, we find confidence knowing we belong to Him. No longer do we live for ourselves, but our desire is that our lives are a reflection of Christ.

"For in Him we live and move and have our being." —Acts 17:28

> "I have been crucified with Christ; it is no longer I who live,
> but Christ lives in me; and the life I now live in the flesh I live
> by faith in the Son of God, who loved me and gave Himself
> for me."　　　　　　　　　　　　　　　—Galatians 2:20

Satan comes as a thief in the night to steal our peace, rob our joy, and convince us we are not enough. But, we can live with the assurance knowing, what Satan came to steal, Christ has overcome.

> *"The thief does not come except to steal, and to kill, and to
> destroy. I have come that you may have life, and that they
> may have it more abundantly."*　　　　　　　—John 10:10

The next time we are tempted to feel "less than", let's remember to whom we belong and live in the strength of our Savior, instead.

> I can do all things through Christ who strengthens me.
> 　　　　　　　　　　　　　　　　　—Philippians 4:13

For they loved the praise of men
more than the praise of God.

John 12:43

We live for an audience of One.
His name is Jesus.

Praise of God

John 12:43

For they loved the praise of men
more than the praise of God

Even though Jesus had done many signs and miracles, many Chief Priests and Jews refused to believe He was the Son of God. They were determined to see Him crucified for proclaiming what they felt was blasphemy. Those that did believe, refused to proclaim Jesus as the Christ because of fear of the Pharisees.

> Nevertheless even among the rulers many believed in Him,
> But because of the Pharisees they did not confess *Him*, lest they
> should be put out of the synagogue for they loved the praise
> of men more than the praise of God.　　—John 12:42-43

When I read this, my first thought was, "Oh Lord, may this never be true in my life. May I be willing to proclaim my belief and love for you regardless of who I am with." Then I thought about how important it is to us all to be accepted by others. We can justify not sharing our beliefs for fear of becoming an offense to others.

What does our Father tell us we are to do?

> *"Come out from among them, and be separate says the Lord."*
> 　　　　　　　　　　　　　　—2 Corinthians 6:17

Jesus walked among the lost, not trying to blend in, nor cower from the Truth, but simply sharing the love of the Father. As we live our lives as a witness for our Lord, we are to do the same.

> THEREFORE be imitators of God as dear children.
> And walk in love, as Christ also has loved us
> and given Himself for us, an offering and a sacrifice
> to God for a sweet-smelling aroma.　　—Ephesians 5:1-2

We live for an audience of One. His name is Jesus. May we live our life pleasing to Him. Only then will we bring Him the glory due His Holy name.

> *"Let your light so shine before men, that they may see your
> good works and glorify your Father in heaven."*　　—Matthew 5:16

Jesus said to her, "Mary!"
She turned and said to Him, "Rabboni!"

John 20:16

Just as Mary was devastated
with grief until she saw
her Savior,
we, too, have times when life
becomes overwhelming.

Turn

John 20:16

Jesus said to her, *"Mary!"*
She turned and said to Him, "Rabboni!"

Three days after Jesus had been crucified, Mary Magdalene, devastated and filled with fear, stood outside the tomb where He had been buried. Seeing the stone rolled away, His cloths lying where Jesus had been, she assumed they had taken her Savior away. Turning, she saw who she thought was the gardener, standing in front of her.

> Jesus said to her, *"Woman why are you weeping? Whom are you*
> *seeking?"* She, supposing Him to be the gardener; said to
> Him, "Sir, if You have carried Him away, tell me where You
> have laid Him, and I will take Him away."
> Jesus said to her, *"Mary!"* She turned and said to Him,
> "Rabboni!" (which is to say, Teacher).   —John 20:15-16

At that moment, Mary knew Jesus was alive, that He had come back as He said He would. In an instant her fears were gone, her sorrow turned to joy.

Do you know Jesus knows your name? Before you were born He knew the color of your eyes, the texture of your hair, how tall you would be, where you would live, the family awaiting your arrival, and what your future would hold. Before you were placed in the arms of your loving mother, Jesus loved you with a never-ending love.

> My frame was not hidden from You,
> When I was made in secret,
> *And* skillfully wrought in the lowest parts of the earth.
> Your eyes saw my substance, being yet unformed.
> And in Your book they all were written,
> The days fashioned for me,
> When *as yet there were* none of them.   —Psalm 139:15-16

Just as Mary was devastated with grief until she saw her Savior, we, too, have times when life becomes overwhelming. When we find ourselves in this place, may we turn toward Jesus. As we do, we will hear Him say, (your name), and our sorrow will be turned to joy, our fears to peace, and we will know He is there, just as He said He would be.

He will not leave you nor forsake you.   —Deuteronomy 31:6b

"*Nevertheless I tell you the truth.
It is to your advantage that I go away;
for if I do not go away,
the Helper will not come to you;
but if I depart, I will send Him to you.*"

John 16:7

With Christ living in us
through the Holy Spirit,
we are one with Him.

The Helper

John 16:7

"Nevertheless I tell you the truth.
It is to your advantage that I go away;
for if I do not go away, the Helper will not come to you;
but if I depart, I will send Him to you."

Gathered with His disciples, Jesus shared how He would be going away. Filled with sorrow the disciples asked no questions, but sat in unbelief in what they were hearing. Understanding their despair, Jesus assured them He would not leave them alone, but would send a Helper to guide them.

"However, when He, the Spirit of truth, has come, He will
guide you into all truth; for He will not speak on His own
authority; but whatever He hears He will speak; and He will
tell you things to come."   —John 16:13

When we accept Christ as our Personal Savior, we, too, receive the Holy Spirit;

Then Peter said to them, "Repent, and let every one
of you be baptized in the name of the Lord Jesus Christ
for the remission of sins; and you shall receive the gift
of the Holy Spirit."   —Acts 2:38

We become new in Him, the Spirit living in us that we might walk in all His ways;

"Then I will give them one heart, and I will put a new spirit
within them, and take the stony heart out of their flesh,
and give them a heart of flesh, that they may walk in My
statutes and keep My judgments and do them; and they
shall be My people, and I will be their God."
                    —Ezekiel 11:19-20

When we receive the Holy Spirit, He takes what is Christ's and declares it to us;

He will glorify Me, for He will take of what is Mine and
declare it to you.   —John 16:14

With Christ living in us through the Holy Spirit, we are one with Him. May we rejoice as we allow Him to have His way in our lives!

Christ in you, the hope of glory.   —Colossians 1:27b

Even a fool is thought to be wise
if he keeps silent, and discerning
if he holds his tongue.

Proverbs 17:28 (NIV)

Too often we share our
opinion before
understanding the situation.

A Wise Man

Proverbs 17:28 (NIV)

Even a fool is thought wise
if he keeps silent, and discerning
if he holds his tongue.

How easy it is for us to speak our mind rather than remain quiet. We deem it important that others know how we feel, and all we know. The Word of God tells us we would show greater wisdom by keeping silent and not saying anything at all.

Set a guard, O LORD, over my mouth;
Keep watch over the door of my lips. —Psalm 141:3

Too often we share our opinion before understanding the situation. We may feel we know what is best, how things should be handled, but we would be wise to keep silent until we have heard all the details. Even then we need to take the situation to the Lord in prayer, asking for His wisdom and direction. What we think on our own means little and can often do more harm than good.

He who answers a matter before he hears it,
It *is* folly and shame to him. —Proverbs 18:13

Better is the poor who walks in integrity
Than *one who is* perverse in his lips, and is a fool. —Proverbs 19:1

There is no greater attribute than integrity. A person of integrity displays honesty, reliability, wisdom, uprightness, and understanding. They are also held in high esteem, for others know they are truthful in all their ways.

As for me, You uphold me in my integrity,
And set me before Your face forever. —Psalm 41:12

Perhaps the next time we feel we must speak, we need to remain silent instead. So many times our actions speak louder than our words.

He who has knowledge spares his words,
And a man of understanding is of a calm spirit. —Proverbs 17:27

To everything there is a season,
A time to keep silent, and a time to speak. —Ecclesiastes 3:1,7b

When You said, "Seek My face,"
my heart said to You,
"Your face, LORD, I will seek."

Psalm 27:8

As we spend time with Him,
our Lord draws us to Himself,
making us complete in Him.

"Seek My Face"

Psalm 27:8

When You said, "Seek My face,"
my heart said to You,
"Your face, LORD, I will seek."

O GOD, You *are* my God; early I will seek You; my soul thirsts for You;
my flesh longs for You. In a dry and thirsty land where there is no water.
—Psalm 63:1

Just as David penned in the Psalms, my greatest desire is to hunger and thirst
for God. My longing is to fall asleep with Him on my mind, wake thinking
of Him, thirst for Him throughout the day, and live for Him in all I do.

How do we acquire such a thirst and hunger for God?

> Then you will call upon Me and go and pray to Me,
> and I will listen to you.
> And you will seek Me, and find *Me*, when you search
> for Me with all your heart.   —Jeremiah 29:12-13

We are to search for Him with a willingness to put every other ambition and
attitude aside, our only aspiration to know Him fully.

> Yet indeed I also count all things loss for the excellence of the
> knowledge of Christ Jesus my Lord, for whom I suffered the
> loss of all things, and count them as rubbish, that I may gain
> Christ.   —Philippians 3:8

David spent hours praying to the Lord as he tended his sheep. Through continual communication he grew to know God, fall in love with Him, and hear
His voice. In return God blessed David, calling him…

> *A man after My own heart*, who will do all My will.   —Acts 13:22

As we, too, spend time with Him, our Lord draws us to Himself, making us
complete in Him. Oh, that it might be!

> Draw near to God, and He will draw near to you. —James 4:8a

> Ask, and it will be given to you; seek, and you will find;
> knock, and it will be opened to you.   —Matthew 7:7

When you pass through the waters,
I *will be* with you;
And through the rivers,
they shall not overflow you.
When you walk through the fire,
you shall not be burned,
Nor shall the flame scorch you.
For I *am* the LORD your God,
The Holy One of Israel, your Savior.

Isaiah 43:2-3

Nowhere does it say we will be overcome.

You Are Mine

Isaiah 43:2-3

When you pass through the waters,
I will be with you;
And through the rivers,
they shall not overflow you.
When you walk through the fire,
you shall not be burned,
Nor shall the flame scorch you.
For *I am* the LORD your God,
The Holy One of Israel, your Savior.

How many times have we gone through trials which have threatened to over-come our very existence? We thought we were strong, our faith solid, and then, like an out of control tornado, the heartache of a lifetime comes roaring through our life. Perhaps it is an unexpected telephone call, a pink slip ending a career, a child refusing to listen to our guidance, a life threatening disease attacking our body. Whatever it may be, trials can send us into depths of despair we never thought possible.

Do you see the word "through" in these Scriptures? When you pass through the waters, through the rivers, through the fire. Nowhere does it say we will be overcome, but instead assures us we will go through the trials of life. Why?

> For *I am* the LORD your God,
> The Holy One of Israel, your Savior.   —Isaiah 43:3

The Holy One of Israel, our Savior, will lead us through the waters, through the rivers, and through the fire.

> Fear not, for *I am* your God.
> I will strengthen you,
> Yes, I will help you,
> I will uphold you with My righteous right hand.   —Isaiah 41:10

The next time trials seem to be winning, let's remember to *whom* we belong and hold tight to the hand of our Savior. He alone will guide us to the other side.

> "Be strong and of good courage, do not fear nor be afraid
> of them; for the LORD your God, He *is* the One who goes
> with you. He will not leave you nor forsake you."
> —Deuteronomy 31:6

He restores my soul;
He leads me in the path of righteousness
For His name sake.

Psalm 23:3

And I will rest in You, the
keeper of my soul.

Keeper of My Soul

Psalm 23:3

He restores my soul;
He leads me in the path of righteousness
For His name sake.

"Lord Jesus, because You tell me"…

> Be anxious for nothing, but in everything by prayer and
> supplication, with thanksgiving, let your requests be made
> known to God; and the peace of God, which surpasses all
> understanding will guard your hearts and minds through
> Christ Jesus.   —Philippians 4:6-7

"I am not going to be anxious about my family, future, or anything else that
threatens to steal my peace. Instead I will rest in You."

"You tell me to be not be afraid, but be strong and courageous"…

> *"Have I not commanded you? Be strong and of good courage;*
> *do not be afraid, nor dismayed, for the LORD your God is*
> *with you wherever you go."*   —Joshua 1:9

"For that reason, when the world is falling apart around me, I will be strong
and of good courage. I will not fear nor be dismayed, but will keep my eyes
focused on you, trusting in the knowledge that You are with me."

"You tell us to look up for our redemption draws near"…

> *"Then they will see the Son of Man coming in a cloud with peace and*
> *and great glory. Now when these things begin to happen, look up and*
> *lift up your heads, because your redemption draws near."*
>   —Luke 21:27-28

"So I will look up, anticipating with great excitement Your coming back as
You have promised. And I will rest in You, the Keeper of my Soul."…

> The LORD *is* your keeper;
> The LORD *is* your shade at your right hand.   —Psalm 121:5

The name of the LORD is a strong tower;
the righteous run to it and are safe.

Proverbs 18:10

Because we belong to

the LORD,

we have no reason to fear.

Fear Not

Proverbs 18:10

The name of the LORD *is* a strong tower;
the righteous run to it and are safe.

What's in a name? Our name identifies who we are. When we hear a person's name we immediately see them in our mind's eye, their appearance and personality, our love for them, or casual acquaintance.

The Scriptures tell us there is no greater name in all of history then the name of our LORD, Jesus Christ. His name is above every name, and at the name of Jesus every knee shall bow.

> Therefore God also has highly exalted Him and given
> Him the name which is above every name,
> that at the name of Jesus every knee should bow,
> of those in heaven, and of those under the earth,
> and *that* every tongue should confess that
> Jesus Christ *is* Lord, to the glory of God the Father.
> —Philippians 2:9-11

Has there been a time in your life when you were afraid? Anxious about a test result from a medical procedure, fearful of what the future might hold now you have lost your spouse, frightened for your children as they enter the world on their own. We live in a world of uncertainties. It seems more and more we have opportunity for fear of tomorrow

Nevertheless, because we belong to the LORD we have no reason to fear. As we run to Him, He promises His protection.

> *In the world you will have tribulation;*
> *But be of good cheer,*
> *I have overcome the world.*   —John 16:33

When fear threatens to overtake us, paralyzing our every thought and action, let's remember to run to Jesus, the name above every name. He alone is our strong tower!

> The LORD *is* my light and my salvation;
> Whom shall I fear:
> The LORD *is* the strength of my life;
> Of whom shall I be afraid?   —Psalm 27:1

But without faith *it is* impossible to please *Him,*
for he who comes to God must believe
that He is, and *that* He is a rewarder of those
who diligently seek Him.

Hebrews 11:6

As we walk by faith,
we walk according to
the Word of God.

Faith

Hebrews 11:6

But without faith *it is* impossible to please *Him*,
for he who comes to God must believe
that He is, and *that* He is a rewarder of those
who diligently seek Him.

How difficult is it to walk by faith? Do we believe the Lord will;
Make all things beautiful in His time   —Ecclesiastes 3:11
Intend for good what Satan meant for evil   —Genesis 50:20
Turn our ashes into beauty —Isaiah 61:3
Keep us in perfect peace —Isaiah 26:3
Work all things together for good   —Romans 8:29
Keep what we've committed to Him
until that Day.   —2 Timothy 1:12

As we walk by faith, we walk according to the Word of God. We believe what it says, seeking His face when we don't understand.

> If any of you lacks wisdom, let him ask of God, who gives to
> all liberally and without reproach, and it will be given to him.
> But let him ask in faith, with no doubting, for he who doubts
> is like a wave of the sea driven and tossed by the wind. For let
> not that man suppose that he will receive anything from the
> Lord; *he is* a double-minded man, unstable in all his ways.
>   —James 1: 5-8

As children of God, we don't see to believe, but believe because we have faith in the Son of God who gave His life for us.

> For we walk by faith, not by sight.   —2 Corinthians 5:7

> But as many as received Him, to them He gave the right to become
> Children of God, to those who believe in His name: who were born,
> not of blood, nor of the will of the flesh, nor of the will of man, but
> of God.   —John 1:12-13

> Now faith is the substance of things hoped for, the evidence of things
> not seen.   —Hebrews 11:1

Faith is a gift given to the children of God that we might walk hand in hand with our Savior. May we walk by faith without doubting, knowing we can trust our Father.

The next day John saw Jesus
coming toward him,
And said, "Behold! The Lamb of God
who takes away the sins of the world!"

John 1:29

Have you ever thought of
what you will do when
you see the Lord Jesus
face to face?

I Want to See Him

John 1:29

The next day John saw Jesus coming toward him,
And said, "Behold! The Lamb of God
who takes away the sins of the world!"

Celebrating the life of a wonderful Christian friend, the pastor told how when he asked Margaret if she wanted to go home, she promptly replied, "I don't want to go home. I want to go see Him!"

How often do we think about seeing Jesus when we pass from this earthly tent to our home in heaven? Often we find comfort in knowing we will be united with loved ones who have gone before. However, do we wait with anticipation for when we will see our Savior?

> One *thing* I have desired of the LORD,
> That will I seek:
> That I may dwell in the house of the LORD
> All the days of my life,
> To behold the beauty of the LORD,
> And to inquire in His temple. —Psalm 27:4

Have you ever thought of what you will do when you see the Lord Jesus face to face? Perhaps you will raise your hands in praise, fall at His feet with over-flowing gratitude, or possibly prostrate before Him, your face to the ground.

> Therefore God also has highly exalted Him and
> given Him the name which is above every name,
> that at the name of Jesus every knee shall bow,
> of those in heaven, and of those on earth, and of
> under the earth, and *that* every tongue should confess
> that Jesus Christ *is* Lord, to the glory of God the Father.
> —Philippians 2:9-11

Regardless of your response when you see your Savior, in that moment every heartache, sickness, trial, and tribulation you have endured will vanish from your life, and you will be in the presence of your Lord forevermore. What a glorious day that will be!

> *Surely I am coming quickly.* " Amen
> Even so, come, Lord Jesus! — Revelations 22:20

The LORD is good to those whose hope
is in Him, to the one who seeks Him.

Lamentations 3:25 (NIV)

We can trust the heart
of our Father when we can't
trace His hand.
He alone knows what is best.

Hope in the Lord

Lamentations 3:25 (NIV)

The LORD is good to those whose hope
is in Him, to the one who seeks Him

Hope is always the right choice. With hope we look forward to the future with anticipation. The glass remains full to overflowing instead of half empty. And, most importantly, our faith in the Father continues to develop into an everlasting trust.

> *I would have lost heart,*
> unless I had believed
> That I would see the goodness of the LORD
> In the land of the living.   —Psalm 27:13

As children of the living God, our hope is in Him alone.

> Blessed *be* the God and Father of our Lord Jesus Christ,
> who according to His abundant mercy has begotten us
> again to a living hope through the resurrection of Jesus
> Christ from the dead.   —1 Peter 1:3

And, just as faith is the evidence of things we cannot see, hope that is seen is not hope.

> For we were saved in this hope,
> but hope that is seen is not hope;
> for why does one still hope for what he sees?
> But if we hope for what we do not see,
> we eagerly wait for *it* with perseverance.   —Romans 8:24-25

When the road is long and we are tempted to give into fear, we have a Father who will renew our strength, giving us hope for the future.

> In the multitude of my anxieties within me,
> Your comforts delight my soul.   —Psalm 94:19

We can trust the heart of our Father when we can't trace His hand. He alone knows what is best. As we place our hope in Him, our heart will be settled, and we will find strength once again for all our tomorrows.

> "The LORD is my portion," says my soul"
> "Therefore I hope in Him!"   —Lamentations 3:24

Delight yourself also in the LORD,
And He shall give you the desires of your heart.

Psalm 37:4-5

God has a plan for each of us
As we travel this journey
called life.

Desires of Your Heart

Psalm 37:4-5

Delight yourself also in the LORD,
And He shall give you the desires of your heart.

When I was younger and began living what I thought was the desire of my heart, it looked as if I would reach my goals as I continued climbing the ladder of success.

However, as I daily studied the Word of God, my heart's desires were changing. What I thought was essential to attain my purpose in life began to diminish in comparison to all I was learning. Then I was asked to lead a Bible Study. Unbeknown to me, the Lord was about to bless me with a fulfillment I had never known. I loved every moment we spent pouring over His Word! This is when I understood the meaning of Psalm 37: 4-5 for the first time. As I delighted myself in the LORD, He began fulfilling what was truly the desire of my heart.

> For I know the plans I have you, says the Lord.
> They are plans for good and not for evil, to give
> you a future and a hope.   —Jeremiah 29:11 TLB

> "For My thoughts *are* not your thoughts,
> Nor *are* your ways My ways, " says the LORD.
> For as the heavens are higher than the earth,
> So are My ways higher than your ways,
> And My thoughts than your thoughts."   —Isaiah 55:8-9

God has a plan for each of us as we travel this journey called life. As we let go of our own goals and ambitions, allowing Him to have His way with our life, we will find He has given us the true desire of our heart.

> I will instruct you and teach you in the way you should go;
> I will guide you with my eye.   —Psalm 32:8

> Your ears shall hear a word behind you, saying,
> "This is the way walk in it," whenever you turn to the
> right hand or whenever you turn to the left.   —Isaiah 30:21

> Trust in the Lord with all your heart, and lean not on your own
> understanding; in all your ways acknowledge Him, and He shall
> direct your paths.   —Proverbs 3:5-6

Be anxious for nothing, but in everything
by prayer and supplication, with thanksgiving,
let your requests be made known to God;
and the peace of God,
which passes all understanding,
will guard your hearts and minds
through Christ Jesus.

Philippians 4:6-7

What does it say?
What does it mean?
What does it mean to
me personally?

Be Anxious for Nothing

Philippians 4:6-7

Be anxious for nothing, but in everything
by prayer and supplication, with thanksgiving,
let your requests be made known to God;
and the peace of God, which passes all understanding,
will guard your hearts and minds through Christ Jesus.

Receiving a disturbing telephone call from one of our children, as I laid down to sleep that night, sleep would not come. My thoughts were consumed with what the future would hold, how the situation could be resolved, and what this meant for all involved.

As I prayed, asking the Lord for guidance, this Scripture came to my mind. As I lay there, I asked the Lord to show me what this meant concerning our heartache. As only the Lord could, He led me through the Scripture by asking what does it say and what does it mean to me personally:

Be anxious (do not worry) *for nothing* (about this situation), *but in everything* (but instead), *by prayer and supplication*, (pray) *with thanksgiving* (being thankful for the gift of prayer), *let your requests be made to God* (tell Me your concerns, your desires) *and the peace of God* (then My peace) *which passes all understanding* (which you cannot understand) *will guard your heart* (will keep your heart from breaking) *and mind* (and mind from fearing the worst) *through Christ Jesus* (because you have given it to Me.)

As I meditated on what He had shown me, I thanked God for His provision of prayer, concern for my fears, and promise of peace in the midst of the turmoil. His assurance that He would keep my heart from breaking and my mind from racing to the worst possible scenario became a healing balm in the midst of my broken heart. As I thanked Him for His faithfulness, His Holy Word, and His peace, I fell asleep, no longer consumed with the situation, but knowing I could rest in Him.

> You will keep *him* in perfect peace,
> *Whose* mind is set *on You,*
> Because he trusts in You.
> Trust in the LORD forever,
> For in YAH, the LORD, *is* everlasting strength.   —Isaiah 26:3-4

"Peace I leave with you, My peace I give to you;
not as the world gives do I give to you.
Let not our heart be troubled,
neither let it be afraid."

John 14:27

As we live our lives focused on
Jesus and all He is in our lives,
we will find a peace
the world does not know.

My Peace I Give

John 14.27
"Peace I leave with you, My peace I give to you;
not as the world gives do I give to you.
Let not your heart be troubled, neither let it be afraid."

What are your first thoughts when you wake in the morning? Are they thoughts of great anticipation for all the day holds, excitement for all you will accomplish? Or, do you have a pit in your stomach, dreading the thought of facing another day? As children of God we can rest in the Truth that we will not walk through the day alone. As we hang on tight to the hand of our Father, He will lead us through every decision, circumstance, heartache, or frustration we might face.

> Whoever listens to me will dwell safely, and will be secure,
> without fear or evil.   —Proverbs 1:33

The Word of God tells us as we live our lives focused on Jesus and all He is in our lives, we will find a peace the world does not know. No longer will we walk in despair and hopelessness, but our lives will become a reflection of our heavenly Father, a sweet fragrance for all to see.

> Now thanks *be* to God who always leads us in triumph in Christ,
> and through us diffuses the fragrance of His knowledge in every
> place.   —2 Corinthians 2:14

I heard a Christian teacher once say, "We get to choose where we look." I have never forgotten these words; they make all the difference in the life of a believer. Do we choose to look at our problems, or do we choose to look at the One who has the answer for every situation we face? It is the difference in living with a pit in our stomach, or hope in our heart.

> You will keep *him* in perfect peace, *whose* mind *is* stayed *on You*,
> because he trusts in You.   —Isaiah 26:3

May we choose to look at Him, and wake each morning praising the Lord for His never-ending love and faithfulness, regardless of what the day might hold.

> This is the day the LORD has made;
> We will rejoice and be glad in it.   —Psalm 118:24

Cast your burden on the LORD,
And He shall sustain you;
He shall never permit the righteous to be moved.

Psalm 55:22

Could it be God allows worries
and concerns to come into our
lives to build our faith
and trust in Him?

Burdens into Blessings

Psalm 55:22

Cast your burden on the LORD,
And He shall sustain you;
He shall never permit the righteous to be moved.

As I visited with a friend concerning a heartache I have endured for some-time, I realized nothing has changed since the last time we talked. The situation remains the same, our conversation has become idle talk, and I leave our time together more discouraged then when we first began.

As I thought about this realization, I wondered what would happen if I prayed about the situation as much as I discuss it with friends. As sympathetic as they are, just as I have no answers, neither do they. I know the only answer is the intervention of God.

The Lord tells us;

> Casting all your cares upon Him for He
> cares for you.   —1 Peter 5:7

Listen to how this same Scripture is translated in the Message;

> Don't fret or worry. Instead of worrying, pray.
> Let petitions and praises shape your worries into prayers,
> letting God know your concerns.   —1 Peter 5:7 (The Message)

Could it be God allows worries and concerns to come into our lives to build our faith and trust in Him? As I turn my worries into prayers, trusting God to answer, no longer will I feel the situation is hopeless, but will find renewed hope and peace in the midst of my heartache. He alone turns our burdens into blessings.

> Be anxious for nothing, but in everything by prayer and
> supplication let your requests be known unto God, and
> the peace of God that passes all understanding will guard
> your hearts and minds through Christ Jesus.   —Philippians 4:7

> "Is anything too hard for God?"   —Genesis 18:14

> There is nothing too hard for You.   —Jeremiah 32:17b

But I *am* like a green olive tree
in the house of God;
I trust in the mercy of God forever and ever.
I will praise You forever,
because you have done *it*,
And in the presence of Your saints
I will wait on Your name, for *it is* good.

Psalm 52:8-9

Our faith is to be built on our
steadfast trust in our Father's
wisdom, and our willingness to
praise Him in the waiting.

Steadfast

Psalm 52:8-9

But I *am* like a green olive tree in the house of God;
I trust in the mercy of God forever and ever.
I will praise You forever, because you have done *it;*
And in the presence of Your saints
I will wait on Your name, for *it is* good.

As I studied this Psalm, the words *trust, praise,* and *wait* stood out to me. Even though David's desires had not come to fruition, he would praise the Lord in the waiting because he trusted in Him.

David compared himself to a green olive tree in the house of God. As I studied the signifance of the olive tree, I found this tree symbolizes faithfulness and steadfastness. Regardless of the weather conditions, the olive tree will continue to live and produce fruit. Even being cut down and destroyed, the roots of the olive tree grow so deeply a new tree will grow back in its place. David was declaring he would be faithful regardless of what happened, standing steadfast in his trust in the Lord.

As I considered my desires, I thought about my faithfulness and never wavering steadfastness before the Lord. Do I stand firm, trusting He will bring it to pass? Do I praise Him in the waiting, knowing His ways are not mine? And, do I trust Him, even when I don't understand what He is doing?

In one of the first Bible Studies I participated in, there was a prayer that went something like this;

> Dear Lord,
> I don't understand it and I don't like it, but; regardless of how I
> feel, or my desires, I will trust You, as I wait on You to do
> what I know is best.
> In Your Precious Name I pray, Amen.

Our faith is not to be built on what we see, nor how we feel. Our faith is to be built on our steadfast trust in our Father's wisdom, and our willingness to praise Him in the waiting. God is never late, and He is never early. He is exactly on time. May we be like David, faithful and steadfast, trusting in the mercy of God forever and ever.

GREAT is the LORD, and greatly to be praised.   —Psalm 48:1

By humility *and* the fear of the LORD
Are riches and honor and life.

Proverbs 22:4

Only what we do for Jesus
is of any importance.

Riches, Honor, & Life

Proverbs 22:4

By humility *and* the fear of the LORD
Are riches and honor and life.

Have you ever known a person blessed with a spiritual gift, and instead of living in gratitude for the gift, used the gift to make a name for themselves? It is a dangerous thing to believe we have anything to do with our God given gifts. The Lord desires for us to use our gifts to bring others to Himself, not to magnify our lives before men.

> Humble yourselves in the sight of the Lord, and He
> will lift you up.   —James 4:10

As we walk humbly before our Lord, we no longer live for ourselves. Instead, we live knowing only what we do for Jesus is of any importance. Riches and fame become strangely dim, and our life becomes about lifting His name on high, becoming a light in the darkness. We realize our life is but a vapor in comparison to eternity, and our desires and purpose in life become heaven focused, living for Christ alone.

> *"Let your light so shine before men, that they may see*
> *your good works and glorify your Father in heaven."*
>   —Matthew 5:16

> For what is life? It is even a vapor that appears for a little
> time and then vanishes away.   —James 4:14

Only as we remain humble before God, remembering all He has done for us, will we live in awe and highest respect for who He is:

> O magnify the LORD with me,
> And let us exalt His name together.   —Psalm 34:3

May we lift His name on high as we live for Him, giving Him the glory due His Holy name! In Him alone are riches, honor, and life:

> O LORD, our Lord,
> How excellent *is* Your name in all the earth,
> Who have set Your glory above the heavens!
>   —Psalm 8:1

Now may the God of hope fill you with all joy and peace in believing, that you may abound in hope by the power of the Holy Spirit.

Romans 15:13

He alone will turn our sorrow into dancing as He draws us to Himself.

Blessings in the Pain

Romans 15:13

Now may the God of hope fill you with all joy
and peace in believing, that you may abound
in hope by the power of the Holy Spirit.

How can it be that blessings sometimes break our heart?

Our loved one runs home to our Father after struggling with cancer, finally out of pain.

Our heart breaks over the loss of losing them.

Our prodigal child hits bottom, finding himself/ herself alone, reaping the consequences of his/her actions.

Our heart breaks to see our child so broken and desperate.

Our friend of 66 years, and at the age of 92, is called home to be with her Lord and Savior, finally at rest after a full life on earth.

Our heart is broken at the thought of not hearing her sweet voice again, sharing our hearts with one another.

We know being free of pain is what we want for our love one. It is not until our child comes to their end they realize the need to run to the Father for help. And just as much, we know we will all die. Nevertheless, what we know is best doesn't keep our heart from breaking.

The Lord does not promise a life free of trials, heartache, or tribulation. What He does promise is that He will walk through our suffering with us.

The Lord is my shepherd; I shall not want.
He makes me to lie down in green pastures;
He leads me beside the still waters.
He restores my soul   —Psalm 23:1-3

In times such as this, may we allow our Father to be our comfort, carrying us through the pain as He heals our broken heart. He alone will turn our sorrow into dancing as He draws us to Himself.

You have turned for me my mourning into dancing;
You have put off my sackcloth and clothed me with gladness.
                                        —Psalm 30:11

Said the Robin

Psalm 55:22

Cast your burden on the LORD
and He shall sustain you.

May we learn from the sparrow:

Said the Robin to the Sparrow
"I should really like to know,
why those gracious human beings
rush around and worry so?"

Said the Sparrow to the Robin
"Friend, I think that it must be
that they have no Heavenly Father
such as cares for you and me."

Author Unknown

"I am the good shepherd. The good shepherd gives His life for the sheep.
__ John 10:11

"Therefore I say to you, do not worry about your life, what you will eat or what you will drink; nor about your body, what you will put on. Is not life more than food and the body more than clothing?

   Look at the birds of the air, for they neither sow nor reap nor gather into barns; yet your heavenly Father feeds them. Are you not of more value than they?

   Which of you by worrying can add one cubit to his stature?

   So why do you worry about clothing? Consider the lilies of the field, how they grow: they neither toil nor spin; and yet I say to you even Solomon in all his glory was not arrayed like one of these.

   Now if God so clothes the grass of the field, which today is, and tomorrow is thrown into the oven, will He not much more cloth you, O you of little faith?

   Therefore do not worry, saying, "What shall we eat?" or "What shall we drink?" or "What shall we wear?"

   For after all these things the Gentiles seek. For your heavenly Father knows that you need all these things.

   But seek first the kingdom of God and His righteousness, and all these things shall be added to you.

   Therefore do not worry about tomorrow, for tomorrow will worry about its own things. Sufficient for the day *is* its own trouble." —Matt. 6:25-34

Therefore God also has highly exalted Him
And given Him the name which
is above every name.

Philippians 2:9

What is it you need
from the Lord?
Jesus is Who
you need Him to be.

Name Above All Names

Philippians 2:9

Therefore God also has highly exalted Him
And given Him the name which is above every name.

What name do you think of when you think of Jesus? Perhaps you think of Savior, Teacher, Lord, Christ, or maybe Abba, Father?

As Hagar sat by a spring of water in the wilderness, fleeing from her home for fear of Sarai, she felt the presence of the Lord come to her.

> The Angel of the LORD said to her, "Return to your mistress,
> and submit yourself under her hand."   —Genesis 16:9

Upon hearing the words of the Lord, Hagar found comfort, knowing the LORD was with her, no longer was she alone.

> Then she called the name of the LORD who spoke to her,
> You-Are-the God-Who- Sees; for she said, "Have I also seen
> Him who sees me?"   —Genesis 16:13

I love that Hagar gave the Lord the name that fulfilled her need. What she needed was for the Lord to see her as she sat alone in the wilderness.

What is it you need from the LORD? Where do you need Him to meet you? Perhaps you need peace in the midst of turmoil. Do you know He is The-God-Who-Gives-Peace?

> "Peace I leave with you. My peace I give to you; not as the world
> gives do I give to you.. Let not your heart be troubled, neither let
> it be afraid?"   —John 14:27

Jesus is Who you need Him to be. The-God-Who-Heals, The-God-Who-Loves, The-God-Who-Comforts. The-God-Who- ————_. You fill in the blank with your need. This is Who He is. Just as He met Hagar in the center of her need, He will meet you in the center of yours. Call on Him today. He promises to meet you there.

> He shall call upon Me, and I will answer him, I *will be* with him
> in trouble; I will deliver him and honor him.   —Psalm 91:15

Without Ceasing

1 Thessalonians 5:17

Pray without ceasing

For whom are you praying that they may come to know Jesus as their Savior? Does it seem your prayers are hitting the ceiling and that God isn't listening?

> And let us not grow weary while doing good,
> For in due season we shall reap if we do not lose heart.
> —Galatians 6:9

While visiting with a friend, whose daughter had strayed during her high school years, my friend told me it had taken ten years of praying for her before her daughter accepted Christ as her Savior. When her husband would become discouraged, she reminded him, "Where does it say in the Bible it will only take two, three, or even five years for our daughter to accept Christ? It doesn't! What it says is to pray without doubting."

> But let him ask in faith, with no doubting, for he who
> doubts is like a wave of the sea driven and tossed by
> the wind. For let not that man suppose that he will receive
> anything from the Lord; *he* is a double-minded man, unstable
> in all his ways. —James 1:6-8

We are a society of instant satisfaction. We expect answers to our questions without hesitation, food to satisfy our hunger simply by driving by a window, text messages to be answered the moment they are received, and prayers answered at our command.

This is not the way of our Father. His desire is that His children would trust His Holy Word, be still in Him, and wait patiently as He works all things out for their good. So often there is so much more to our prayer request then we can see. There may be hearts to soften, hurt feelings to heal, and lifestyles to redirect, before our prayers can be answered. In the waiting may we know our Father is not slow in His answer, but patient with all those involved. His ways our perfect, may we trust in Him.

> The Lord is not slack concerning *His* promise, as some count
> slackness, but is longsuffering toward us. —2 Peter 3:9

I was formerly a blasphemer, a persecutor,
and an insolent man; but I obtained mercy
because I did *it* ignorantly in unbelief.

1 Timothy 1:13

We no longer live under the
bondage of past sins,
lies from Satan,
or shackles from our past.

That Was Then

1 Timothy 1:13

I was formerly a blasphemer, a persecutor,
and an insolent man; but I obtained mercy because
I did *it* ignorantly in unbelief.

In writing to Timothy, Paul explained to him there was a time in Paul's life when he was a blasphemer, a persecutor, and chief among sinners.

As I read this portion of scripture, the word "formerly" stood out. Paul was telling Timothy this is who he was before coming to Christ. Because of the mercy and longsuffering of Christ, Paul recognized he had been set free from who he had been and was now new in Christ.

> This is the faithful saying and worthy of all acceptance, that Christ
> Jesus came into the world to save sinners, of whom I am chief.
> However, for this reason I obtained mercy, that in me first Jesus
> Christ might show all longsuffering, as a pattern to those who are
> going to believe on Him for everlasting life.   —1 Timothy 1:15-16

When we accept the saving grace of Jesus, we are made new in Him. No longer do we consider ourselves as we use to be, but our identity is found in Christ alone, and children of the living God, joint heirs with Christ.

> The Spirit Himself bears witness with our spirit that we
> are children of God, and if children, then heirs with Christ.
> —Romans 8:16-17

We no longer live under the bondage of past sins, lies from Satan, or shackles from our past. When He died on the cross, Christ made us new in Him. Old things were passed away.

> Therefore, if anyone *is* in Christ, *he is* a new creation; old things
> have passed away; behold, all things have become new.
> —2 Corinthians 5:17

What are you hanging on to that keeps you from being free in Christ? Will you open your hands and let go of that which you hold so tightly? Just as Paul, that is who you formerly were. No longer must you live in those chains. Through the mercy of Christ you are free indeed.

"Therefore if the Son makes you free, you shall be free indeed." —John 8:36

"I did not know Him,
but He who sent me to baptize
with water said to me,
"Upon whom you see the Spirit
descending, and remaining on Him,
this is He who
baptizes with the Holy Spirit."
John 1:33

As I walk by faith, I must not
only believe His Word,
but also live it out.

Walk By Faith

John 1:33

"I did not know Him, but He who sent me to baptize
with water said to me, "Upon whom you see the Spirit
descending, and remaining on Him, this is He who
baptizes with the Holy Spirit."

John the Baptist had been sent to the desert to proclaim the coming of Christ.
When asked by the priests and Levites who he was, he promptly declared he
was not the Christ, but announced:

> "I am 'The voice of one crying in the wilderness:
> Make straight the way of the LORD."   —John 1:23

Even though John had not seen Christ, his desire was to walk in faith, being
obedient to his calling. Considering the faith of John the Baptist, I couldn't
help but ponder how willing I am to walk in faith.

> Now faith is the substance of things hoped for,
> the evidence of things not seen.   —Hebrews 11:1

> But without faith *it is* impossible to please *Him,* for he
> who comes to God must believe that He is, and *that*
> He is a rewarder of those who diligently seek Him.
>   —Hebrews 11:6

Do I believe I will receive the blessings of God as I diligently seek Him? As
I walk by faith, I must not only believe His Word, but also live it out. My
heart's desire must be to seek the Lord with all my heart, mind, and soul.

> Jesus said to him, *"You shall love the LORD your God with all your
> heart, with all your soul, and with all your mind."*   —Matthew 22:37

May we not only admire those who came before, but also be willing to learn
from their example. As John the Baptist walked by faith, may we do the same.

> Therefore we also, since we are surrounded by so great a cloud
> of witnesses, let us lay aside every weight that so easily ensnares
> *us*, and let us run with endurance the race set before us, looking
> unto Jesus, the author and finisher of *our* faith   —Hebrews 12:1-2a

Through the tender mercy of our God,
With which the Dayspring from on
high has visited us;
To give light to those who sit in darkness
and the shadow of death,
To guide our feet into the way of peace.
Luke 1:78-79

As believers, our lives should reflect Jesus as brightly as the Morning Star.

Dayspring

Luke 1:78-79

Through the tender mercy of our God,
With which the Dayspring from on high has visited us;
To give light to those who sit in darkness and the shadow of death,
To guide our feet into the way of peace.

There is nothing more beautiful then watching the morning sun rise over the horizon, leaving the darkness of night behind.

As I considered Jesus being referred to as the Dayspring, I thought how He is light to us each morning. Just as the sun rises to give light for the day, Christ becomes our light giving us purpose beyond ourselves, direction for each new day, and life eternal. The word Dayspring in the dictionary is defined as "up-rising." What a wonderful comparison to Jesus, as just as the morning sun replaces the darkness of the night, Jesus replaces the darkness of our soul with the light of His love.

In Him was life, and the life was the light of men.   —John 1:4

In Revelation Jesus refers to Himself as *"the bright and morning star,"*

I, Jesus, have sent My angel to testify to you these things in the churches.
I am the Root and the Offspring of David, the Bright and Morning Star."
—Revelation 22:16

As believers, our lives should reflect Jesus as brightly as *the Morning Star.* As we live our lives in the will of our Father, we will become a reflection of His light to others.

"You are the light of the world. A city that is set on a hill cannot be hidden.
Nor do they light a lamp and put it under a basket, but on a lampstand,
and it gives light to all who are in the house.
Let your light so shine before men, that they may see your good works and
glorify your Father in heaven.   —Matthew 5:14-16

As you rise each morning, fix your eyes on the Dayspring, our Bright and Morning Star. You will find peace in the midst of turmoil, direction in place of confusion, and confidence where there once was despair.

This is the day the Lord hath made,
Let us rejoice and be glad in it.   —Psalm 118:24

"Let not our heart be troubled;
you believe in God, believe also in Me."

John 14:1

Peace is not the absence
of trouble,
but the presence of God.

The Presence of God

John 14:1

"Let not your heart be troubled;
you believe in God, believe also in Me."

Peace is not the absence of trouble, but the presence of God.

It should come as no surprise we will face pain and suffering. The Lord warns of such times.

In the world you will have tribulation; but be of good cheer.
I have overcome the world." —John 16:33b

When tribulations come, where does our faith lie in the face of such trials? Will we succumb to despair, desperate to find a solution, or will we look to our Father, the author and finisher of our faith?

Looking unto Jesus, the author and finisher of *our* faith,
who for the joy that was set before Him endured the cross,
despising the shame, and has sat down at the right hand of
the throne of God. —Hebrews 12:2

Only as we remember nothing catches God by surprise, will we run to our Father for the answer, comfort, and hope we so desperately need.

He gives power to the weak,
And to *those who have* no might He increases strength.
Even the youths shall faint and be weary,
And the young men shall utterly fall,
But those who wait on the LORD
Shall renew *their* strength;
They shall mount up with wings like eagles,
They shall run and not be weary,
They shall walk and not faint. —Isaiah 40:29-31

The next time you find yourself in the midst of trials and tribulation, instead of succumbing to despair, run to your Father, and holding tight to His hand, rest in Him.

"Peace I leave with you, My peace I give to you;
not as the world gives do I give to you.
Let not your heart be troubled, neither let it be afraid." —John 14:27

The way of the LORD is
strength for the upright.

Proverbs 10:29

May we never take for granted
all He continues to bestow so
abundantly upon us.

Strength for the Upright

Proverbs 10:29

The way of the LORD *is* strength for the upright.

Have you ever considered the rewards we receive as we walk upright before the Lord? No longer do we face each day without purpose. When we know Jesus as our Savior, we live our life for the One who made the sun for our day, told the oceans where to stop, and the mountains how high to climb. He is the One who gives strength to the weary, comfort to the sick, and will never leave nor forsake His children.

> You *are* my hiding place and my shield;
> I hope in your word.   —Psalm 119:114

Through Christ we have forgiveness of our sins and are made clean before the throne of God. No longer must we walk in fear, but in time of need are given the gift of unshakable peace, confident we are never alone.

> In Him we have redemption through His blood, the forgiveness
> of sins, according to the riches of His grace.   —Ephesians 1:7

> All we like sheep have gone astray;
> We have turned every one, to his own way;
> And the LORD has laid on Him the iniquity of us all.
>   —Isaiah 53:6

> Be anxious for nothing, but in everything by prayer and
> supplication, with thanksgiving, let your requests be made
> known to God; and the peace of God that passes all under-
> standing will guard your hearts and minds through Christ Jesus.
>   —Philippians 4:6-7

Yes, there certainly is strength for those who walk upright before the LORD. Where would we be without Him? May we never take for granted all He continues to bestow so abundantly upon us.

> Bless the LORD, O my soul;
> And all that is within me, *bless* His holy name!
> Bless the LORD, O my soul,
> And forget not all His benefits   —Psalm 103:1-2

And we know that all things work together
for good to those who love God, to those who are
called according to *His* purpose.

Romans 8:28

May we trust His Word
and allow Him to use the hard
places in our lives for our good
and for His glory.

Spiritual Blessings

Romans 8:28
And we know that all things work together for good to those
who love God, to those who are called according to *His* purpose.

How can all things work together for good? A young child is taken home before he has lived life to its fullest. A mother is called home, leaving her children behind. A father decides he doesn't want to be a part of the family, leaving his wife and children alone. How can these, and oh, so many more heartaches, work together for good?

We live in a fallen world where disease and sin run rapid. Not until Jesus comes back will we find reprieve from the heartache threatening to engulf our very existence.

> If in this life only we have hope in Christ, we are of all
> men the most pitiable.   —1 Corinthians 15:19

If not for God, there would be no purpose in pain. But God promises He will take what Satan meant for evil and turn it for good.

> But as for you, you meant evil against me; *but* God meant
> it for good.   —Genesis 50:20

When my younger sister, battling breast cancer, called me dissolved in tears, all I could do was cry with her. However, my older sister, who had fought breast cancer seven years earlier, was able to give her words of encouragement, promising her she would get through all she was feeling. She needed reassurance from one who understood and had been in the same place in her life.

> Blessed *be* the God and Father of our Lord Jesus Christ, the
> Father of mercies and God of all comfort, who comforts us
> in all our tribulation, that we may be able to comfort those
> who are in any trouble, with the comfort with which we
> ourselves are comforted by God.   —2 Corinthians 1:3-4

We may never know the why's to heartaches we face this side of heaven. However, we know Our Father loves us, and will never leave us to face our sorrows alone. May we trust His Word, and allow Him to use the hard places in our lives for our good, and for His Glory.

> He heals the brokenhearted and binds up their wounds.
> —Psalm 147:3

Gideon said to them, "I would like to make
a request of you that each of you would give me
the earrings from his plunder."
Then Gideon made it into an ephod
and set it up in his city Ophrah.
And all Israel played the harlot with it there.
It became a snare to Gideon and to his house.

Judges 8:24a, 27

An idol is anything or
anyone who takes the place
of God being first place
in our life.

Idols

Judges 8:24a, 27

Gideon said to them, "I would like to make a request of you,
that each of you would give me the earrings from his plunder."
Then Gideon made it into an ephod and set it up in his city Ophrah.
And all Israel played the harlot with it there.
It became a snare to Gideon and to his house.

Let me ask you a question, "What, or who is the most important thing or person in your life?" Is it your children? Surely it can't be wrong to hold our children in a place of most importance in our lives? Or perhaps it's your spouse. You are sure life could not go on without him or her. Possibly it is your career. You are proud of how hard you have worked, your title, and the prestige of your position. Your career defines who you are.

Did you know an idol is anything or anyone who takes the place of God being first in our life? Of course, we hold our family in utmost importance. And our God given ability can be why we are successful in our career. However, when we believe we cannot live without these, they become an idol, taking first place over God.

Idol: an object of extreme devotion

For you shall worship no other god, for the LORD, whose name *is* Jealous, *is* a jealous God. —Exodus 34:14

"And you shall love the LORD our God with all your heart with all your soul, with all your mind, and with all your strength."
This *is* the first commandment. —Mark 12:30

When we consider someone or something in our lives more important to us than God…they become a snare in our devotion to God. As long as all is well, our family safe and happy, our career going as we hoped it would, it is easy to trust God, feel He is first in our devotion. However, when our world comes crashing in, if we have not worshipped the Lord above all else, we will blame God rather than trust Him to carry us through the heartache. Only as we keep the LORD first in our lives will we understand what it means to live in His perfect peace, trusting Him unconditionally.

"For where you treasure is, there your heart will be also." —Matthew 6:21

"But now he is dead; why should I fast?
Can I bring him back again?
I shall go to him, but he shall not return to me."

2 Samuel 12:23

Yes, there is hope,
even in death.

They Are in Our Future

2 Samuel 12:23

"But now he is dead; why should I fast?
Can I bring him back again?
I shall go to him, but he shall not return to me."

David's child was sick unto death:

> David therefore pleaded with God for the child, and David
> fasted and went in and lay all night on the ground.
> —2 Samuel 12:16

When David was given the devastating news his child had died, he anointed himself, changed his clothes, and went into the house of the Lord and worshiped. When his servants asked him how he could do this, David's reply was not one of despair, but of hope.

> And he said, "While the child was alive, I fasted and wept;
> for I said, "Who can tell *whether* the LORD will be gracious
> to me, that the child may live?"
> "But now he is dead; why should I fast? Can I bring him back
> again? I shall go to him, but he shall not return to me."
> —2 Samuel 12:22-23

David lived with the assurance although his child had died, he would see him again. "I shall go to him," he told his servants. David's child was no longer just in his past, but he was now in David's future.

When we, as Christians, lose a loved one to death we don't live as those without hope, but with the blessed promise we will see them again. Just as David, we have the assurance they are no longer in our past alone, but they are now in our future. We shall go to them, but they will not return to us.

> But I do not want you to be ignorant, brethren, concerning
> those who have fallen asleep, lest you sorrow as others who
> have no hope. For if we believe that Jesus died and rose again,
> even so God will bring with Him those who sleep in Jesus.
> —1 Thessalonians 4:13-14

Yes, there is hope, even in death. We weep for our loss, but in our loss we also rejoice. We will see our loved ones again!

"Look up and lift your heads, because your redemption draweth near."
— Luke 21:28

"For I have given you an example,
that you should do as I have done to you."

John 13:15

Only through Christ will our
life be a reflection of our
Heavenly Father.

Our Example

John 13:15

"For I have given you an example,
that you should do as I have done to you."

As children of the Living God, our Father has gone before us, setting an example for us to follow. As He died on the cross, forgiving us of our sins, He set the ultimate example in what it means to forgive. We did nothing to deserve His forgiveness, yet He freely gave. This is the kind of forgiveness He asks of us in forgiving one another.

And be kind to one another, tenderhearted, forgiving
one another, even as God in Christ forgave you.   —Ephesians 4:32

The last night Jesus was with His disciples, He poured water in a basin and began washing their feet. In doing this, He showed humility. We are not greater than another, but all children of God.

"Most assuredly, I say to you, a servant is not greater than his master;
nor is he who is sent greater than he who sent him."   —John 13:16

Lest we feel justified to judge others, when the scribes and Pharisees brought a woman caught in adultery to Jesus to be condemned, Jesus knelt down and began writing on the ground:

So when they continued asking Him, He raised Himself up
and said, *"He who is without sin among you, let him throw a stone*
at her first." When Jesus had raised Himself up and saw no
one but the woman, He said to her, *"Woman, where are those*
accusers of yours? Has no one condemned you?" She said,
"No one, Lord; and Jesus said to her, *"Neither do I condemn you;*
go and sin no more."   —John 8:7,10-11

When trials come, through the compassion Jesus has for us, we are shown the compassion we are to have toward others.

Therefore, as the *elect* of God, holy and beloved, put on tender
mercies, kindness, humility, meekness longsuffering;
—Colossians 3:12

Only through Christ will our life be a reflection of our Heavenly Father. May we follow His example that our lives might be as His.

"If anyone loves Me, he sill keep My word,
and My Father will love him,
and We will come to him
and make Our home with him."

John 14:23

In Him I find
all that I need
and strength for each
new day.

Home with Christ

John 14:23

"If anyone loves Me, he will keep My word, and My Father will love him, and We will come to him and make Our home with him."

As I read this Scripture, I thought about what it means to have Christ make His home with me. I know what it means to live in my home, all it brings into my life. I wondered if they are in anyway alike:

I find love in my home, being accepted for who I am.
"Yes, I have loved you with an everlasting love;
Therefore with loving kindness I have drawn you.
—Jeremiah 31:3

I find nourishment as I sit around the dinner table with my family:

Your words were found, and I ate them,
And Your word was to me the joy and rejoicing of my heart;
For I am called by Your name,
O LORD God of hosts.   —Jeremiah 15:16

In my home I find my most rewarding work. As I care for those the Lord has blessed me with, I find pleasure and fulfillment:

Therefore, my beloved, as you have always obeyed, not as in my presence only, but now much more in my absence, work out your own salvation with fear and trembling; for it is God who works in you both to will and to do for *His* good pleasure.   —Philippians 2:12-13

I find sweet fellowship with my loved ones. We laugh and cry together, and celebrate special events in each of our lives:

God is faithful, by whom you were called into the fellowship of His Son, Jesus Christ our Lord.   —1 Corinthians 1:9

And I find rest in my home, reprieve from the busyness of the day, and much needed rest for the night:

"Come to Me, all you who labor and are heavy laden, and I will give you rest. Take My yoke upon you and learn from Me, for I am gentle and lowly in heart, and you will find rest for your souls."   —Matthew 11:28-30

Yes, living in my home with those I love is much like dwelling with Christ. In Him I find all that I need and strength for each new day:

LORD, everything you have given me is good. You have made my life secure.   —Psalm 16:5 NIRV

Therefore, if anyone *is* in Christ,
he is a new creation;
old things have passed away;
behold, all things have become new.

2 Corinthians 5:17

As children of the Living God,
our lives become a reflection of
who we are in Christ.

In Christ

2 Corinthians 5:17

Therefore, if anyone *is* in Christ,
he is a new creation; old things have passed away;
behold, all things have become new.

Have you considered the changes that take place in our lives when we accept Jesus as Savior? Not only are we forgiven of our sins, but we become a new creation through Christ.

When we accept Christ as our Savior, we receive a renewed heart. The hardened heart, full of resentment and bitterness, is replaced with a heart of compassion and forgiveness.

> "I will give you a new heart, and put a new spirit within you;
> I will take the heart of stone out of your flesh and give you a
> heart of flesh."　　　　　　　　　　　—Ezekiel 36:26

Our mind is renewed; giving us a new thought life. Instead of thinking on things of discouragement and disgrace, we begin thinking thoughts pleasing to Christ.

> And do not be conformed to this world, but be transformed by the
> renewing of your mind, that you may prove what is that good and
> acceptable and perfect will of God.　　　　　—Romans 12:2

> Finally, brethren, whatever things *are* true, whatever things *are* noble,
> whatever things *are* just, whatever things *are* lovely, whatever things
> *are* of good report, if *there is* any virtue and if *there is* anything
> praiseworthy; meditate on these things.
> 　　　　　　　　　　　　　　　—Philippians 4:8

No longer are our bodies our own, but we become the temple of the Holy Spirit.

> Or do you not know that your body is the temple of the Holy Spirit
> *who is* in you, whom you have from God, and you are not your own?
> For you were bought at a price; therefore glorify God in your body
> and in your spirit, which are God's.　　　　—1 Corinthians 6:19-20

As children of the Living God, our lives become a reflection of who we are in Christ. May we live a life holy, pleasing to Him.

> Search me Oh God, and know my heart;
> Try me, and know my anxieties; and see *if there is* any wicked way in
> me, and lead me in the way everlasting.　　　—Psalm 139:23-24

I will seek what was lost
and bring back what was driven away,
bind up the broken and strengthen what was sick.

Ezekiel 34:16

We become so consumed
with our heartache,
we forget Who
holds our heart.

I Will

Ezekiel 34:16

I will seek what was lost
and bring back what was driven away,
bind up the broken and strengthen what was sick.

Do you need to read this Scripture again? I know I did. This is a Scripture that needs to be memorized, put on a plaque, and hung for all to read. We all have things in our lives, whether a broken spirit, sickness, or broken relationships, that need restoring. In each of these situations, we can stand on the Word of God. The Lord did not say, "I will try" or " possibly," but, He promised, "I will seek." Our Father is a promise keeper. We can stand on His Word.

> Every word of God *is* pure
> He *is* a shield to those who put their trust in Him. —Proverbs 30:5

How easily we forget how big God is. We become so consumed with our heartache that we forget who holds our heart. Regardless of how impossible the situation may appear, God is bigger. We must know that we know; whatever our concern, God is in control and nothing is too hard for Him.

> Then the word of the LORD came to Jeremiah, saying,
> "Behold *I am* the LORD, the God of all flesh.
> Is there anything too hard for Me?" —Jeremiah 32:26-27

Where does our confidence come from? Does it come from peaceful circumstances, our loved ones living as we had hoped, and a problem free life? Or, does it come from our unshakeable trust in the Lord? When we come to know we can trust our Father, and what He said He would do, He will do, we will find a peace only He can give.

> You will keep *him* in perfect peace,
> *Whose* mind is stayed *on You,*
> Because he trusts in You. —Isaiah 26:3

> "God *is* not a man, that He should lie,
> Nor a son of man, that He should repent,
> Has He said, and will He not do?
> Or has He spoken, and will not make it good? —Numbers 23:19

Stand strong my friend. God has spoken. His promise; "I Will!"

*"For it is not you who speak,
but the Spirit of your Father
who speaks in you."*
Matthew 10:20

It can be a scary thing to be asked questions we do not know how to answer. Fear Not! The Lord is with you!

He Speaks

Matthew 10:20

"For it is not you who speak,
but the Spirit of your Father
who speaks in you."

Sitting across the table from a forever friend, she looked at me and what seemed like from nowhere said, "You can't tell me that Jesus is the only way to get to heaven. What about all the other religions? Could they all really be wrong?"

My first thought was, "What do I say? How can I defend what I know to be truth? What I say could change how she believes forever." So I did the only thing I knew to do. I prayed. I asked the Lord to give me His words, to speak through me, to help me say what my friend needed to hear.

"If Jesus isn't the only way, why did He have to die such a horrible death? Why would He do that except for the Truth that He did this to save us from our sins? In all the other religions are their "saviors" alive today? Jesus is alive! He rose on the third day and came back to earth. And when He left to sit at the right hand of the Father, He sent the Holy Spirit to live with those who believe in Him. We are not alone, we have the Holy Spirit living in us!"

I knew those were not my words, but the Lord's. She did not argue, dispute, or disagree. She simply said to me, "I remember learning about the Father, Son, and Holy Ghost in youth group. Is that what that means?"

The Lord had spoken, and the Lord was in total control. I could rest in Him for the results. She did not pray the sinner's prayer that day, accepting Jesus as her Savior, but as we parted ways I had the assurance my words had not gone away void. Why? They were not my words.

> So shall My word be that goes forth from My mouth;
> It shall not return to Me void,
> But it shall accomplish what I please,
> And it shall prosper *in the thing* for which I sent it.   —Isaiah 55:11

It can be a scary thing to be asked questions we do not know how to answer. Fear not! The Lord is with you! As I was taught; hide behind the Word of God. "I didn't say it, God did!" Who can argue with that?

"For I was hungry and you gave Me food;
I was thirsty and you gave me drink;
I was a stranger and you took Me in;
I was naked and you clothed Me;
I was sick and you visited Me;
I was in prison and you came to Me."

Matthew 25:35-36

The world is hurting
and we have the answer.

Compassion of Jesus

Matthew 25:35-36

"For I was hungry and you gave Me food; I was thirsty
and you gave Me drink; I was a stranger and you took Me in;
I was naked and you clothed Me; I was sick and you visited Me;
I was in prison and you came to Me."

Wouldn't it be wonderful to be a reflection of Jesus to those we meet along the way? There are so many hurting people in this world that are in need of the compassion of Jesus. Through Christ, we can give them what they need. We can be there for the lonely, the broken, and the hurting. We can feed the hungry, drive the sick to their doctor appointment, and listen to the hurting as they pour out their heart. We can show them Jesus.

> *"Then the righteous will answer Him saying, "Lord when did we see*
> *You hungry and feed You, or thirsty and give You drink?*
> *And the King will answer and say to them, "Assuredly, I say to you,*
> *inasmuch as you did it to one of the least of these My brethren, you*
> *did it to Me."* —Matthew 25: 37, 40

"Where do I find those in need?", you ask. Ask Jesus to bring them into your life. He alone knows who needs a touch of love and grace from one of His children. Seek His face and He will lead. And in His leading, and your obedience, you will not only bless others, but you too, will be blessed.

> In all your ways acknowledge Him,
> And He shall direct your paths. —Proverbs 3:6

In listening to a message from Joni Earekson Tada, she defined a person of compassion as one willing to live as Jesus lived, with a willingness to pour out their life for another. Joni has certainly done this as she has ministered to the disabled throughout the world.

The world is hurting and we have the answer. May we be the hands and feet of Christ as through His compassion and love, we live our lives as a reflection of Him. What a privilege we have been given.

> But when He saw the multitudes, He was moved with compassion
> for them, because they were weary and scattered, like sheep having
> no shepherd. —Matthew 9:36

Trust in Him at all times,
you people;
Pour out your heart before Him;
God is a refuge for us.

Psalm 62:8

Get to know your Savior.
Jesus is all you need.

Our Refuge

Psalm 62:8

Trust in Him at all times,
you people;
Pour out your heart before Him;
God *is* a refuge for us.

We have all had times in our life when we were in need of refuge from the demands of this world. The stress of work, struggle of never-ending bills, concern for our children, and the chaos of this world, can send us into feelings of despair and frustration.

When we get to know our Savior, we have the assurance we can run to Him, regardless of how we are feeling. Jesus is our safe haven in times of trouble, comfort when we are hurting, joy when prayer has been answered, and guidance when we are lost. Jesus is all we need. When we are in the arms of our Father we need not fear, but rest in knowing He will protect us from all that comes against us.

> The LORD also will be a refuge for the oppressed,
> A refuge in times of trouble.   —Psalm 9:9

> From the end of the earth I will cry to You,
> When my heart is overwhelmed;
> Lead me to the rock that is higher than I.   —Psalm 61:2

The more I study the Word of God, the more I understand the character of Jesus. Our Father is faithful to His children. He loves us with an everlasting love, and waits with open arms for us to run to Him. When we realize God is our greatest advocate, we will look to Him regardless of what we are facing. He is closer then our breath and loves us more then life itself. Get to know your Savior. Jesus is all you need.

> God is our refuge and strength,
> A very present help in trouble.
> Therefore we will not fear,
> Even though the earth be removed,
> And though the mountains be carried into the midst of the sea;
> *Though* its waters roar *and* be troubled,
> *Though* the mountains shake with its swelling.   Selah
> —Psalm 46:1-3

I will instruct you and teach you
in the way you should go;
I will guide you with My eye.

Psalm 32:8

He not only has today
on His heart,
but He cares about
our forever future.

Forever Future

Psalm 32:8

I will instruct you and teach you
in the way you should go;
I will guide you with My eye.

As I read this Psalm I wondered; what does it mean God will guide me with His eye? As I prayed about this, I felt this Scripture was saying that not only will God guide all our tomorrows, but He will guide foreseeing what lies ahead. We can trust the Lord as He directs our path, knowing He not only has today on His heart, but He cares about our forever future.

> Trust in the LORD with all your heart,
> And lean not on your own understanding;
> In all your ways acknowledge Him,
> And He shall direct your paths.   —Proverbs 3:5-6

That made me wonder what I have missed by not allowing Him to guide my every step. What has He known was ahead for my life, but because I did not listen, I missed?

> *You* stiff-necked and uncircumcised in heart and ears!
> You always resist the Holy Spirit; as your fathers *did*,
> so *do* you.   —Acts 7:51

We bring heartache into our lives simply because we refuse to do things God's way. Instead of believing we can trust God, even when we don't understand, we walk away from the will of our Father, deciding to live life based on our own logic and desires. Then, in our despair, we cry out to the Lord. He shows such mercy, as He lifts us out of the miry clay.

> He inclined to me,
> And heard my cry.
> He also brought me up out of the horrible pit,
> Out of the miry clay,
> And set my feet upon a rock,
> And established my steps.   — Psalm 40:1-2

May we trust our Father and lean not on our own understanding. He alone knows what is best, now and forevermore.

> The LORD shall preserve
> your going out and your coming in
> From this time forth,
> and even forevermore.   —Psalm 120:8

Search me, O God, and know my heart;
Try me, and know my anxieties;
And see if *there is any* wicked way in me,
And lead me in the way everlasting.

Psalm 139:23

When we humble ourselves before
the Lord, asking for guidance,
we will find the help we need.

Forgiveness

Psalm 139:23

Search me, O God, and know my heart;
Try me, and know my anxieties;
And see if *there is any* wicked way in me,
And lead me in the way everlasting.

What do you do when someone holds a grudge against you? We have all had times in our lives when we see things differently than another. Instead of coming to an understanding, both parties become bitter, holding resentments and blaming the other person. Unfortunately, when we hold resentments and bitterness, we also harden our heart, making it impossible to praise the Lord, study His Word, or have true fellowship with others.

Thirty-six years ago a person in my life entered the doors of Alcoholics Anonymous. The steps he learned to remain sober were life changing. They would make the difference of life or death. As children of Christ, we need to take the Word of God just as seriously. Just as he learned to make a searching and fearless inventory of himself, promptly admitting when he was wrong, we need to ask the Lord to search our heart and see if there be any wicked thing in us, and then be willing to take ownership for our faults.

Search me, O God, and know my heart;
Try me, and know my anxieties;
And see if *there is any* wicked way in me,
And lead me in the way everlasting.   —Psalm 139:23

The next step in AA was to make amends to those he had offended. Asking for forgiveness is never easy. However, without this step we often find the hard feelings created in the disagreement remain the same. The Lord asks we be willing to ask for forgiveness when we have wronged another.

Confess *your* trespasses to one another, and pray for one another,
that you may be healed. The effective, fervent prayer of a righteous
man avails much.   —James 5:16

When we humble ourselves before the Lord, asking for guidance, we will find the help we need. May we follow His leading, that we might be set free.

Stand fast therefore in the liberty by which Christ has made us free,
and do not be entangled again with a yoke of bondage. —Galatians 5:1

But you, O Lord,
are a God merciful and gracious,
slow to anger
and abounding in steadfast love
and faithfulness.

Psalm 86:15

When God is in control,
and it seems
nothing is happening,
we can be sure
something is happening.

Our God Is Faithful

Psalm 86:15

But you, O Lord, *are* a God merciful and gracious,
slow to anger and abounding in steadfast love
and faithfulness. (NIV)

What prayer are you waiting for God to answer? Is it beginning to feel as if you have been praying in vain?

God is faithful; He can be trusted. As impossible as a situation may seem, God is bigger. As we wait on Him our faith is tested, our trust in God strengthened, and our need for Him increased. We can trust Him to work all things for our good and for His glory.

> And we know that all things work together for good to those who love God, to those who are called according to *His* purpose. For whom He foreknew, He also predestined *to be* conformed to the image of His Son. —Romans 8:28-29a

When God is in control, and it seems nothing is happening, we can be sure something is happening. He is faithful regardless of what we see.

> Now faith is the substance of things hoped for, the evidence of things not seen. —Hebrews 11:1

When our prayer request involves another person, not only does God conform our hearts to His ways, but we can be sure He is also working in their life. It is hard to wait for a prodigal child to return, a broken relationship to be healed, a misunderstanding to be resolved, but we can trust God in every situation. He is our Father and He loves us.

> "For My thoughts *are* not your thoughts,
>   Nor *are* your ways My ways," says the LORD.
> "For *as* the heavens are higher than the earth,
>   So are My ways higher than your ways,
>   And My thoughts than your thoughts." — Isaiah 55:8-9

When you can't trace His hand, may you trust His heart.

> Wait on the LORD;
> Be of good courage,
> And He shall strengthen your heart;
> Wait, I say, on the LORD! —Psalm 27:14

For whatever things were written
before were written for our learning,
that we through the patience and comfort
of the Scriptures might have hope.

Romans 15:4

Our only hope in hard places
is found in the Word of God.

Hope in Him

Romans 15:4

For whatever things were written
before were written for our learning,
that we through the patience and comfort
of the Scriptures might have hope.

While leading a Ladies Sunday School Class, one of the members came into the room dissolved in tears. "What do you do when your stepchildren won't listen to you? How do you make them understand you love them and only want what is best for them?" Being a class of mothers, many of us understood. Nothing hurts quite like a mother's broken heart. Immediately, women started sharing advice, explaining how they handled such a situation. It was precious to see the love and concern everyone felt for her.

As I left the class that day, I felt such confusion. I knew that regardless of the great advice and kindness the ladies offered, only the Lord knew the answer to her heartache. How could I help them understand our only hope in hard places is found in the Word of God?

Be still and know that I *am* God.   —Psalm 46:10a

Our God is so faithful! (Can I get an Amen?) Before going to church, the following Sunday, I was reading my daily devotional. The last Scripture for the day was Romans 15:4:

That we through the patience and comfort of the Scriptures
might have hope.   —Romans 15:4b

This is what I had been praying for all week. As only our God could, He brought the answer though the Holy Scriptures! As I left for church I could hardly wait to share this truth with the ladies. Our hope is found in the Scriptures, written for our learning.

Where do you need hope? Would you cry out to the Lord and open the Scriptures, asking the Lord to answer through His Holy Word? Through comfort found, only in the Scriptures will we find our hope. God is a God of promise. May we trust His Holy Word.

For all the promises of God in Him *are* Yes, and in Him Amen,
to the glory of God through us.   —2 Corinthians 1:20

But Simon Peter answered Him,
"Lord to whom shall we go?
You have the words of eternal life."

John 6:68

Jesus will carry us when we
cannot walk,
give us peace that passes
all understanding,
and the strength we need
to face each new day.

Where Would We Go?

John 6:68

But Simon Peter answered Him,
"Lord to whom shall we go?
You have the words of eternal life."

Jesus had just proclaimed to the multitudes that He is the bread of life, through Him alone they would find eternal life.

> *"Most assuredly, I say to you, he who believes in Me has*
> *everlasting life. I am the bread of life."*   —John 6:47-48

Because they knew Jesus' earthly parents, many were offended. How could Jesus, who grew up among them and worked as a carpenter with His father, proclaim He is the bread of life, the One who gives eternal life?

> From that *time* many of His disciples went back and walked
> with Him no more.   —John 6:66

Watching them leave, Jesus turned to the twelve and asked:

> *"Do you also want to go away?"*   —John 6:67

As I sat in church, I noticed the mother of a friend of mine, who has been missing for four years, sitting in church next to her grandson, whom she is now raising. The heartache this mother has had to endure is more than most of us can imagine. Not knowing where your child is, or what has happened to him or her, would cause anyone to fall into depths of despair. Not so with my friend's mom. She has hung on to Jesus, drawing strength to face each new day, and lived her life knowing only through her Savior will she find peace that passes all understanding. What a testimony she is to all who know her.

Just as Simon Peter answered Jesus, "Lord to whom shall we go?" we, too, can respond in the same way. When life holds unbearable heartache and pain, Jesus will carry us when we cannot walk, give us peace that passes all understanding, and the strength we need to face each new day.

> My flesh and my heart fail;
> *But* God *is* the strength of my heart
> And my portion forever.   —Psalm 73:26

> When my heart is overwhelmed;
> Lead me to the rock that is higher than I.   —Psalm 61:2b

Therefore they said to Him,
"What sign will You perform then,
that we may see it and believe You?
What work will You do?"

John 6:30

Do we love Jesus
for what He can do for us,
or do we love Him
simply for Who He is?

What Work Will You Do?

John 6:30

Therefore they said to Him,
"What sign will You perform then,
that we may see it and believe You?
What work will You do?"

After healing the sick at the Pool of Bethesada, Jesus traveled to the Sea of Galilee, where a multitude of 5,000 followed Him. Seeing the people were hungry, Jesus took five barley loaves and two small fish, and when He had given thanks, distributed *them* to the disciples. The disciples gave as much food to the people as they wanted.

The next day, when the people were standing on the other side of the sea, and seeing that Jesus was not there, they crossed the sea to Capernaum looking for Him. It is here we find Jesus speaking to the multitudes, explaining He does only what His Father in heaven tells Him to do.

> *"This is the work of God, that you believe in Him whom He sent."*
> —John 6:29

Instead of falling on their knees in gratitude for how He had fed the multitudes, and in awe of who Jesus was, the people demanded He prove Himself as the Son of God.

> Jesus answered them and said, *"Most assuredly, I say to you,
> you seek Me, not because you saw the signs, but because you ate of
> the loaves and were filled."* —John 6:26

How easy it is for us to read this and wonder how they could ask such a thing of Jesus. Didn't they realize from what He had just done for them He truly was the Son of God?

Before we judge too quickly, it would behoove us to ask the same question of ourselves. After all Jesus has done for us… died on the cross for our sins, given us eternal life, blessed us with family and friends, and goodness beyond what we deserve, don't we sometimes question God?

May we be willing to ask the hard question: Do we love Jesus for what He can do for us, or do we love Him simply for Who He is? If He never did another thing for us, would what He has done already be enough for us to trust Him to the end? Jesus is the Lord, may that be enough!

> "For the Lord your God *is* God of gods and Lord of lords,
> the great God, mighty and awesome." —Deuteronomy 10:17

The joy of the Lord is your strength.

Nehemiah 8:10b

Satan comes as a thief
in the night
to steal our peace,
rob our joy,
and convince us
we are not enough.

The Joy of the Lord

Nehemiah 8:10b

The joy of the Lord is your strength.

In a world filled with self-assured strong people, it is easy for us to feel unsure of ourselves. We feel "less than" and thus, live our lives trying to prove to ourselves, and to others, we are enough.

As children of the Living God, we have no need to feel or live this way. In our weakness we find strength in the Lord.

> And He said to me, *"My grace is sufficient for you, for My strength is made perfect in weakness.* Therefore, most gladly I will boast in my infirmities, that the power of Christ may rest upon me.
>
> —2 Corinthians 12:9

When we live in the joy of the Lord and all He has done for us, we find confidence knowing we belong to Him. No longer do we live for ourselves, but our desire is that our lives are a reflection of Christ.

"For in Him we live and move and have our being."—Acts 17:28

> I have been crucified with Christ; it is no longer I who live,
> but Christ lives in me; and the life I now live in the flesh I live
> by faith in the Son of God, who loved me and gave Himself
> for me. —Galatians 2:20

Satan comes as a thief in the night to steal our peace, rob our joy, and convince us we are not enough. But, we can live with the assurance knowing, what Satan came to steal, Christ has overcome.

> The thief does not come except to steal, and to kill, and to
> destroy. I have come that you may have life, and that they
> may have *it* more abundantly. —John 10:10

The next time we are tempted to feel "less than", let's remember to whom we belong, and live in the strength of our Savior instead.

> "I can do all things through Christ who strengthens me."
>
> —Philippians 4:13

> O my soul, march on in strength!
>
> —Judges 5:21

"For the LORD you God *is* He
who goes with you, to fight for you
against your enemies to save you."

Deuteronomy 20:4

Victory is ours
as we wait on Him.

Strong in the Battle

Deuteronomy 20:4

"For the LORD your God *is* He
who goes with you, to fight for you
against your enemies to save you."

As the Israelites prepared for battle, Moses reminded the people God would go before them to fight their enemies. He knew how important it was they enter the battle confident of victory.

As I thought about this, I thought of the many battles life holds. It is true that most of us will never enter a physical battle against the enemy, but just as real, we face battles in many ways.

> Beloved, do not think it strange concerning the fiery trial
> which is to try you, as though some strange thing happened
> to you.   —1 Peter 4:12

In times such as this, we, too, need to remember who goes before us to fight our battles. Never do we enter a problem or heartache alone. As we lean on Jesus, holding tight to His hand, He goes before us, comforting, leading, and assuring our victory. Peace in the midst of battle is not the absence of conflict, but the presence of God.

> Be anxious for nothing, but in everything by prayer and supplication,
> with thanksgiving, let your requests be made known to God; and the
> peace of God, which surpasses all understanding, will guard your
> hearts and minds though Christ Jesus.   —Philippians 4:6-7

If God has allowed a trial to come into our lives, as we allow Him to fight the battle for us, He will employ what Satan meant for evil and use it for our good. We can stand strong in the battle, knowing who it is who goes before us! Victory is ours as we wait on Him.

> The horse is prepared for the day of battle,
> But deliverance *is* of the LORD.   —Proverbs 21:31

> Finally, my brethren, be strong in the Lord and in the power of
> His might.   —Ephesians 6:10

> Watch, stand fast in the faith, be brave, be strong.
>   —1 Corin. 16:13

But I *am* like a green olive tree
in the house of God;
I trust in the mercy of God forever and ever.
I will praise You forever,
because you have done *it,*
And in the presence of Your saints
I will wait on Your name, for *it is* good.

Psalm 52:8-9

Our faith is to be built on our steadfast trust in our Father's wisdom, and our willingness to praise Him in the waiting.

Steadfast

Psalm 52:8-9

But I *am* like a green olive tree in the house of God;
I trust in the mercy of God forever and ever.
I will praise You forever, because you have done *it;*
And in the presence of Your saints
I will wait on Your name, for *it is* good.

As I studied this Psalm, the words *trust, praise,* and *wait* stood out to me. Even though David's desires had not come to fruition, he would praise the Lord in the waiting because he trusted in Him.

David compared himself to a green olive tree in the house of God. As I studied the significance of the olive tree, I found this tree symbolizes faithfulness and steadfastness. Regardless of the weather conditions, the olive tree will continue to live and produce fruit. Even being cut down and destroyed, the roots of the olive tree grow so deeply a new tree will grow back in its place. David was declaring he would be faithful regardless of what happened, standing steadfast in his trust in the Lord.

As I considered my desires, I thought about my faithfulness and never wavering steadfastness before the Lord. Do I stand firm, trusting He will bring it to pass? Do I praise Him in the waiting, knowing His ways are not mine? And, do I trust Him, even when I don't understand what He is doing?

In one of the first Bible Studies I participated in, there was a prayer that went something like this:

Dear Lord,
I don't understand it and I don't like it, but; regardless of how I feel, or my desires, I will trust You, as I wait on You to do what I know is best.
In Your Precious Name I pray,

Amen

Our faith is not to be built on what we see, nor how we feel. Our faith is to be built on our steadfast trust in our Father's wisdom, and our willingness to praise Him in the waiting. God is never late, and He is never early. He is exactly on time. May we be like David, faithful and steadfast, trusting in the mercy of God forever and ever.

GREAT is the LORD, and greatly to be praised   —Psalm 48:1

If we confess our sins,
He is faithful and just to forgive us our sins
and cleanse us from all unrighteousness.

1 John 1:9

As children of the Living God,
there is no place
in our lives for pride.

Freedom

1 John 1:9

If we confess our sins,
He is faithful and just to forgive us *our* sins
and to cleanse us from all unrighteousness.

A little boy gets caught taking a cookie out of the cookie jar as his mama is making dinner: "Johnny, did you take a cookie?" his mama asks. Without giving it a second thought, Johnny looks up at his mama, and with big brown eyes and cookie crumbs on his face, promptly says, "No mama, I didn't take a cookie."

This sounds like an innocent little story; nevertheless, it shows how hard it is for us all, from the youngest to oldest, to admit when we are wrong. We want to be right, even if when what we have done is wrong. Why is that?

Could it be we feel shame? And with shame comes embarrassment and humiliation. We feel caught, found out, and shameful for our actions.

Or could it be pride? We feel we are above reproach, our reputation at stake. As children of the living God, there is no place in our lives for pride. The Word of God is clear concerning the consequences of choosing pride over humility:

> Pride *goes* before destruction,
> And a haughty spirit before a fall.
> Better *to be* of a humble spirit with the lowly,
> Than to divide the spoil with the proud.   —Proverbs 16:18-19

The Lord desires humility in His children, a meekness of heart:

> The humble He guides in justice,
> And the humble He teaches His way.   —Psalm 25:9

When we are willing to humble ourselves, confessing our wrong, it is not shame we find, but the promise of cleansing and forgiveness. No longer are we held in the shackles of sin, but praise God, with repentance comes freedom. Freedom in Christ and freedom from all condemnation.

> *There is* therefore now no condemnation to those who are
> in Christ Jesus, who do not walk according to the flesh, but
> according to the Spirit.   —Romans 8:11

> *Therefore if the Son makes you free, you shall be free indeed.*
> —John 8:36

In this the love of God was manifested toward us, that God has sent His only begotten Son into the world, that we might live through Him.

1 John 4:9

When Christ lives through us everything changes.

Through Him

1 John 4:9

In this the love of God was manifested toward us,
that God has sent His only begotten Son into the world,
that we might live through Him.

As I read 1 John 4:9, the word "through" stood out among the rest. When the love of God was manifested toward us, it was for the purpose of Christ living through us. Only as we die to our own ambitions and desires, living instead through Christ, do we live our life according to the creation of God.

> Put off, concerning your former conduct, the old man which grows corrupt according to the deceitful lusts, and be renewed in the spirit of your mind, and that you put on the new man which was created according to God, in true righteousness and holiness. —Ephesians 4:22-24

As Christians, Christ lives in us; old things are passed away;

> Therefore, if anyone *is* in Christ, *he is* a new creation; old things have passed away; behold all things have become new. —2 Corinthians 5:17

When Christ lives through us everything changes. Our thought life, which was once corrupt, becomes obedient to the thoughts of Christ:

> We demolish arguments and every pretension that sets itself up against the knowledge of God, and we take captive every thought to make it obedient to Christ. —2 Corinthians 10:5 NIV

We are called to a higher calling; a life lived for the glory of God.

> And *whatever* you do in word or deed, *do* all in the name of the Lord Jesus, giving thanks to God the Father through Him.
> —Colossians 3:17
> Therefore, whether you eat or drink, or whatever you do, do all to the glory of God. —1 Corinthians 10:31

What a privilege we have been given. May we be willing to die, that Christ may live!

> For to me, to live *is* Christ, and to die is gain.
> —Philippians 1:21

Do all things without complaining
and disputing; that you may become blameless,
children of God without fault in the midst
of a crooked and perverse generation,
among whom you shine as lights in the world.

Philippians 2:14-15

Jesus became the light of the
world to make a way
for us in the darkness.

Light in the Darkness

Philippians 2:14-15

Do all things without complaining and disputing;
that you may become blameless, children of God
without fault in the midst of a crooked and perverse
generation, among whom you shine as lights in the world.

This little light of mine, I'm going to let it shine
This little light of mine, I'm going to let it shine
Let it shine, let it shine, let it shine!

How well I remember singing this song with all my little friends in Sunday school. We would hold up our pointer finger pretending it was our light that would never go out. We were going to shine for Jesus forever!

"I am the light of the world. He who follows Me shall not walk in darkness, but have the light of life."   —John 8:12

Jesus became the light of the world to make a way for us in the darkness. Without Christ in our lives we are lost, like sheep without a shepherd. We live our lives without hope, and with no promise for the future.

Before coming to Christ, my life was without purpose. I simply did the same thing over and over every day, for no other reason than to pay my bills. Life seemed so mundane. Then I heard a pastor speak and it was like he was speaking just to me: "You can't know your purpose until you know the One who made you." His words got my attention! He then went on to introduce the audience to Jesus Christ. At that point in my life I knew Jesus as the Son of God, the One to whom we prayed and sang about in church. However, I didn't know we could know Him personally. That day I confessed I was a sinner, asked for His forgiveness, and invited Him into my heart as my Lord and Savior. By faith I was saved. My life has not been the same since. I have purpose where I once had confusion, light where I once walked in darkness, and hope for all my tomorrows.

If you confess with your mouth the Lord Jesus and believe in
your heart that God has raised Him from the dead, you will be
saved. For with the heart one believes unto righteousness, and
with the mouth confession is made unto salvation. —Romans 10:9-10

Wait on the LORD; be of good courage,
and He shall strengthen your heart;
Wait, I say, on the LORD!

Psalm 27:14

Wait on the Lord.
And in your waiting,
trust the words of your Father.
His promises are true.

Wait

Psalm 27:14

Wait on the LORD; be of good courage,
and He shall strengthen your heart;
Wait, I say, on the LORD!

Is your heart full of gratitude for all the blessings bestowed upon you and hopeful for what lies ahead? Or is your heart broken, shattered beyond what you could ever imagine? Are you singing praises to the Lord, basking in His goodness? Or are you simply trying to hold back the floodgate of tears, ready to fall at any moment from a heart aching like it has never ached before?

Our Father meets us exactly where we are. He knows our comings and go-ings, our victories and failures, and He knows all about our broken heart. He sees each tear that falls, and knows our anxious thoughts. Our Lord gives strength when we are weak, words when we don't know what to speak, and direction when we are lost. What a comfort to know, as we hold tight to our Father's hand, nothing will come against us that will overtake our lives.

"I will pray to the Father, and He will give you another Helper, that He may abide with you forever." —John 14:16

"I will not leave you as orphans; I will come to you." —John 14:18

In the day when I cried out, You answered me,
And made me bold *with* strength in my soul. —Psalm 138:3

The eyes of the LORD *are* on the righteous,
And His ears *are open* to their cry. —Psalm 34:15

Are you weak, heavy laden, spent beyond what you can bear? Wait on the Lord! And in your waiting, trust the words of your Father. His promises are true. As you wait, you will find strength for your heart and courage for each new day.

Our soul waits for the LORD;
He *is* our help and our shield.
For our heart shall rejoice in Him,
Because we have trusted in His holy Name.

—Psalm 33:20-21

Therefore, we also, since we are surrounded
by so great a cloud of witnesses, let us lay
aside every weight, and the sin that so easily
ensnares us, and let us run with endurance
the race that is set before us.

Hebrews 12:1

How we see God will determine
how much we trust God.

Let Us Run the Race

Hebrews 12:1

Therefore, we also, since we are surrounded
by so great a cloud of witnesses, let us lay
aside every weight, and the sin that so easily
ensnares *us*, and let us run with endurance
the race that is set before us.

Hebrews 11 has often been referred to as "The Roll Call of the Heroes of Faith". As we read this chapter, we will find name after name of saints who have gone before us, standing in faith as they trusted their God. These are the cloud of witnesses we are surrounded by spoken of in Hebrews 12. As we read of their faith, we are encouraged to run with endurance the race they have set before us.

Those listed among the faithful were men and women like you and I. They had struggles, questions, fears, and apprehension much like we do today. Yet, though many did not see the outcome of what they believed, they stood in faith, trusting His promises to be true.

> Those all died in faith, not having received the promises,
> but having seen them afar off were assured of them,
> embraced *them* and confessed that they were strangers
> and pilgrims on the earth.   —Hebrews 11:13

Faith in the Word of God means we believe what we cannot see. We believe because the Lord has told us it is Truth.

> Now faith is the substance of things hoped for, the evidence
> of things not seen.   —Hebrews 11:1

How we see God will determine how much we trust God. Do we see Him as loving, caring, and working all things for our good? Or do we see Him as harsh, ready to condemn us at any moment? Only as we trust God for who He is, our loving Father, will we be able to walk in faith, regardless of what we see.

May we run with endurance the race they have set before us:

> But without faith *it is* impossible to please *Him*, for he who
> comes to God must believe that He is, and *that* He is a rewarder
> of those who diligently seek Him.   —Hebrews 11:6

"So We Prayed"

1 Thessalonians 5:17

Pray without Ceasing

Recently I received a Christmas letter from my cousin telling how she and her husband had come to a crossroad in their lives. They didn't know if they should move closer to their adult children, or remain where they were. She wrote, "So we prayed."

We are told to bring our requests before the Lord. Nevertheless, I wonder how many times we pray and actually leave our requests at the feet of Jesus. Too often we ask Him to direct our path, but instead of waiting for His direction, attempt to figure things out on our own.

> Be anxious for nothing, but in everything by prayer and
> supplication, with thanksgiving, let your requests be made
> known to God; and the peace of God which surpasses all
> understanding, will guard your hearts and minds through
> Christ Jesus.   —Philippians 4:6-7

In the book of Isaiah, the Lord told the people their strength would come as they sat quietly before Him. Nevertheless, they would not listen, but did as they saw fit in their own eyes. Consequently, they were left powerless and fainthearted.

> For thus says the LORD GOD, the Holy One of Israel:
> "In returning and rest you shall be saved;
> In quietness and confidence shall be your strength."
> But you would not."   —Isaiah 30:15

The Lord blessed my cousin and her husband, giving them opportunity beyond what they could have hoped for. They knew He had directed their path and answered their prayer. Quietness and confidence became their strength!

> Now to Him who is able to do exceedingly abundantly
> above all that we ask or think, according to the power that
> works in us, to Him *be* glory in the church by Jesus Christ
> to all generations, forever and ever. Amen
> —Ephesians 3:20-21

*"Let your light so shine before men,
that they may see your good works
and glorify your Father in heaven."*

Matthew 5:16

As children of the living God,
our single purpose in life is to
bring glory to our Father.

Shine

Matthew 5:16

"Let your light so shine before men, that they may
see your good works and glorify your
Father in heaven."

Addressing the multitudes, Jesus exhorted the people to be a light in a dark world. *"Don't hide your light under a basket,"* He spoke, *"but let it shine."*

> *"You are the light of the world. A city that is set on a hill cannot*
> *be hidden. Nor do they light a lamp and put it under a basket,*
> *but on a lampstand, and it gives light to all who are in the house."*
> —Matthew 5:14-15

While Jesus walked among the multitudes as the light of the world, He set an example for those who followed Him to be a light in the darkness.

> *"I am the light of the world. He who follows Me shall not walk in*
> *darkness, but have the light of life."*   —John 8:12

As I thought about this, I realized His light will only shine in my life as I follow Christ, living my life in such a way:

> my words might be His words
> my thoughts His thoughts
> my intentions and motives His delight
> and my life lived solely through Him.

As children of the living God, our single purpose in life is to bring glory to our Father. As we let our light so shine before men, allowing the Holy Spirit to live through us, only then will they see our good works and glorify Our Father in Heaven. May we be willing to die to ourselves that He might live!

> *"Most assuredly, I say to you, unless a grain of wheat falls into the ground and*
> *dies, it remains alone; but if it dies it produces much grain."*   —John 12:24

> *"If anyone serves Me, let him follow Me; and where I am, there My servant*
> *will be also. If anyone serves Me, him My Father will honor."* —John 12:26

I have been crucified with Christ; it is no longer I who live, but Christ who lives in me; and the *life* which I now live in the flesh I live by faith in the Son of God, who loved me and gave Himself for me.
>
> —Galatian 2:20

You were bought at a price;
do not become slaves of men.

1 Corinthians 7:23

We were bought at a price.
May we walk worthy
of the cost.

Slaves

1 Corinthians 7:23

You were bought at a price;
do not become slaves of men.

How do we live in this world, and yet not become a slave to the ways of men? First of all, we must realize how easy it is to fall into the trap of living as the world lives.

As I considered this, I thought of some ways this could happen:

— Compromise our beliefs to keep others happy
for they loved the praise of men more than the
praise of God.   —John 12:43

— Make peace at any cost
Saying, "Peace, peace!" When *there is* no peace.
             —Jeremiah 6:14b

— Succumb to fear of tomorrow rather than trusting God
"In this world you will have tribulation; but be of
good cheer, I have overcome the world." —John 16:33b

So then, how do we flee from living as the world, but instead live in the freedom which is ours through Christ? The Word of God is clear in how we are to live.

— Put on the new man, living in true righteousness and holiness;
Be renewed in the spirit of your mind, and that you put on
the new man which was created according to God, in true
righteousness and holiness.   —Ephesians 4:23-24

— Be aware of the warning concerning the evil of this world;
Be sober, be vigilant; because your adversary the devil
walks about like a roaring lion, seeking whom he may
devour. Resist him, steadfast in faith.   —1 Peter 5:8-9a

— Become grounded in the Word of God
Study to show yourself approved unto God, a workman
that needs not be ashamed, rightly dividing the word of
truth.   —2 Timothy 2:15

We were bought at a price. May we walk worthy of the cost.

Jesus said to him,
"I am the way, the truth, and the life.
No one comes to the Father
except through Me."

John 14:6

The character of Jesus
never changes.

I AM

John 14:6

Jesus said to him,
"I am the way, the truth, and the life.
No one comes to the Father
except through Me."

During the three years Jesus walked with His disciples, they sat at His table, walked where He walked and learned from His teachings. They grew to love Him and understood it was through Jesus, alone, they would come to the Father.

As Jesus taught His disciples, He teaches us today. As we get to know the Father through the pages of His Holy Word, we can rest on the assurance that as He was then, He is today. The character of Jesus never changes.

Jesus Christ *is* the same yesterday, today, and forever.
—Hebrews 13:8

Jesus taught His disciples, and He teaches us:

I AM
The bread of life	—John 6:35
The light of the world	—John 8:12
The good shepherd	—John 10:11
The true vine	—John 15:1
And the life	—John 14:6

Just as our Father never changes in who He is, He never changes in what He will do for His children. The disciples knew they could trust Him with their lives and we, too, can trust Him with ours. As He loved His disciples, He loves us with an everlasting love, rejoicing over us with singing.

The LORD your God in your midst,
The Mighty One, will save;
He will rejoice over you with gladness,
He will quiet *you* with His love,
He will rejoice over you with singing.   —Zephaniah 3:17

Behold, what manner of love the Father
has bestowed on us, that we should be called
children of God!   —1 John 3:1a

We should no longer be children,
tossed to and fro and carried about with
every wind of doctrine, by the trickery of men,
in the cunning craftiness of deceitful plotting.

Ephesians 4:14

Knowing Christ,
and the power of His
resurrection,
trumps everything else in life.

Satisfied

Ephesians 4:14

We should no longer be children,
tossed to and fro and carried about with
every wind of doctrine, by the trickery of men,
in the cunning craftiness of deceitful plotting.

What is it that keeps us from being satisfied in God?
Worldly Success
Pleasures of this world
Ridicule from others in our beliefs
Not knowing who we are in Christ
Other ways?

In his book, "Desiring God," John Piper states, "Christ is most glorified when we are most satisfied in Him." If this is the case, shouldn't our lives reflect a life of contentment and fulfillment because of who we are in Christ?

Satan's goal is to persuade Christians that Christ isn't enough, that there is more to life than living for Him. The Word of God warns us to be aware of such lies, and flee from the temptations of this world.

> Test all things; hold fast what is good.
> Abstain from every form of evil.   —1 Thessalonians 5:21

> But each one is tempted when he is drawn away
> by his own desires and enticed.
> Then, when desire has conceived, it gives birth to sin;
> And sin, when it is full-grown, brings forth death. —James 1:14-15

Knowing Christ, and the power of His resurrection, trumps everything else in life. We are children of the King of Kings and Lord of Lords. How could anything keep us from being completely satisfied in Him?

> Yet indeed I also count all things loss for the excellence of the
> knowledge of Christ Jesus my Lord, for whom I have suffered
> the loss of all things, and count them as rubbish, that I may gain
> Christ, and be found in Him, not having my own righteousness
> which is from God by faith; that I may know Him and the power
> of His resurrection, and the fellowship of His suffering, being
> conformed to His death.   —Philippians 3:8-10

My voice You shall hear in the morning,
O LORD;
In the morning I will direct *it* to You,
And I will look up.

Psalm 5:3

When we meet with the Lord
in the morning,
He gives us direction
and strength for each new day.

Strength for the Day

Psalm 5:3

My voice You shall hear in the morning,
O LORD;
In the morning I will direct *it* to You,
And I will look up.

When do you have your quiet time with the Lord? Perhaps you ponder over your devotional during your lunch hour at work. Possibly it is last thing at night, before you turn off the light. Maybe it is different each day, finding time when you can sit quietly before the Lord.

As Jesus walked this earth He set an example for us to follow. He rose early, and going alone, went to a quiet place.

> Now in the morning, having risen a long while before daylight,
> He went out and departed to a solitary place; and there He prayed.
> —Mark 1:35

When we meet with the Lord in the morning, He gives us direction and strength for each new day. To walk out the door knowing we have spent time alone with our Father gives us a Christ confidence we will not find on our own.

> Your Word *is* a lamp unto my feet
> And a light to my path.   —Psalm 119:105

> Oh, satisfy us early with Your mercy,
> That we may rejoice and be glad all our days!   —Psalm 90:14

As we meet with the Lord before beginning our day, He will prepare our hearts for what the day may bring. Our response to someone who speaks a harsh word sounds a little different after we have spent time with the Lord. Direction for the day seems less rattled and more peaceful when we know we are in the Father's will. The task set before us no longer seems impossible. As we begin our day with Lord, and then continue with Him through the day, we will find life is easier, and despair replaced with hope for what lies ahead.

> O GOD, You *are* my God;
> Early I will seek You;
> My soul thirsts for You
> My flesh longs for You
> In a dry and thirsty land
> Where there is no water.   —Psalm 63:1

Let your speech always be with grace,
seasoned with salt.

Colossians 4:6a

I want to be an encouragement
to others believers.
I want to remind them how
much our Father loves them.

Speaking Words of Grace

Colossians 4:6a

Let your speech always be with grace,
seasoned with salt.

Teaching the multitudes as they sat humbly before Him, Jesus called the multitudes, *"the salt of the earth."* He beseeched them to let their speech always be seasoned with grace.

> *"You are the salt of the earth; but if the salt loses its flavor, how shall it be seasoned? It is then good for nothing but to be thrown out and trampled underfoot by men."* —Matthew 5:13

While attending a conference at the COVE in North Carolina, I arrived an hour before the conference was to begin. After getting settled in my room, I decided to go find something to drink before the teaching began. As I came into the lounge area, a sweet employee of the COVE approached me and with a smile as big as the room said to me,

> "I was talking to our Father about you today. I asked Him to give you a wonderful time while you are here and bless you with all you have come to receive. He loves you, you know, and has something very special for you while you are here."

I could hardly believe my ears. What did she say? Was she telling me she had prayed for me before I got to the conference?

The entire weekend I was blessed by her words. If this sweet lady had prayed to "our Father" about me, I was sure He had heard her prayer. Let your speech always be with grace, seasoned with salt. (Col. 4:6a). This is exactly what she had done for me.

I want to be an encouragement to other believers. I want to remind them how much our Father loves them. What if each day we spoke to our Father about those we would meet during the day, and then as we saw them, told them what we had done? I can tell you from experience, they will be blessed, and your speech will be seasoned with grace.

> Pleasant words *are like* a honeycomb,
> Sweetness to the soul and health to the bones. —Proverbs 16:24

How will you do in the floodplain of the Jordan?

Jeremiah 12:5

As we sit at His feet,
He gives us confidence in
Who it is that holds all
our tomorrows.

Floodplain of Jordan

Jeremiah 12:5

How will you do in the floodplain of the Jordan?

In time of harvest, the Jordan River overflowed its banks, threatening to flood the entire area. Those who stood strong in the Lord overcame the floodplain. Those overcome with fear, perished.

Like the banks of the Jordan River, our lives can begin to overflow with circumstances that are totally out of our control. How we respond to such times will greatly depend on how we live our lives before this happens. Will we plant our feet firmly in the Word of God, growing more in His love each day, or will we live our lives for the moment?

> *The rain descended, the floods came, and the winds blew*
> *and beat on that house; and it did not fall, for it was founded*
> *on the rock.* —Matthew 7:25

> *The rain descended, the floods came, and the winds blew,*
> *and beat on the house; and it fell. And great was its fall.*
> —Matthew 7:27

Recently, I heard a Christian who had just been diagnosed with cancer say: "I would rather worship the Lord than wail in the misery." This did not just happen. Unbeknown to her, as she daily sat at the feet of Jesus, He was preparing her heart for such a time as this. When the diagnoses came, her first response was to run to her Father rather than succumb to despair.

> In the fear of the LORD there is strong confidence, and His
> children will have a place of refuge. —Proverbs 14:26

> I will sing of Your power; yes, I will sing aloud of Your mercy
> in the morning; for You have been my defense and refuge in the
> day of my trouble. —Psalm 59:16

The Lord beseeches us to built our lives on the Rock. As we sit at His feet, He gives us confidence in Who it is that holds all our tomorrows.

> Fear not, for I *am* with you;
> Be not dismayed, for I *am* your God.
> I will strengthen you. Yes, I will help you,
> I will uphold you with My righteous right hand. —Isaiah 41:10

Jesus said to her,
"Woman, why are you weeping?
Whom are you seeking?'"

John 20:15

While Mary was seeking Jesus,
He was also seeking her.

Seeking

John 20:15

Jesus said to her, *"Woman, why are you weeping?*
Whom are you seeking?"

While doing a bible study on the book of John, I came to this Scripture and realized: while Mary was seeking Jesus, He was also seeking her. Mary had come to the empty tomb, and in total despair, thinking someone had taken her Lord, turned from the tomb to leave. It was then she saw someone she thought to be the gardener. Not until He spoke her name did she realize it was Jesus.

Jesus said to her, *"Mary!"*   —John 20:16

How different would our prayer life be if when we came to the Lord we knew He was meeting us as well? No longer were we alone, pouring out our heart and hoping He was listening. Instead, we could see in our mind's eye our Lord and Savior coming to us just as He came to Mary. As I considered this thought, it made me want to run to Him, pour out my heart to the only One who truly understands everything about me.

> "Call to Me, and I will answer you, and show you great and
> mighty things, which you do not know."   —Jeremiah 33:3

I then began considering the many Scriptures affirming Jesus meets us in prayer:

> In my distress I called upon the LORD,
> And cried out to my God;
> He heard my voice from His temple,
> And my cry came before Him, *even* to His ears.   —Psalm 18:6

> The LORD is near to all who call upon Him,
> To all who call upon Him in truth.   —Psalm 145:18

The next time you call on the Lord in prayer, rest assured that He is not only hearing your prayer, but just like He approached Mary in the garden, He approaches you as He calls out your name, "——, whom are you seeking?"

> Then you will call upon Me and go and pray to Me, and I will
> listen to you.   —Jeremiah 29:12

There is therefore now no condemnation
to those who are in Christ Jesus,
who do not walk according to the flesh,
but according to the Spirit.

Romans 8:1

As children of God,
we can live our lives with our
head held high,
skip in our step, and assurance
in our heart our Father holds us
in the palm of His hands.

Free Indeed

Romans 8:1

There is therefore now no condemnation
to those who are in Christ Jesus,
who do not walk according to the flesh,
but according to the Spirit.

Attending the wedding of the daughter of a well-known Christian author, I was amazed at the love of Christ radiating from the face of his wife. There was no mistake she understands the love her Father has for her, and in return her love is the same. Her face absolutely glowed with the love of the Lord. I want that glow! I want others to look at me and see the love of Christ.

I have thought much about this since that day, pondered how she could radiate the love of God just by her countenance. I think I know her secret. I believe it is because she lives the life the Lord died on the Cross to give us all. She lives free in Him! No longer does she live under condemnation or guilt. No longer does she live with anxiety, nor fear. She lives her life completely absorbed in the love of her Father. She understands how much He loves her, how she can trust Him for all her tomorrows, that He will never leave her nor forsake her, and He is all she needs.

"Therefore if the Son makes you free, you shall be free indeed." —John 8:36

Coming to this place in our lives requires complete trust in our Father. When He tells us to:

Cast all our cares on Him because He cares for us.

—1 Peter 5:7

We cast all our cares on Him. We don't help Him carry them, worry about how He will take care of them, nor continue to take our cares back. We give all our cares to our Father and walk in the love we know He has for us.

As children of God, we can live our lives with our head held high, skip in our step, and assurance in our heart our Father holds us in the palm of His hand. And as we do, we, too, will glow with the love of the Lord.

See, I have inscribed you on the palms of *My hands;*
Your walls *are* continually before Me.   —Isaiah 49:16

But You, O LORD, *are* a shield for me,
My glory and the One who lifts up my head.   —Psalm 3:3

Your faith toward God has gone out,
so that we do not need to say anything.

1 Thessalonians 1:8b

When others observe us being
kind and patient
in difficult situations,
our faith toward God
has gone out.

Living Faith

1 Thessalonians 1:8b

Your faith toward God has gone out,
so that we do not need to say anything.

As I read this Scripture, I was reminded of watching a friend explain to others standing near us, "We are followers of Jesus Christ." With those words her faith toward God went out. Those all around knew we were Christians.

I remember thinking, "Am I that bold? Would I make such a statement to complete strangers? The answer to that question should always be, "Yes! Without a doubt I would proclaim my love for the Lord."

> For I am not ashamed of the gospel of Christ, for it is the power of God to salvation for everyone who believes, for the Jew first and also for the Greek.　　　　　—Romans 1:16

We have heard the phrase "Your actions speak so loudly I can't hear what you are saying." When others see us being kind and patient in difficult situations, our faith toward God has gone out. They see a difference in our response.

> Be kind to one another, tenderhearted, forgiving one another, even as God in Christ forgave you.　　　　　—Ephesians 4:32

Just as my friend proclaimed her love for Jesus, we can show the love of Christ toward others in how we respond to their actions. When others speak unkind words to us, do we respond with the love of Christ, rather then react in anger?

> Kind words are like honey – sweet to the soul and healthy for the body.　　　　　—Proverbs 16:24NLT

When others fall into the temptation of talking about others, do we join in, allowing our flesh to control our speech, or do we flee in obedience?

> Keep your tongue from evil,
> And your lips from speaking deceit.　　　　—Psalm 34:13

Your faith toward God has gone out! May those words be spoken of us!

Simon, Simon! Indeed Satan has asked for you,
that he may sift you as wheat.
But I have prayed for you,
that your faith should not fail.

Luke 22:31-32

Could it be, as we cry out to
Jesus, our Abba,
He prays for us, and in praying
sends angels to strengthen us?

Holy Prayers

Luke 22:31-32

Simon, Simon! Indeed Satan has asked for you,
that he may sift you as wheat.
But I have prayed for you, that your faith should not fail.

Jesus sat with the disciples, sharing all that was about to happen as He faced the cross. Not wanting to believe Jesus, Peter cried out to Him,

> "Lord, I am ready to go with You, both to prison
> and to death."   —Luke 22:33

Jesus knew Peter would deny Him three times. He also knew Peter would need protection from Satan when he realized what He had done. He knew Peter would be distraught because of denying his Lord, and that Satan would love to take his faith from him.

> *"But I have prayed for you, that your faith should not fail."*

Reading these words caused me to consider: does Jesus pray for me when I am tempted, discouraged, or confused? Does He pray for me when I am hurting and brokenhearted? Does He see when my faith is hanging on with a thread?

As I read, further, regarding Jesus praying at the Mount of Olives, knowing what He was about to face, and then the Scripture to follow, I felt certain the answer is Yes indeed, Jesus does pray for me, for you, for all His children as they cry out to Him.

> *"Father, if it is Your will, take this cup away from Me;*
> *nevertheless not My will, but Yours be done."*
> Then an angel appeared to Him from heaven,
> strengthening Him.   —Luke 22:42-43

Could it be that as we cry out to Jesus, our Abba, He prays for us, and in praying, sends angels to strengthen us? When we are discouraged, and after praying feel encouraged, strengthened, and filled with hope, could it be our Abba has sent angels to minister to our soul? I believe He has. I believe Jesus is praying for us, that our faith will not fail.

> For He shall give His angels charge over you,
> To keep you in all your ways.   —Psalm 91:11

*For as many of you as were baptized
into Christ have put on Christ.*

Galatians 3:27

We must take off our clothes
of flesh and clothe
ourselves instead in Christ.

Put on Christ

Galatians 3:27

For as many of you as were baptized
into Christ have put on Christ.

As I read this Scripture, I couldn't help but wonder, "What does it mean to put on Christ?" I know what it means to believe in Christ, to accept Christ as Lord and Savior. I know what it means to follow Christ and His Holy Word. But, is that the same as putting on Christ?

When I think of putting something on, my mind immediately goes to putting on clothes. Covering myself. Could putting on Christ mean much the same? Could it mean we are to cover ourselves with Christ? If so, how?

The Word of God tells us that when we accept Christ we are a new creation, old things are passed away;

> Therefore, if anyone *is* in Christ, *he is* a new creation; old things
> have passed away; behold, all things have become new.
> —2 Corinthians 5:17

And that we are to set our mind on things above, not on things on earth;

> Set your mind on things above, not on things on earth.
> For you died, and your life is hidden with Christ in God.
> —Colossians 3:2-3

As I considered these Scriptures, it became obvious what we must do. We must take off our clothes of flesh, letting go of how we once lived, and clothe ourselves, instead, in Christ. We must truly die that He might live. Only then will others see our covering as Christ and Christ alone.

> And let the peace of God rule in your hearts, to which also
> You were called in one body; and be thankful.   —Colossians 3:15

> Walk in wisdom toward those *who are* outside, redeeming the time.
> *Let* your speech always be with grace, seasoned with salt, that you
> may know how you ought to answer each one.   —Colossians 4:5-6

> But above all these things put on love, which is the bond of
> perfection.   —Colossians 3:14

Give us this day our daily bread.

Matthew 6:11

As we feast on the Word of God
we receive manna for our soul.

Manna from Heaven

Matthew 6:11

Give us this day our daily bread

As I considered this Scripture given in the Lord's prayer, I thought of the manna sent from heaven for the Israelites. Complaining to Moses and Aaron, the children of Israel said to them,

"Oh, that we had died by the hand of the LORD in the
land of Egypt, when we sat by the pots of meat *and* when
we ate bread to the full!
Then the LORD said to Moses, "Behold, I will rain bread
from heaven for you. And the people shall go out and gather
a certain quota every day, that I may test them, whether they
will walk in My law or not.　　　　—Exodus 16:3a-4

In much the same way, the Lord sends manna to us each day. As we feast on the Word of God, we receive instruction from the Lord and encouragement for the day. We receive manna for our soul.

Your words were found, and I ate them,
And Your word was to me the joy and rejoicing of my heart;
For I am called by Your name, O LORD God of hosts.
　　　　　　　　　　　　　　　　　—Jeremiah 15:16

The Lord also sends manna daily, as He bestows His mercies upon us.

Through the LORD's mercies we are not consumed.
Because His compassions fail not.
They are new every morning; great is His faithfulness.
"The Lord *is* my portion, says my soul,
"Therefore I hope in Him!"　　　　—Lamentations 3:22-24

The next time we are tempted to become like the Israelites, complaining of our hardships, let's look to the Lord instead and receive His manna. Just as the Israelites found with their manna, we will find in God's faithfulness manna from heaven and nourishment for our soul.

Every day I will bless You,
And I will praise Your name forever and ever.
Great *is* the LORD, and greatly to be praised;
And His greatness *is* unsearchable.　　　　—Psalm 145:2-3

We give thanks to God always for you all,
mentioning of you in our prayers,
remembering without ceasing your work of faith,
labor of love, and patience of hope
in our Lord Jesus Christ
in the sight of our God and Father.

1 Thessalonians 1:2-3

This is grace in action;
loving others as we
have been loved.

Grace in Action

1 Thessalonians 1:2-3

We give thanks to God always for you all,
mentioning of you in our prayers, remembering
without ceasing your work of faith, labor of love,
and patience of hope in our Lord Jesus Christ
in the sight of our God and Father

Paul wrote a letter of thanksgiving and prayer to the church at Thessalonica, commending them for their work of faith, labor of love, and patience of hope. He recognized how they worshipped and worked together, building each other up in the faith, becoming a church of community.

As I read this Scripture, I couldn't help but wonder if this would describe my church. Do we gather to grow in our faith, showing one another unconditional love, encouraging one another, and building each other up in the faith? Do we grow in confidence in who we are in Christ because we have been with our community of sisters and brothers?

> And let us consider one another in order to stir up love and good works, not forsaking the assembling of ourselves together, as *is* the manner of some, but exhorting *one another*, and so much more as you see the Day approaching. —Hebrews 10:23-25

When we feel genuinely loved, we are free to be ourselves. There is no need to be self-conscious or timid in our faith, but rather we are free to express our love for the Lord and for each other. In a community such as this, there is no room for judging. We realize we have all sinned and are in need of a Savior. If we should stumble in our walk we have the assurance that those with whom we worship will gather us to themselves in love and assurance, giving us the confidence we need to walk once again in the grace of Christ. This is grace in action—loving others as we have been loved.

> *"A new commandment I give to you, that you love one another; as I have loved you, that you also love one another. By this all will know that you are My disciples, if you have love for one another.* —John 13:34-35

The church of Thessalonica set an example for us all to follow. May we be willing to live a life of grace in action, encouraging one another in our community of believers, as together we grow in our love and faith in Jesus Christ, our Lord and Savior.

For to me, to live is Christ,
and to die is gain.

Philippians 1:21

Paul knew letting Christ
have His way in his life,
allowing Him to *be* his life,
was finding true freedom.

Alive In Christ

Philippians 1:21

For to me, to live *is* Christ,
and to die is gain.

Paul was in prison, a place from which most people would desperately want to escape. Not so for Paul. He saw this as an opportunity to praise His Lord—share Christ with others.

> But I want you to know, brethren, that the things
> *which happened* to me have actually turned out for
> the furtherance of the gospel, so that it has become
> evident to the whole palace guard, and to all the rest,
> that my chains are in Christ.   —Philippians 1:12-13

Why wasn't Paul consumed with fervor to prove his innocence, to make others see he didn't belong in prison? Paul had determined long before he was sent to prison his life belonged to Christ. He made the decision Christ wouldn't just be a part of his life, someone he prayed to in addition to all his other daily activities, but he would breath, eat, and sleep Christ. He would seek His face for every decision he would make, go only where Christ would lead, and do only what he felt Christ was encouraging him to do.

How easy is it to worship Jesus, pray for direction in our lives, and wisdom in our decisions, but then actually die to self and allow Him to have His complete way with our lives? What if we can't go where we use to go, do what we want to do?

Let's look at Paul's response to such an attitude. "For to me, to live *is* Christ, and to die is gain." Paul knew letting Christ have His way in his life, allowing Him to *be* his life, was finding true freedom. Paul was no longer responsible for where his life would take him, what he would eat, or where he would sleep. Whether to live or die, Paul knew in living for Christ, it would be gain.

"To die is gain." May we be willing to die to ourselves today, and live in Christ alone. Only then will we find true freedom.

"If anyone desires to come after Me, let him deny himself, and take up his cross daily, and follow me."   —Luke 9:23

But if we hope for what we do not see,
we eagerly wait for it with perseverance.

Romans 8:25

Because we know who holds us
in His hands,
we wait with assurance,
confident He will do
what is best.

Hope

Romans 8:25

But if we hope for what we do not see,
we eagerly wait for *it* with perseverance

As children of God our hope is not based on positive thinking or false hope. Our hope is centered on the promises of God. We establish our beliefs on:

> Who our Father is,
> What our Father promises He will do,
> Why we know we can hope with assurance

Our Father is God Almighty

> *"I am the Alpha and Omega, the Beginning and the End,*
> *the First and the Last"* —Revelations 22:13

> *"I am the Root and the Offspring of David, the Bright and*
> *Morning Star."* —Revelations 22:16

Our Father promises to take care of our every need and concern.

> O LORD, *You are* the portion of my inheritance
> and my cup; You maintain my lot. —Psalm 16:5-6

> Be of good courage,
> And He shall strengthen your heart,
> All you who hope in the LORD —Psalm 31:24

> Trust in Him at all times, you people;
> Pour out your heart before Him;
> God *is* a refuge for us. Selah —Psalm 62:8

And because we know who holds us in His hands, we wait with assurance, confident He will do what is best.

> See, I have inscribed you on the palms of *My hands;*
> Your walls *are* continually before Me. —Isaiah 49:16

> "Is anything too hard for the LORD?" —Genesis 18:14

> For I know the thoughts that I think toward you, says the
> Lord, thoughts of peace and not of evil, to give you a future
> and a hope. —Jeremiah 29:11

Therefore I exhort first of all that
supplications, prayers, intercessions,
and giving of thanks be made for all men.

1 Timothy 2:1

The Lord calls us to go out
among the hungry, lost,
and desperate
and show them Jesus.

Only One

1 Timothy 2:1

Therefore I exhort first of all that
supplications, prayers, intercessions, *and*
giving of thanks be made for all men.

Have you ever considered that you might be the only one praying for some-one? There are those who do not come from a Christian background, have never darkened the door of a church, and have no idea what it means to walk in the freedom of Christ. Nevertheless, they, too, have walked with heavy hearts, not knowing which way to turn. They have felt the pain of loneliness, weariness, and desperation. Yet, during these times, they have no one in their circle of friends or acquaintances praying for them.

The Lord calls us to go out among the hungry, lost, and desperate and show them Jesus. And He calls us to pray for those who do not yet know Him as their Savior.

> *"For I was hungry and you gave Me food; I was thirsty and you gave*
> *Me drink; I was a stranger and you took Me in;*
> *Then the righteous will answer Him saying, "Lord, when did we see*
> *You hungry and feed You, or thirsty and give You drink?*
> *When did we see you a stranger and take You in or naked and clothe You?*
> *And the King will answer and say to them, "Assuredly, I say to you,*
> *inasmuch as you did it to one of the least of these My brethren, you did*
> *it to Me."* —Matthew 25:35,37-38,40

> The Lord is not slack concerning *His* promise, as some count
> slackness, but is longsuffering toward us, not willing that any
> should perish but that all should come to repentance.
> —2 Peter 3:9

As we go about our busy days, let's not become so busy that we neglect to notice the cashier at the register where we buy our milk, or the saleslady that helps us pick out the perfect outfit. Let's lift our children's teacher up in prayer each morning, and let's be willing to pray for the waitress as we thank the Lord for our food. In doing so, we may be praying for one of the least of these.

> Then He said to His disciples, *"The harvest truly is plentiful, but the*
> *laborers are few. Therefore pray the Lord of the harvest to send out laborers*
> *into His harvest.* —Matthew 9:37-38

You shall love the LORD your God
with all your heart, with all your soul,
and with all your strength.

Deuteronomy 6:5

When we give our heart,
we choose to give the very core
of our being.

I Give My Heart

Deuteronomy 6:5

You shall love the LORD your God
with all your heart, with all your soul,
and with all your strength.

Attending a weekend conference, the theme of the event was "Believe". As the speaker shared gems of wisdom and insight into the meaning of "believe", she taught that the word "believe" can be summed up with one wonderful, life changing truth—the word believe can be replaced with I give my heart.

I believe in Jesus—I give my heart to Jesus

I believe in God—I give my heart to God

I believe in the Holy Spirit—I give my heart to the Holy Spirit

I believe in prayer—I give my heart to prayer

I believe the promises of God—I give my heart to the promises of God

When we give our heart, we choose to give the very core of our being. No longer do we come first in our lives, but the One in whom we give our heart comes first. No longer do we demand our own way, but we allow the One to whom we give our heart to direct our path. We are willing to let go of our heart of stone and allow the One to whom we give our heart to replace it with His heart.

> "I will give you a new heart and put a new spirit within you; I will take the heart of stone out of your flesh and give you a heart of flesh."   —Ezekiel 36:26

> "Then I will give them a heart to know Me, that I *am the LORD;* and they shall be My people, and I will be their God, for they shall return to Me with their whole heart."   —Jeremiah 24:7

Lord,
   I give my heart to you! Have your way in me I pray.
                In Your precious name I pray,
                        Amen

Yet, for all of that, you did not
believe the LORD your God.

Deuteronomy 1:32

May we decide today
to walk with God,
holding tight to the hand
that will never let go.

Yet, For All of That

Deuteronomy 1:32

Yet, for all of that, you did not
believe the LORD your God.

Leading the Israelites, Moses spoke to the people the words God had spoken to him in regard to entering the promise land.

> "See, I have set the land before you; go in and possess the land
> which the LORD swore to your fathers, Abraham, Isaac, and
> Jacob, to give them and their descendants after them."
> —Deuteronomy 1:8

Let's consider what had taken place before these words. By the commands of God, Moses had led the people from Egypt, far from the slavery they had known for so long. From there he led them across the Red Sea, and through the wilderness, where they were led by a pillar of cloud by day and a light of fire by night.

> Marvelous things He did in the sight of their fathers,
> In the land of Egypt, in the field of Zoan.
> He divided the sea and caused them to pass through;
> And He made the waters stand up like a heap.
> In the daytime also He led them with the cloud,
> And all the night with a light of fire.   —Psalm 78:12-14

Yet, after sending twelve men to check out the land, when all but two men brought back reports of woe, they refused to go in. They chose, instead, to believe the reports of ten men over the Word of God.

How often that sounds like us. We know what the Word of God tells us. We know all the Lord has done for us until now. Yet, for all of that, when life comes crashing in around us, we refuse to walk in His Truth, but choose instead to believe the lies of Satan.

May that not be! May we decide today, regardless of where He leads, to walk with God, holding tight to the hand that will never let us go.

> Fear not, for I *am* your God.
> I will strengthen you,
> Yes, I will help you,
> I will uphold you with My righteous right hand.
> —Isaiah 41:10

Walk as children of light.

Ephesians 5:8

We are to be light
in the midst of darkness.

Children of Light

Ephesians 5:8

Walk as children of light.

Jesus is light:

> Then Jesus spoke to them again, saying,
> *"I am the light of the world. He who follows Me shall not walk in
> darkness, but have the light of life."* —John 8:12

The Word of God is light:

> Your Word *is* a lamp to my feet
> And a light to my path. — Psalm 119:105

We are the light of the world:

> *"You are the light of the world. A city that is set on a hill
> cannot be hidden."* —Matthew 5:14

We all know the world is a place of darkness. Each night on the evening news, we hear of crime after crime committed, continual chaos throughout the world, and enemies turning against enemies.

It is in the midst of all of this, as children of the living God, that we are called to be light. We are to show love to our neighbors, help to the hurting, and kindness to our enemy. We are to be light in the midst of darkness.

> *"Let your light so shine before men, that they may see your good works
> and glorify your Father in heaven."* —Matthew 5:16

How do we do this? How do we set ourselves apart to be different than the world around us? We look to our Father. We read His love letter and we follow where He leads.

> Trust in the Lord with all your heart,
> And lean not on your own understanding;
> In all your ways acknowledge Him,
> And He shall direct your paths.
> Do not be wise in your own eyes;
> Fear the LORD and depart from evil.
> It will be health to your flesh,
> And strength to your bones. —Proverbs 3:5-7

In the midst of a dark and hopeless world, we walk as children of light that others might see our good works and glorify our Father in heaven.

Then the LORD spoke to Moses and Aaron,
"Because you did not believe Me,
to hallow me in the eyes of the children of Israel,
therefore you shall not bring this assembly
into the land which I have given them.

Numbers 20:12

God delights in our obedience.
It is always for our good,
and for His glory.

The Cost of Disobedience

Numbers 20:12

Then the LORD spoke to Moses and Aaron,
"Because you did not believe Me, to hallow Me in the eyes
of the children of Israel, therefore you shall not bring this
assembly into the land which I have given them.

Have you ever wondered why Moses didn't enter the promise land? After talking to God face to face, and leading the people for forty years, God grew so angry with Moses that He refused to allow Him to cross over with the people. What did Moses do to make God so angry?

It began with an assembly of the people complaining to Moses:

> "And why have you made us come up out of Egypt, to bring us to this evil place? It is not a place of grain or figs or vines or pomegranates; nor is there any water to drink." —Numbers 20:5

Leaving the assembly, Moses and Aaron fell on their faces before the Lord. It is here the Lord spoke to Moses, telling him what he was to do:

> "Take the rod; you and your brother Aaron gather the congregation together. Speak to the rock before their eyes, and it will yield its water; thus you shall bring water for them out of the rock, and give drink to the congregation and their animals." —Numbers 20:8

Instead of obeying the word of the Lord, Moses decided to take things into his own hands, do things his way:

> And Moses and Aaron gathered the assembly together before the rock; and he said to them, "Hear now, you rebels! Must we bring water for you out of this rock?" Then Moses lifted his hand and struck the rock twice with his rod; and water came out abundantly, and the congregation and their animals drank.   —Numbers 20:10-11

When did the Lord tell Moses to hit the rock? When did God say it would be Moses and Aaron bringing forth water? He did not. He told Moses to speak to the rock, in order that they might see the holiness of God and it would yield water. Moses did it his way instead and his disobedience cost him dearly.

God delights in our obedience. It is always for our good and for His glory.

> "Has the LORD *as great* delight in burnt
>   offerings and sacrifices,
>   As in obeying the voice of the LORD?
>   Behold, to obey is better than sacrifice.   —1 Samuel 15:22

Let us therefore come boldly
to the throne of grace,
that we may obtain mercy and grace
to help in time of need.

Hebrews 4:16

This scripture is not referring
to arrogance,
nor is it telling us to
demand what we desire.

Come Boldly

Hebrews 4:16

Let us therefore come boldly to the throne of grace,
that we may obtain mercy and find grace
to help in time of need.

As I read this Scripture, the word boldly stood out amongst the rest. So often the word "boldly" refers to someone who is conceited. They convey a sense of arrogance, as if they deserve what it is they desire.

As children of God, we have received more than any of us deserve. Because of the gracious love of our Father, we have been given grace and blessings beyond compare.

> As it is written:
> *There is none righteous, no, not one;*
> *There is none who understands;*
> *There is none who seeks after God.*
> *They have all turned aside;*
> *They have together become unprofitable;*
> *There is none who does good, no, not one.* —Romans 3:10-12

This Scripture is not referring to arrogance, nor is it telling us to demand what it is we desire. It is teaching us to approach the throne of grace with confidence. We are to come to the throne of grace in humility and meekness, but also with confidence, knowing our Father hears our prayers.

> I LOVE the Lord, because He has heard
> My voice *and my supplications.*
> Because He has inclined His ear to me,
> Therefore I will call *upon Him* as long as I live.
> —Psalm 116:1-2

> But blessed is the man who trusts in the LORD
> Whose confidence is in Him. —Jeremiah 17:7 NIV

We can rest in the assurance that as we approach the throne of grace with boldness, in whom it is we come, our Father sees our heart and hears our prayers. He alone is able to help in time of need.

> I sought the LORD, and He heard me,
> And delivered me from all my fears. —Psalm 34:4

Surrender yourself to the LORD
And wait patiently for Him.

Psalm 37:7 (GW)

As we surrender all to Him,
He goes through our all with us.

Surrender All

Psalm 37:7

Surrender yourself to the LORD
And wait patiently for Him. (GW)

When we are faced with heartaches and problems we know demand a answer, it is hard to wait on the Lord for direction.

As our loved one faces the uncertainty of tomorrow, not knowing if they will be healed of the disease engulfing their body, it can be so hard to wait for what lies ahead. When finances run low and we have no idea how we are going to pay our bills, we can easily surrender to fear rather than God.

> Fear not, for I *am* with you;
> Be not dismayed, for I *am* your God.
> I will strengthen you,
> Yes, I will help you,
> I will uphold you with My righteous right hand.
> —Isaiah 41:10

How easy it is to sing the song, "I Surrender All." However, when we must surrender our prodigal child, trusting God will do whatever it takes to bring him or her home, uncertainty can pull at our heartstrings.

Life is full of uncertainties and heartaches. No one escapes life unscathed. However, we need not walk alone. If we will call upon the One who is there for us, we will find the peace we so desperately need.

> *"In the world you will have tribulation; but be of good cheer,*
> *I have overcome the world."* —John 16:33b

> *"Peace I leave with you. My peace I give to you; not as the world gives*
> *do I give to you. Let not your heart be troubled, neither let it be afraid.*
> —John 14:27

As we surrender all to Him, He goes through our all with us. He does not leave us nor forsake us, but works all things out in ways only He can. What are you facing today that requires an open hand and surrendered heart? Be willing to trust His heart when you can't trace His hand.

> Surrender your heart to God, turn to Him in prayer.
> —Job 11:13 CEV

And they glorified God in me.

Galatians 1:24

Accepting Christ as our Savior
is a heart issue.
From the heart one believes,
and is saved.

What Do You See?

Galatians 1:24

And they glorified God in me.

Reading Galatians, concerning Paul proclaiming Jesus as his Savior, I marveled at the response of those to whom He preached.

> And I was unknown by face to the churches of Judea which
> *were* in Christ.
> But they were hearing only, "He who formerly persecuted us
> now preaches the faith which he once *tried to destroy.*"
> And they glorified God in me. —Galatians 1:22—24

Aware of Paul's past, how easily it would have been for them to refuse to listen to him, but instead send him away. What we find in its place is acceptance and rejoicing in Paul's new found faith.

What a blessing it is when one lost in their sins turns from their sinful ways, and repenting, accepts Christ as their Savior.

> *"What man of you, having a hundred sheep, if he loses one of them,*
> *does not leave the ninety—nine in the wilderness, and go after the one*
> *which is lost until he finds it?*
> *"And when he has found it, he lays it on his shoulders, rejoicing."*
> —Luke 15:4-5

Accepting Christ as our Savior is a heart issue. From the heart one believes and is saved.

> If you confess with your mouth the Lord Jesus and believe
> in your heart that God has raised Him from the dead, you
> will be saved.
> For with the heart one believes unto righteousness, and with
> the mouth confession is made unto salvation.
> —Romans 10:10—11

As those to whom Paul preached did not consider his past, but rejoiced in his salvation, may we do the same regardless of where our Christian brothers and sisters have once walked. The ground is level at the foot of the cross. We all come the very same way—broken.

God uses the church to exalt the humble, as well as humble the exalted.

"Therefore whoever hears these sayings of Mine, and does them, I will liken him to a wise man who built his house on the rock."

Matthew 7:24

What does it look like to build your life on the Rock?

Built on the Rock

Matthew 7:24

"Therefore whoever hears these sayings of Mine,
and does them, I will liken him to a wise man
who built his house on the rock

Dear Friends,

What does it look like to you to build your life on the Rock?

As I read the parable concerning building your life on the rock, I considered what it would look like to build my life on the Rock. What exactly does that mean? Rather than answer the question myself, I sent out a group text to my friends asking this question. The answers I received were thought provoking and exciting.

> "To me it means that my heart is bent toward Him, and
> that I examine my heart in every thought, decision,
> and behavior. Of course, I am still being sanctified, so I
> am not close to that. But it is my prayer."

> "Daily choosing to follow Christ."

> "Jesus is the Rock. When you follow Him, asking, "What would
> Jesus do?" in every decision you will build your life on the Rock."

> "To me it is building my life on the solid foundation of Jesus. He
> alone is my unmovable and everlasting foundation."

So what would you say? What would it look like to build your life on the Rock? Would you, along with my friends, agree it is a life built on our unmovable and everlasting Father? Would you concur it is choosing to follow Christ with your heart bent toward Him, asking in every decision, "What would Jesus do?" This is a thought for every believer to ponder and strive toward. Jesus is our Rock, may we build our lives on Him.

> The LORD is my rock and my fortress, and my deliverer;
> My God, my strength, in whom I will trust;
> My shield and the horn of my salvation, my stronghold.
> —Psalm 18:2

> My soul finds rest in God alone; my salvation comes from him.
> He alone is my rock and my salvation; he is my fortress,
> I will not be shaken. —Psalm 62:1-2 (NIV)

Then, when Mary came where Jesus was,
and saw Him, she fell down at His feet,
saying to Him, "Lord, if You had been here,
my brother would not have died."

John 11:32

Nothing catches God
by surprise.

Trust

John 11:32

Then, when Mary came where Jesus was,
and saw Him, she fell down at His feet,
saying to Him, "Lord, if You had been here,
my brother would not have died."

Four days before coming to Bethany, Mary's brother, Lazarus, had died. Mary and her sister, Martha, mourned for their brother. They knew if only Jesus had been there, Lazarus would still be alive. Why hadn't He come? Why hadn't He healed their brother? Why did Lazarus have to die?

The Scriptures tell us that when Mary came to Jesus she fell at His feet. With her head down, tears falling, she asked her Lord the question we have all asked, when life doesn't make sense, "Why?" "Why didn't You do what only You can do?" "Why didn't you step in before it was too late?"

How we see God will determine how much we will trust God. Do we see Him as a compassionate Father, One who feels our pain, understands our confusion? Or do we see Him as our Judge and Jury, allowing hurt to come into our lives with no rhyme or reason?

> "Therefore, when Jesus saw her weeping, and the Jews who came
> with her weeping, He groaned in the spirit and was troubled. And
> He said, *"Where have you laid him?"* They said to Him, Lord come
> and see. Jesus wept.   —John 11:33-35

When Jesus saw Mary weeping, He felt her pain, understood her confusion, and He wept.

> As a father has compassion on *his* children,
> So the LORD has compassion on those who fear Him.
> For He knows our frame;
> He remembers that we *are* dust.   —Psalm 103:13-14

When we know the character of our Heavenly Father we can rest in His love, knowing although we don't understand the "why," we can trust Who it is that holds our lives in His hands. Nothing catches God by surprise. He alone can take what Satan meant for evil and through His infinite wisdom and grace, use it for our good and for His Glory.

> Blessed *is* the man who trusts in the LORD,
> And whose hope is the LORD.   —Jeremiah 17:7

To give them beauty for ashes.
Isaiah 61:3

What feels like heartache
could be the very tool
God uses to take us to the
next place in our walk
with Him.

Beauty for Ashes

Isaiah 61:3

To give them beauty for ashes.

Attending the wedding of my nephew, tears of joy could not be contained as I witnessed, first-hand, the love and faithfulness of God. I expected to look into the star lit sky and see written for all to read, "I turn ashes into beauty." It was obvious this was exactly what God had done in my nephew's life. As he stood before the guests, he proclaimed, "I thank God every night for how He has blessed me." Yes, God had taken what once looked like a life of sadness and despair and replaced it with blessings beyond his greatest expectations.

> To give them beauty for ashes,
> The oil of joy for mourning,
> The garment of praise for the spirit of heaviness;
> That they may be called trees of righteousness,
> The planting of the LORD, that He may be glorified.
> —Isaiah 61:3

More and more the Lord is teaching me to wait on Him, and in the waiting trust Him. If only we could see behind the scene of how God is working in each of our lives. He has a plan for our lives and He alone knows what must take place to bring this plan to pass. What feels like heartache could be the very tool God uses to take us to the next place in our walk with Him.

> What then shall we say to these things? If God *is* for us,
> who *can be* against us?   —Romans 8:31

> Wait on the LORD; be of good courage,
> And He shall strengthen your heart;
> Wait, I say, on the LORD!   —Psalm 27:14

> For I know the thoughts that I think toward you says the LORD,
> thoughts of peace and not of evil, to give you a future and a hope.
> —Jeremiah 29:11

I want to wait on the Lord. I want to know that I can trust Him to work all things out, and in the working, turn the ashes of my life into beauty. I know He will. I saw it written across the sky!

> And we know that all things work together for good to those who
> love God, to those who are called according to *His* purpose.
> —Romans 8:28

For I *am* the LORD your God,
The Holy One of Israel, your Savior.

Isaiah 43:3

How can we trust God,
if we never have a reason
to put our faith in Him.

I Am the Lord Your God

Isaiah 43:3

For I *am* the LORD your God,
The Holy One of Israel, your Savior.

The LORD your God is in your present. He was in your past, He will be in your future; but more importantly, He is in your present. He is in your today and all it entails.

What are you facing today that seems too heavy to carry? God is in this burden with you. He has not left you to carry it alone, nor to find a solution. He is in your today to go through the waters with you.

> When you pass through the waters, *I will be* with you;
> And through the rivers, they shall not overflow you.
> When you walk through the fire, you shall not be burned,
> Nor shall the flame scorch you.   —Isaiah 43:2

So often we pray for the hard places of life to pass us by. We long to be problem and worry free. If only our lives would go as we planned. Much to our dismay, there is not a Scripture written promising us a worry and problem free life. Instead, we are told of the heartaches and turmoil the people faced as they lived their lives. Why do you suppose this is? Could it be the Lord wants to teach us what it means to trust Him? How can we trust God if we never have a reason to put our faith in Him? How can we realize His faithfulness if we never need to wait on Him? How can we feel our Father's peace if we are never fearful? Could it be God wants to show us He is in our present? Could it be He wants us to understand His faithfulness, compassion, and the love He has for us today?

> "Fear not, for I have redeemed you;
>   I have called *you* by your name;
> You *are* Mine."   —Isaiah 43:1

God alone puts purpose in our pain as we wait on Him. He will carry us when we cannot walk, and turn the impossible into the possible.

> Fear not, for I *am* with you;
> Be not dismayed, for I *am* your God.
> I will strengthen you, Yes I will help you,
> I will uphold you with My righteous right hand.   —Isaiah 41:10

Walk worthy of the LORD, fully pleasing *Him*,
being fruitful in every good work and increasing
in the knowledge of God.

Colossians 1:10

Only what we do for Jesus
will count for all eternity.

Our Legacy

Colossians 1:10

Walk worthy of the LORD, fully pleasing *Him,*
being fruitful in every good work and increasing in
the knowledge of God.

Writing to Timothy, Paul encouraged him to continue to walk in the faith that dwelt first in his grandmother Lois and then in his mother Eunice.

> I call to remembrance the genuine faith that is in you,
> which dwelt first in your grandmother Lois and your
> mother Eunice, and I am persuaded is in you also.
> —2 Timothy 1:5

As I read this scripture, I couldn't help but consider who my life is influencing, as they witness my faith in God. Do they see my trust in God remains steady, regardless of what life may hold? Do they feel the love of Christ as we spend time together? Do they realize I have committed my life to Christ, walking daily hand in hand with my Lord?

What legacy are we leaving to our children, and to others in whom we love? Do they see Jesus, and know without a shadow of a doubt our life has been built on the love of our Savior? Paul referred to Timothy's grandmother, Lois, and his mother, Eunice, as he commended him for his walk with the Lord. Paul knew it was because of the example set before him that Timothy remained fruitful in every good work.

Our life is but a vapor, here today and gone tomorrow. Only what we do with Jesus will matter for all eternity. May our love for Him so shine that others will see Christ in us. Only then will our legacy count for Him.

> Trust in the Lord, and do good;
> Dwell in the land, and feed on His faithfulness.
> Delight yourself also in the LORD,
> And He shall give you the desires of your heart.   —Psalm 37:3-4

> For what is your life?
> It is even a vapor that appears for a little time
> And then vanishes away.   —James 4:14

Peter siad to Him,
"You shall never wash my feet!"
Jesus answered him,
"If I do not wash you,
you shall have no part with Me."

John 13:8

Peter must be willing to
submit himself before Jesus,
or have no part with Him.

Wash My Feet

John 13:8

Peter said to Him, "You shall never wash my feet!"
Jesus answered him,
"If I do not wash you, you shall have no part with Me."

The night before Jesus was to be crucified, He and the twelve disciples convened in the Upper Room. After supper, Jesus, taking a basin of water, poured the water over the disciples' feet, then wiped them with a cloth.

Why would the Son of God kneel before men and wash their feet? Shouldn't they be doing everything possible to honor Him? As Jesus came to Peter, he became outraged. "You shall never wash my feet!" he told Him. Jesus' reply caused me to sit up and take notice. What did He mean when He told Peter, *"If I do not wash you, you shall have no part with Me."*

Examining this Scripture closer, I realized Jesus was telling Peter He <u>must</u> wash his feet. This was not something He would reconsider. Peter must be willing to submit himself before Jesus or have no part with Him.

As we come to Jesus we must do the same. We must humble ourselves, admit we are sinners, and allow Christ to wash us clean by His shed blood. Likewise, until we are willing to let go of our own agenda and allow Christ to have His way in our lives, like Peter, we will have no part in Christ.

> Purge me with hyssop, and I shall be clean;
> Wash me, and I shall be whiter than snow. —Psalm 51:7

> *"God resists the proud, but gives grace to the humble"*
> Therefore humble yourselves under the mighty hand of God,
> that He may exalt you in due time. —1 Peter 5:5-6

> He has shown you, O man, what *is* good;
> And what does the LORD require of you
> But to do justly,
> To love mercy,
> And to walk humbly with your God? —Micah 6:8

As I thought of my life, my willingness to humble myself with my actions and attitude, my prayer became: "Lord show me where I refuse to bow before You. May I allow You to wash my feet, that I may be clean in You!" In Jesus' Precious Name I pray, Amen & Amen

*"Or have you not read in the law
that on the Sabbath the priests
in the temple profane the Sabbath,
and are blameless?"*

Matthew 12:5

May we be as swift to praise
our brothers and sisters
as we are to criticize.

Blameless

Matthew 12:5

"Or have you not read in the law that on the Sabbath
the priests in the temple profane the Sabbath, and are blameless?"

As I studied this Scripture, I was totally confused as to how anyone, at any-time, could profane the Sabbath, and yet be blameless.

Let me explain the setting in which this statement was spoken by Jesus. It was the Sabbath and the disciples became hungry. Walking through grain fields, they began plucking off heads of grain to eat. Becoming enraged, the Pharisees said to Jesus,

> "Look, Your disciples are doing what is not lawful to do
> on the Sabbath!"   —Matthew 12:2

As I read this, I couldn't help but be amused as I imagined the Pharisees seizing the moment to "tattle" on the disciples. How much we are like this! We are so quick to find fault with others, judging them as they fall short of our standards as a Christian. We then share their shortcomings with others. Jesus warns strongly against this.

> These six *things* the LORD hates,
> Yes, seven *are* an abomination to Him;
> A false witness, *who* speaks lies,
> And one who sows discord among brethren.
> —Proverbs 6:16,19

Digging deeper into this Scripture, what I found was Jesus explaining to the Pharisees, just as the priests broke the law by working on the Sabbath by slaying the lambs given as a sacrifice, they were considered blameless because it was a requirement of their position as priests. Likewise, the disciples were blameless in plucking off heads of grain to eat on the Sabbath because it was necessary they be nourished to continue their positions as disciples of Christ. What appeared wrong to the Pharisees was as right as them performing duties on the Sabbath.

How quickly we come to wrong conclusions before knowing all the facts. May we be as swift to praise our brothers and sisters as we are to criticize.

> *"This is My commandment, that you love one another as I have loved you."*
> —John 15:12

Thus says the LORD to you:
"Do not be afraid nor dismayed
because of this great multitude,
for the battle *is* not yours, but God's."

2 Chronicles 20:15b

The battle belongs to the Lord, and the Lord always wins!

The Battle Belongs to the Lord

2 Chronicles 20:15b

Thus says the LORD to you:
"Do not be afraid nor dismayed because of this great
multitude, for the battle *is* not yours, but God's."

Standing in church with a heavy heart, the congregation began singing "The Battle Belongs to the Lord". When we are in the midst of a crisis, our heart broken, the feeling of hopelessness consuming our very being, these words become our lifeline. They are words of comfort in the midst of despair, giving us renewed faith in the One to whom we belong. When we realize our battle is too big for us, but not for the Lord, we find a new strength that had once been taken from us. No longer must we walk in defeat, consumed with worry, but as we release the crisis to the Lord, we find hope and strength for what lies ahead.

> "Have I not commanded you? Be strong and of good courage;
> do not be afraid, nor be dismayed, for the LORD your God *is*
> with you wherever your go."   —Joshua 1:9

As the congregation finished singing, I found myself holding on to these words. This battle really did belong to the Lord. We had done all we knew to do, spent in strength, left only with defeat. I knew I must release our heartache to the Lord. As I opened my hands and lifted my heart to Him, I felt a peace I had not known for so long. We could stop looking for an answer, trying are best to come up with a plan. We could let go and let God fight the battle.

Then the thought came to me:

> This battle belongs to the Lord, and the Lord always wins!

I knew at that moment the crisis would end. I didn't know how, or when, but I did know when we crossed the finish line, it would end in victory in Jesus. HE would fight and He would win.

What is your battle? Will you give it to Jesus? He will fight for You! The battle belongs to the Lord. And, He always wins!!

> "Be strong and of good courage, to not fear nor be afraid of them;
> for the LORD your God, He *is* the One who goes with you. He will
> not leave you nor forsake you."   —Deuteronomy 31:6

"The thief does not come except to steal,
and to destroy.
I have come that they may have life
and that they may have it more abundantly."

John 10:10

Nothing gives Satan more satisfaction then when he succeeds in taking our eyes off Jesus, and instead succumb to defeat.

Choose This Day

John 10:10

*"The thief does not come except to steal,
and to destroy. I have come that they may have life
and that they may have it more abundantly."*

How often have you been having a wonderful day, all is as it should be, and then like a thief in the night, something happens and your joy is immediately replaced with despair and frustration. *"The thief does not come except to steal, and to destroy."*

As followers of Christ we have a chose whether to stoop to the lies of Satan, walking in defeat, or stand on the word of God, knowing what He tells us is truth. Just as He spoke to the multitudes, He speaks to us of the thief who comes to steal our joy, destroy our peace, and ploy to steal our faith and trust in our Savior. Nothing gives Satan more satisfaction then when he succeeds in taking our eyes off Jesus, and instead succumb to defeat. My mom tells me at times like this he is sitting in the corner clapping, knowing he has won.

How do we stand on the Word of God when everything around us seems to be moving toward defeat? How do we trust in what we do not see? We stand in faith. We believe the Word of God over the evidence before us.

> Now faith is the substance of things hoped for, the
> evidence of things not seen.   —Hebrews 11:1

Faith is a chose. It cannot be forced, nor can it be replaced. Faith and fear cannot exist as one. We either choose to walk in faith or allow fear to steal our peace. Who will we believe, our Savior or our enemy?

> "I call heaven and earth as witnesses today against you, *that* I have set
> before you life and death, blessings and cursing; therefore choose life
> that both you and your descendants may live; that you may love the
> LORD your God, that you may cling to Him, for He *is* your life and the
> length of your days.   —Deuteronomy 30:19

Let's choose this day to stand on the Word of God, allowing Satan to stoop in the corner, not clapping this time, but with his head hung low in defeat.

> *"I have come that they may have life and that they may have it
> more abundantly."*   —John 10:10

Draw near to God and He will draw near to you. Cleanse *your* hands, *you* sinners; and purify *your* hearts, *you* double-minded.

James 4:8

The dross of our heart is that which keeps us from living a Christ centered life.

Purify Your Heart

James 4:8

Draw near to God and He will draw near to you.
Cleanse *your* hands, *you* sinners; and purify *your* hearts,
you double minded.

"Purify your hearts," James commanded. Make your heart pure, without imperfections, hardness of heart or bitterness of any kind.

As I pondered James instruction, the Lord brought to my remembrance the Scripture concerning the taking of dross from silver:

> Take away the dross from silver,
> And it will go to the silversmith *for* jewelry   —Proverbs 25:4

And of the silversmith as he purified the silver:

> He will sit as a refiner and a purifier of silver.   —Malachi 3:3

The dross of our heart is that which keeps us from living a Christ centered life. Just as dross on silver must be removed before it can be used for silver, so the dross of our heart must be removed before we can live a life purified before Christ.

> Let all bitterness, wrath, anger, clamor, and evil speaking
> be put away from you, with all malice. And be kind to one
> another, tenderhearted, forgiving one another, even as God
> in Christ forgave you.   —Ephesians 4:31-32

But how do we do this? How do we put away such things as keep us from living the abundant life in Christ? Just as the silversmith sat as a refiner of silver looking into the fire until the dross was removed, we seek the face of God, asking Him to remove the dross from our heart. As we submit to His ways, obeying His teachings, and allow Him to work in our hearts, He will walk with us through the process of letting go of all that keeps us from having a heart purified before Him.

> Search me, O God, and know my heart;
> Try me, and know my thoughts;
> And see if *there is any* wicked way in me,
> And lead me in the way everlasting.   —Psalm 139:23-24

> If we confess your sins, He is faithful and just
> to forgive us *our* sins and to cleanse us from
> all unrighteousness.   —1 John 1:9

Your ears will hear a word behind you, saying,
"This is the way, walk in it,"
Whenever you turn to the right hand
Or whenever you turn to the left.

Isaiah 30:21

God is our Father,
and He cares
about His children.
If it concerns us,
it concerns Him.

Lord, Go Before Us

Isaiah 30:21

Your ears shall hear a word behind you, saying,
"This is the way, walk in it,"
Whenever you turn to the right hand
Or whenever you turn to the left.

Coming home from Estes Park, after a wonderful weekend of wedding festivities, our family found our strength wavering, our bones weary, and exhaustion chasing us down. How would we make it through the stress of finding our way through airports, making the necessary connections, and home to our place of refuge?

At times like this, how often do we stop and ask the Lord to guide our steps, clear the way, and direct our path? So often, instead of asking for His help, we simply buck up, determined to make it through the day.

"The steps of a *good* man are ordered by the LORD,
And He delights in his way.   —Psalm 37:23

He gives power to the weak,
And to *those who have* no might
He increases strength.   —Isaiah 40:29

God *is* our refuge and strength,
A very present help in trouble.   —Psalm 46:1

We feel to ask the Lord for such trivial help is foolishness. Aren't there enough big problems in the world that need His attention without us asking Him to get us through the airport? Yes, yes there are. But God is our Father and He cares about His children. If it concerns us, it concerns Him.

And because you are sons, God has sent forth the
Spirit of His Son into your hearts, crying out,
"Abba, Father!"   —Galatians 4:6

The next time you find yourself weary in body, your strength spent, call out to your Father. Ask Him to go before you, then watch as He orders your steps and prepares the way.

Then God said to Noah,
"Come out of the ark,
you and your wife and your sons
and their wives."

Genesis 8:15-16

Do I move because I *think*
I've heard from God,
or do I wait until I *know*
I've heard from God?

Walking with God

Genesis 8:15-16

Then God said to Noah, "Come out of the ark,
you and your wife and your sons and their wives."

As I read the account of Noah on the ark, I was amazed that at the first glance of dry land he didn't leave the ark, but stayed until he heard from God.

> By the first day of the first month of Noah's six hundred and first year, the water had dried up from the earth. Noah then removed the covering from the ark and saw that the surface of the ground was dry. By the twenty-seventh day of the second month the earth was completely dry. —Genesis 8:13-14 (NIV)

Then I thought; "How willing I am to wait on God? Do I move because I *think* I have heard from God, or do I wait until I *know* I've heard from God?"

Attending a Christian conference, one of the attendees shared how she had just broken off a relationship because, even though everything was fine, she knew it was not the will of God. "I have always settled for the crumbs, but this time I'm going to wait on God because I know He has the very best for me," she said.

> "I will instruct you and teach you in the way you should go;
> I will counsel you and watch over you." —Psalm 32:8 (NIV)

After living within the the four walls of an ark, surrounded by animals of every kind, I'm sure at the first glimpse of dry land I would want to leave the ark. Not so for Noah. He waited until he heard from God. He knew without the leading of God, he would surely lose his way.

> Noah was a righteous man, blameless among the people of his time, and he walked with God. —Genesis 6:9 (NIV)

"And he walked with God." Oh, how I want that to be said of my life! May I be willing to listen for His voice, that where He leads I may follow.

> For *You* are my rock and my fortress;
> Therefore, for Your name sake,
> Lead me and guide me. —Psalm 31:3 (NIV)

The angel of the LORD encamps around
those who fear Him, and He delivers them.

Psalm 34:7

As we replace our worries
with His presence,
our choices with His will,
and our heartache
with His peace,
we will find
the answer will come.

He Dances Over You

Psalm 34:7

The angel of the LORD encamps around
those who fear Him, and He delivers them.

There have been times in all of our lives when we had decisions to make, problems to solve, and relationships to mend, yet felt powerless over what we were to do. During these times, the Lord encamps His angels around those who fear Him.

> Taste and see that the LORD is good,
> Blessed is the man who takes refuge in Him.   —Psalm 34:8 (NIV)

When all we want to do is solve the problem, make the difficult decision, or find harmony in the midst of strife, before we do anything, it would behoove us to listen to the counsel of the Lord.

> The eyes of the LORD are on the righteous,
> And his ears are attentive to their cry.   —Psalm 34:15 (NIV)

> The LORD is close to the brokenhearted
> And saves those who are crushed in spirit.   —Psalm 34:18 (NIV)

> A righteous man may have many troubles,
> But the LORD delivers him from them all.   —Psalm 34:19 (NIV)

As we replace our worries with His presence, our choices with His will, and our heartache with His peace, we will find the answer will come. No longer will we feel alone, desperate to know what to do, but we will know the goodness of the Lord, and feel the deliverance only He can bring.

> "The LORD your God is with you,
> He is mighty to save.
> He will take great delight in you,
> He will quiet you with his love,
> He will rejoice over you with singing."   —Zephaniah 3:17 (NIV)

Take refuge in the Lord. He encamps His angels around you with His love, rejoicing over you with singing. He alone has the answer.

> "Be still and know that I am God."   —Psalm 41:10 (NIV)

"Am I Enough?"

Habakkuk 3:17-18

Though the fig tree may not blossom,
Nor fruit be on the vines;
Though the labor of the olive may fail,
And the fields yield no food;
Though the flock may be cut off from the fold,
And there be no herd in the stalls----
Yet I will rejoice in the LORD,
I will joy in the God of my salvation.

Sitting on my basement floor painting a rocking chair for my grandson, tears ran down my face that would not stop. "Why Lord? I don't understand. Why don't you do something about this heartache that never seems to go away?" Battling feelings of betrayal and confusion, nothing seemed to make sense. Didn't we do all we could to prevent this heartache? Was there no reward for walking close to the Lord, leaning on Him for every decision? "God, where are you? Do You care that I am hurting?"

It wasn't spoken words I heard, ones others would hear had they been in the room. It was an inner voice, deep in my soul; "Cyndy, am I enough for you? If all else falls away and you are left with only Me, am I enough?" How I wanted to shout, "Yes, Lord! You know You are!" But, before I could speak, I knew I couldn't say yes. At that moment, I knew this wasn't about the heartache we were facing. It wasn't about unanswered prayers. This wasn't even about Satan having havoc with my life. It was all about my coming face to face with the truth that I expected the Lord to hear my prayers and come to my rescue, taking away the heartache. It was about my realizing that I found joy in my salvation, and peace that passes all understanding, only when all was well in my life.

This is not what Jesus wants for His children. He wants us to know He is enough even when life is not peaceful and all is well. He wants us to want Him and Him alone. From the words of John Piper, "God is most glorified when we are most satisfied in Him." Am I satisfied in Him? Is He enough? Oh, Lord, may I shout "Yes!" and know that it is true!

Though the fig tree may not blossom,
Nor fruit be on the vines,
Yet I will rejoice in the LORD
I will joy in the God of my salvation.

Delight yourself in the Lord
and He will give you the desires of your heart.

Psalm 37:4

Gaze upon His goodness
and we will find a heart
hungry for Him.

Delight Yourself in the Lord

Psalm 37:4

Delight yourself in the Lord
and He will give you the desires of your heart.

As I studied the Psalms, coming upon this familiar verse, I considered the definition of "delight." When I looked it up in my Thesaurus, I was surprised to find delight also means appreciate.

Appreciate the Lord and He will give you the desires of your heart.

This brought me back to a Psalm I had previously read:

I was young and *now* am old;
Yet I have not seen the righteous forsaken,
Nor his descendants begging bread.   —Psalm 37:25

Do I appreciate all the Lord has and continues to do for me? Do I live my life with a posture of thankfulness and a grateful heart? How true it is the Lord has never forsaken me.

Gaze upon His goodness and we will find a heart hungry for Him. Gaze upon the heartaches of our lives and we will find despair and frustration meeting us at every turn. It has been said we are to gaze at Jesus and glance at our problems. How often are we guilty of doing the opposite? We glance at Jesus and gaze, actually dwell, on our problems.

Therefore submit to God
Resist the devil and He will flee from you.   —James 4:7

Draw near to God
and He will draw near to you.   —James 4:8a

We have heard it called many things; markers, wall of remembrance, God sights, but they all mean the same. Let us not forget all the Lord has done for us in the past. We serve a loving Father. Never will He forsake us.

"The LORD your God, He *is* the One who goes with you.
He will not leave you nor forsake you."   —Deuteronomy 31:6b

"You did not choose Me,
but I chose you and appointed you that you
should go and bear fruit,
and that your fruit should remain,
that whatever you ask the Father in
My name He may give you."

John 15:16

God desires a relationship with
His children.
As we abide in Him,
we live a life purposed
for our good and for His Glory.

Chosen

John 15:16

"You did not choose Me, but I chose you
and appointed you that you should go and bear fruit,
and that your fruit should remain,
that whatever you ask the Father in My name
He may give you."

Sitting in the Atlanta airport, I couldn't help but hear the conversation of a couple and their pastor sitting next to me.

"Don't you wonder why God chose us?' asked the woman.

Having asked this same question myself, her question piqued my interest. "We are chosen for His glory," answered the Pastor without hesitation.

The plane arrived, we took our place on board, and that was the end of the conversation. But for me, it was the beginning of meditating upon the answer to her question. Our lives as His children are to bring God glory. What does that mean? How do we glorify God?

"Behold, obedience is greater than sacrifice."   —1 Samuel 15:22

To glorify God is to obey His Holy Word. He doesn't want our sacrifices yet disobedience. He wants our lives to be a reflection of Him.

"Let your light so shine before men, that they may see
your good works and glorify your Father in heaven."
—Matthew 5:16

To glorify God is to abide in Him, that we may bear much fruit. As we die to ourselves, allowing God to have His way in our lives, we bring Him glory.

"I am the vine, you are the branches. He who abides in Me, and I in him,
bears much fruit; for without Me you can do nothing." —John 15:5

God desires a relationship with His children. As we abide in Him, we live a life purposed for our good and for His Glory.

"You did not choose Me, but I chose you." What a privilege! What a gift! May our lives glorify God, giving Him the praise He alone deserves.

"Peace I leave with you, My peace I give you;
not as the world gives do I give to you.
Let not your heart be troubled,
neither let it be afraid."

John 14:27

With each step you take,
each heartache you face,
when you cannot walk,
He will carry you.

My Peace

John 14:27

"Peace I leave with you, My peace I give you;
not as the world gives do I give to you.
Let not your heart be troubled, neither let it be afraid."

Jesus and the disciples had gathered in the Upper Room before the crucifixion of Christ. Having finished supper, Jesus stood, and pouring water into a basin, began washing the feet of the disciples. It was in this setting Jesus began explaining to His disciples what was about to happen. He wanted them to understand this would not be the end, but only the beginning.

"Peace I leave with You, My peace I give you; not as the world gives do I give you,"

He spoke to His disciples. Regardless of the unrest all about, in Him they could have peace.

So often we base our peace on what is happening in our lives. A family member becomes ill and we lose our peace. In its place we become fearful of what lies ahead. A financial crisis comes crashing into our life and our peace is immediately replaced with worry of how we will pay our bills. We struggle with a rebellious child and begin asking why.

Just as Jesus told His disciples in the midst of their despair, He tells us, *"My peace I give you, not as the world gives do I give to you".* Because His peace is based on who He is, not on our circumstances, we can rest in Him, regardless of what is happening in our lives.

"Let not your heart be troubled, neither let it be afraid." How? By resting in the only One who has the answer for what lies ahead. You are not alone today, you will not be alone tomorrow. With each step you take, each heartache you face, when you cannot walk, He will carry you.

> You will keep Him in perfect peace,
> *Whose* mind is stayed *on You,*
> Because he trusts in You.
> Trust in the LORD forever
> For in YAH, the LORD, is everlasting strength. —Isaiah 26:3-4

> The LORD will give strength to His people;
> The LORD will bless His people with peace. —Psalm 29:11

What will you do with Jesus?

Romans 1:16

For I am not ashamed of the gospel of Christ,
for it is the power of God to salvation for everyone
who believes, for the Jew first and also for the Greek.

As I kissed my sister goodbye this side of eternity, it became clear our bodies are but a shell. Only what we do with Jesus will matter.

My oldest sister, Barbara, had struggled with cancer for four years when the doctors told the family it was time to call Hospice. Barb was fine with calling them, we were not. How would we ever live without our daughter, our sister, our friend? As the end drew near we gathered at Barb's home. Daily hospice would visit to do what they could. As so many others, Barb loved her Hospice nurse. One day as Kristen sat visiting with Barb she mentioned going on a mission weekend. Barb's first response to her was, "You do know you need to ask Jesus into your heart don't you? You have done that, right?" Kristen assured her she had and Barb sighed with relief. No longer was Barb concerned about what she was wearing, how her hair looked, nor her makeup. All she cared about was others understood the importance of accepting Christ as their Savior.

The Sunday before Barb ran home to our Father's house, Hospice sent a pastor they referred to as the "Singing Pastor." Her name was Patty, a total delight. As only Barb could, she said to Patty, "I hear you sing. Are you going to sing to me today?" "Well, yes I am," was Patty's reply. "What would you like me to sing?" Without hesitation, Barb asked if she would sing Amazing Grace. After visiting with Barb about what grace means, Patty began to sing. And as she sang, as if she couldn't hold back, Barb began singing along, harmonizing with total perfection. It was as if we had entered the Holy of Holies. Jesus was in our midst. There was not a dry eye in the room.

Our bodies are but a shell, our lives, but a vapor. Today is the day of salvation.

> For what is life? It is even a vapor that appears for a little time
> and then vanishes away.   —James 4:14

"You do know you need to ask Jesus into your heart don't you? You have done that, right?"

Stand fast therefore in the liberty by which Christ has made us free, and do not be entangled again with a yoke of bondage.

Galatians 5:1

It is for freedom Christ
died on the cross.
No longer must we fall for the
lies of Satan, plunging into the
deception set before us.

Yoke of Bondage

Galatians 5:1

Stand fast therefore in the liberty by which
Christ has made us free, and do not be entangled
again with a yoke of bondage.

Speaking to the churches of Galatia, Paul encourages the Galatians to stand fast in their Christian liberty, and not become entangled once again in a yoke of bondage.

As I considered this passage, I thought of ways we as Christians become entangled again with a yoke of bondage. Unfortunately, the list quickly filled my mind; bitterness, refusing to forgive, inferiority, fear, anxiousness, hopelessness, defeat. And I'm sure there are more.

Why is it that even though we know we have been set free, we continue to walk in such bondage? Could it be we are unaware of the enemy's determination to set before us a yoke of bondage? Satan knows exactly what he is doing when he causes a root of bitterness to spring up within us? No longer are we an effective witness for our Lord. Where there once was peace, we now have turmoil. When we pray, we don't feel the freedom we once held dear. Everything changes. We are entangled with a yoke of bondage.

> Pursue peace with all *people*, and holiness,
> without which no one will see the Lord;
> looking carefully lest anyone fall short of the
> grace of God; lest any root of bitterness springing
> up cause trouble, and by this many become defiled.
> —Hebrews 12:14-15

It is for freedom Christ died on the cross. No longer must we fall for the lies of Satan, plunging into the deception set before us. Instead, we can stand fast in the liberty by which Christ has made us free.

> *"Therefore, if the Son makes you free, you shall be free indeed."*
> —John 8:36

> I thank God---through Jesus Christ our Lord!
> So then, with the mind I myself serve the law of God,
> but with the flesh the law of sin.
> —Romans 7:25

For we walk by faith, not by sight.

2 Corinthians 5:7

Faith is an action word.
Only as we step out, putting
action to our words,
do we demonstrate our faith.

Step Out

2 Corinthians 5:7

For we walk by faith, not by sight.

Faith is an action word. Only as we step out, putting action to our words, do we demonstrate our faith. Many great men of the Bible demonstrated their confidence in God as they stepped out in faith, knowing God would be with them.

Abram stepped out in faith when he left his country:

> Now the LORD had said to Abram:
> "Get out of your country, from your family and from your father's house, to a land I will show you." —Genesis 12:1

Moses stepped out as he stretched out his hand over the Red Sea:

> "But lift up your rod, and stretch out your hand over the sea and divide it. And the children of Israel shall go on dry *ground* through the midst of the sea." —Exodus 14:16

David stepped out as he came before Goliath with just a stone:

> "that all the earth may know that there is a God in Israel" —1 Samuel 17:46

The women with the issue of blood stepped out in faith as she made her way through the crowd to touch the border of Jesus' garment.

> A woman came from behind and touched the border of His garment. And immediately her flow of blood stopped. —Luke 8:44

Peter stepped out in faith as he got out of the boat, making his way toward Jesus.

> And Peter answered Him and said, "Lord, if it is You, command me to come to You on the water."
> So He said, "*Come.*" —Matthew 14:28-29

What has the Lord asked you to do, but you are hesitant? Will you trust the Lord to be with you and step out? Only as Peter took his eyes off Jesus did he fall into the water. Keep your eyes on Jesus and allow Him to use you for your good and to bring Him glory. We walk by faith.

"Near to the Brokenhearted"

Psalms 34:18

"The Lord is near to the broken hearted
and saves the crushed in spirit."

Two weeks after losing my sister to cancer, the most incredible thing happened…It had been a particularly hard day for me emotionally, tears ran at the very thought of her. My husband and I were shopping for a new ceiling fan when a darling lady, with a security dog by her side, walked in and starting looking at fans, also. As she stood there, her dog, Angel, laid down. She was finished. The sweet lady looked at me and said, "I guess she has had enough shopping." This began a conversation I did not expect. She told us she had the dog because she could not hear. Angel helped her with anxiety and hearing. Then she went on to tell us ten years earlier her 17 year old daughter died unexpectedly, six months after that she lost her hearing, and six months after that her relatives home was invaded and two were murdered. As I listened all I could think was, "How can she be so sweet and kind when she has been through so much?"

When I walked into the store that night my heart was broken, my spirit crushed. But, as we stood and talked to this sweet lady I knew I would not feel like this forever. Life would go on, and the joy and sweet memories of my sister would return. The Lord was near and He had sent this precious lady to be a comfort to me. When my husband told her I had just lost my sister, she was so caring. "She will always be in your heart. A day won't go by you won't think of her. But, as time goes by, memories will become what you cherish." "Today", she continued, "I have my hearing aids, my family found me Angel, and my relative who survived the break in has remarried and has a darling little three year old boy. Life is good!"

Our Father is so faithful to His children. He loves us with a never-ending love. When our hearts are broken, He sends a sweet lady to encourage us. When we find our lives out of control, He sends a way of escape. And when the future looks bleak and we find ourselves afraid of what lies ahead, ever so gently He speaks,

"Fear not, for I am with You.
Be not dismayed, for *I am* your God.
I will strengthen you,
Yes, I will help you,
I will uphold you with My righteous right hand." —Isaiah 41:10

Wait on the LORD;
Be of good courage,
And He shall strengthen your heart;
Wait, I say, on the LORD!

Psalm 27:14

Is God a God of good times only,
or is He a God of all times?

God of All Times

Psalm 27:14

Wait on the LORD;
Be of good courage,
And He shall strengthen your heart;
Wait, I say, on the LORD!

Do you ever pine over how you thought things would be versus how things are? In all our lives we live with anticipation for how we believe our lives will be, and we do all we can to make our dreams a reality. We attend the necessary schooling to achieve the job of our dreams. We raise our children in a way we feel will result in well adjusted, God fearing adults. We dream for them a life of happiness and success. We live today for how we hope tomorrow will be.

Then life happens. A tragedy fills our lives, a decision is made that results in heartache, a turn of events sends our lives spinning out of our control. We are left wondering how our well laid plans could have taken flight, and in its place left us with despair.

Is God a God of good times only, or is He a God of all times? As children of the living God, we love the blessings our Father so abundantly bestows upon us. We appreciate His never changing grace, His mercy overflowing, the love He showers on us without ending. However, when confusion and despair come tumbling into our lives do we cry out, "God where are You?" or do we know in our heart He is walking with us through what lies ahead?

I *would have lost heart*, unless I had believed
That I would see the goodness of the LORD
In the land of the living.   —Psalm 28:13

Our Father can be trusted. He will make good out of tragedy and bring our lives to a new height of understanding as we lay at His feet what we hoped would be, choosing instead to trust Him. It is here we find courage for our tomorrows and strength for each new day.

The LORD *is* my strength and my shield;
My heart trusted in Him, and I am helped;
Therefore my heart greatly rejoices,
And with my song I will praise Him.   —Psalm 28:7

Now the LORD came and stood
and called as at other times,
"Samuel, Samuel!"
And Samuel answered,
"Speak, for Your servant hears."

1 Samuel 3:10

As we open the Word of God,
asking the Holy Spirit to teach
us all truths,
we must believe He will
meet us there.

The Voice of God

1 Samuel 3:10

Now the LORD came and stood
and called as at other times,
"Samuel, Samuel!"
And Samuel answered,
"Speak, for Your servant hears."

Two times the Lord called to Samuel, "Samuel, Samuel," and each time, Samuel, not knowing the Lord, ran to Eli, "Here I am, for you called me."Both times Eli replied with the same answer, "I did not call; lie down again." And he went and lay down. Finally, the third time the Lord called out to Samuel and Eli, realizing it must be the Lord who called out to the boy, instructed Samuel:

"Go, lie down; and it shall be, if He calls you that you must say,
"Speak, LORD, for your servant hears."   —1 Samuel 3:9

Does the Lord still speak today? Most certainly He does. He speaks through the Holy Spirit:

"But the Helper, the Holy Spirit, whom the Father will send in
my name, He will teach you all things, and bring to your
remembrance all things that I said to you."   —John 14:26

And He speaks through His Word:

For the word of God *is* living and powerful, and sharper than
any two-edged sword, piercing even to the division of soul
and spirit, and of joints and marrow, and is a discerner of the
thoughts and intents of the heart.   —Hebrews 4:12

As we open the Word of God, asking the Holy Spirit to teach us all truths, we must believe He will meet us there. Some say when they hear Him speak it is like the Word of God jumps off the page, letting them know this Word is for them. Others say is it a quickening in their heart, an assurance they have heard from the Lord. Yet others say it is a peace that passes all understanding, a passage addressing exactly what is on their heart. Regardless of how He speaks, as we read the Word of God, we must expect to hear from God. Just as He spoke to Samuel, He will speak to us today.

Your word is a lamp to my feet
And a light to my path.   —Psalm 119:10

O GOD, You *are* my God;
Early will I seek You;
My soul thirsts for You;
My flesh longs for You
In a dry and thirsty land
Where there is no water.

Psalm 63:1

Sometimes we forget
we are not alone.
Everywhere we are, He is.
This is our God.

An Everyday God

Psalm 63:1

O GOD, You *are* my God;
Early will I seek You;
My soul thirsts for You;
My flesh longs for You
In a dry and thirsty landWhere there is no water.

Is there someone in your life, when you see them a calmness comes over you, an assurance all is well, simply because they are in your midst?

God can be that someone in your life in every way, everyday. His greatest desire is that we will seek His face, lean on Him, and allow Him to guide our path. He didn't surrender all on the cross so that we would continue to walk in the bondage of this world. He came that we might be set free.

> *"Therefore, if the Son makes you free, you shall be free indeed."*
> —John 8:36

Sometimes we forget that we are not alone. We carry anxiety on our shoulders like a heavy winter coat, allowing it to weigh us down—our bodies weary from the load. This need not be. Jesus is in our ordinary days. He meets us as our feet touch the floor in the morning and tucks us into bed at night. He walks with us through every appointment we have through the day, and sits with us in the quiet. Everywhere we are, He is. This is our God.

> He shall call upon Me,
> and I will answer him;
> I *will* be with him in trouble;
> I will deliver him and honor him.
> With long life I will satisfy him,
> And show him My salvation   —Psalm 91:15-16

The next time we feel if we could only have that special someone in our midst all would be well, let's remember Jesus is with us and there is nothing we need He cannot give.

> Fear not, for I *am* with you;
> Be not dismayed, for I *am* your God.
> I will strengthen you,
> Yes, I will help you,
> I will uphold you with My righteous right hand.
> —Isaiah 41:10

As for me, I will see Your face in righteousness;
I shall be satisfied when
I awake in Your likeness.

Psalm 17:15

Is Jesus my personal
sovereign preference?
Do I prefer Him over all else?

Sovereign Preference

Psalm 17:15

As for me, I will see Your face in righteousness;
I shall be satisfied when I awake in Your likeness.

Reading Romans in my morning devotions, I read the following Scripture:

And do not be conformed to this world, but be
transformed by the renewing of your mind that
you may prove what is that good and acceptable
and perfect will of God.   —Romans 12:2

My first thought was; how do I renew my mind? Understanding renew means to make new, I realized this Scripture is telling me I must let go of things not pleasing to the Lord, replacing them with pleasing actions and thoughts. I know this can only happen as I surrender my life to Christ.

In his devotional, "My Utmost for His Highest," Oswald Chambers defines total surrender in this way; "genuine total surrender is a personal sovereign preference for Jesus Christ Himself." Considering this, I asked myself, "Is Jesus my personal sovereign preference? Do I prefer Him over all else?"

As I studied this Scripture further, I realized not only am I to surrender my life to Christ, but I am to be changed into His likeness. On my own, I cannot do this. I know how quickly, left to myself, I fall back into my old nature. As I pondered this thought I felt like Paul as he spoke to the Romans:

For what I am doing, I do not understand.
For what I will to do, that I do not practice;
but what I hate, that I do.   —Romans 7:15

Then I understood; only as I surrender my life to Christ, allowing Him to transform me from the inside out, will I be able to prove what is that good and acceptable and perfect will of God. He is the potter I am the clay.

But now, O LORD, You *are* our Father;
We *are* the clay, and You our potter;
And all we *are* the work of Your hand.   —Isaiah 64:8

Search me , O God, and know my heart;
Try me, and know my anxieties;
And see if *there is any* wicked way in me,
And lead me in the way everlasting.   —Psalm 139:23-24

In quietness and confidence
shall be your strength.

Isaiah 30:15

What is your impossible
situation that it can defy
the living God?

Our Strength

Isaiah 30:15

In quietness and confidence shall be your strength.

Sometimes we receive phone calls we wish had never come. I received that call yesterday. While at the Children's Museum with my six year old grandson, my phone rang and it was my doctor telling me my biopsy had come back positive. I have breast cancer.

As I've had time to process this, I realize this did not catch God by surprise, nor is it too hard for Him. God is still on His throne. What Satan is trying to do for evil, I know God will turn for my good and His glory.

Because of this, I want to share with you what the Lord showed me during my quiet time this morning. I've been reading through 1 Samuel and this morning I was in Chapter 17, when David went before the giant, Goliath. While the entire army of Israel ran from Goliath, David said to them:

> "For who *is* this uncircumcised Philistine,
> that he should defy the armies of the living God?" —1 Samuel 17:16b

I could hear God asking me, *"Cyndy, what is cancer that it should defy Me?"*

This is not just for me. It is for every believer. So let me ask you,

> "What is your impossible situation that it can defy the living God?"

…is it finances, relationships, illness, you fill in the blank. I'm sure you know exactly what the giant is in your life. Should it defy the Living God?

> "For with God nothing will be impossible."   —Luke 1:37

Next I read in my devotional reading:

> For thus says the LORD GOD, the Holy One of Israel:
> In quietness and confidence shall be your strength. —Isaiah 30:15

Through this cancer I want to walk in confidence that I might have His strength. I trust Him to fight this Goliath in my life. I know He will win!

> The Lord *is* my strength and my shield;
> My heart trusted in Him, and I am helped;
> Therefore my heart greatly rejoices,
> And with my song I will praise Him.   —Psalm 28:7

He chose us in Him before the
foundation of the world, that we should
be holy and without blame before Him in love.

Ephesians 1:4

We do not earn our way into the
Kingdom of God,
nor are we so smart
we finally got it.

Chosen

Ephesians 1:4

He chose us in Him before the
foundation of the world, that we should
be holy and without blame before Him in love.

Have you considered why Christ chose you to be His child? Do you suppose it was because He saw something in you that would be of value to His Kingdom? Perhaps it was because He knew you would be obedient to His leading. Or possibly it was because He loves you and wanted to shower upon you the gift of His salvation. I believe it was the latter. God doesn't need any of us. He got along just fine before He drew us to Himself.

We do not earn our way into His kingdom. Nor are we so smart we finally got it. We are children of the living God for one reason only; He chose us in Him before the foundation of the world. And why did He choose us? He chose us that we should be holy and without blame before Him in love.

How do we do this? How do we become holy and without blame in love? We humble ourselves daily, obedient to His leading.

> Therefore, humble yourselves under the mighty hand of God,
> that He may exalt you in due time.   —1 Peter 5:6

> "Call to me, and I will answer you, and show you great and mighty
> things, which you do not know.   —Jeremiah 33:3

And we remain teachable, seeking wisdom and instruction as hidden treasures.

> Take firm hold of instruction, do not let go;
> Keep her, for she *is* your life.   —Proverbs 4:13

> Get wisdom! Get understanding!
> Do not forget, nor turn away from the words of my mouth.
> Do not forsake her, and she will preserve you;
> Love her, and she will keep you.
> Wisdom *is* the principal thing;
> *Therefore* get wisdom.
> And in all your getting, get understanding.   —Proverbs 4:5-7

We are chosen for one purpose; that we should be holy and without blame before Him in love. May we walk worthy of our calling.

"For *the* Lord *does* not *see* as man sees;
for man looks at the outward appearance,
but the LORD looks at the heart."

1 Samuel 16:7b

We speak from our heart.
What's in our heart will make
all the difference.

He Looks at Our Heart

1 Samuel 16:7b

"For *the LORD does* not *see* as man sees;
for man looks at the outward appearance,
but the LORD looks at the heart."

While studying the book of 1 Samuel, I read how God sent Samuel to Jesse, the Bethlehemite, to choose a king to replace King Saul. When Jesse presented his son Eliab to Samuel, because of Eliab's physical stature and appearance, he perceived in his heart this was surely to be the anointed one.

> But the LORD said to Samuel, "Do not look at his appearance
> or at his physical stature, because I have refused him."
> —1 Samuel 16:7a

Unfortunately, we do the same today. Our first impression of anyone is his or her appearance. How often have we thought:

> I want to marry a man tall, dark, and handsome.
> Of course she's successful, I would be, too, if I looked like her.
> I wish I had a model figure. Why do I have to be so short?
> Some people get all the breaks! Look at her/him.

We have all heard the saying, "You never have a second chance to make a first impression." However, this is not how God sees us. He doesn't look at our outward appearance. He looks at our heart. This is why He tells us;

> Keep your heart with all diligence,
> For out of it *spring* the issues of life.   —Proverbs 4:23
>
> For as he thinks in his heart so *is* he.   —Proverbs 23:7
>
> As in water face *reflects* face,
> So a man's heart *reveals* the man.   —Proverbs 27:19

Out of one's heart such things as bitterness, envy, and strife our born. In the same way, such things as kindness, meekness, and peace come forth. We speak from our heart. What's in our heart will make all the difference.

> *"A good man out of the good treasure of his heart brings forth evil; and an
> evil man out of the treasures of his heart bring forth evil. For out of the
> abundance of the heart his mouth speaks."*   —Luke 6:45

The LORD is my shepherd; I shall not want.
He makes me to lie down in green pastures;
He leads me beside the still waters.

Psalm 23:1-2

Never will there be a time
He will allow His children to
be overcome by the storm.

My Shepherd

Psalm 23:1-2

The LORD is my shepherd; I shall not want.
He makes me to lie down in green pastures;
He leads me beside the still waters.

If you are like me, you are so familiar with this Scripture you know it by memory. That is, I thought I knew it by memory until I read it this morning. As I read these words in my daily devotional, I noticed two words I have not noticed before.

The first word I noticed was leads. "He leads me beside the still waters." As I contemplated this word, I realized the only way I will come to the still waters is by His leading. He doesn't point the way, leaving me to find still waters on my own. No, our Shepherd leads the way. And where He leads, I must follow. Only as I follow His lead will I find peace in the midst of turmoil, rest in the midst of weariness, and confidence in the midst of doubt.

> *"And when he brings out his own sheep, he goes before them;*
> *and the sheep follow him, for they know his voice."* —John 10:4

The second word was "still." Have you ever known Jesus to lead His children into the raging waters, waves tossing them to and fro? It is true; Jesus allows heartache to come into our lives. At times like this we can feel not only are we being tossed about, life totally out of control, we can feel we are drowning. This is when we find Jesus putting purpose in our pain. As we call on Him, just as He put his hand out to Peter and said, "Come," He stretches out His hand to us. Never will there be a time He will allow His children to be overcome by the storm.

> As for me, I will call upon God,
> And the LORD shall save me.
> Evening and morning and at noon
> I will pray and cry aloud,
> And He shall hear my voice.
> He has redeemed my soul in peace
> From the battle *that was* against me.   —Psalm 55:16-18

He leads me beside the still waters. Where He leads, I will follow.

> For You *are* my rock and my fortress;
> Therefore, for Your names' sake
> Lead me and guide me.   —Psalm 31:3

Perfect Peace

Isaiah 26:3

You will keep *him* in perfect peace,
Whose mind *is* stayed *on You,*
Because he trusts in You.

Not able to sleep, I decided to do what I love most—meditate upon a Scripture asking the three questions:

What does it say,
What does it mean,
What does it mean to me personally?

This is how the conversation went in my mind:

"You will keep him in perfect peace"

What does <u>perfect</u> mean? It means without flaw, complete.
So I could say, "You will keep him in complete peace"

"Whose mind is stayed on You"

What does <u>stayed</u> mean? It means constant, always thinking on
the same thing. So I could say,
"Whose mind is constantly on the Lord."

"Because he trusts in You"

What does <u>trust</u> mean? It means believes completely, or as I
learned at a Women's Retreat; believe means "I give my heart."
So I could say, "Because he gives his heart to You."

Putting this all together, I thought again about this Scripture in light of how
I had taken it apart:

You will keep him in complete peace
Whose mind is constantly on You,
Because he gives his heart to You.

I realized why my peace had wavered—my mind wasn't constantly on the
Lord, but filled with anxiety and frustration. I knew at that moment I needed
to change my thoughts and give my heart to God. Only then would I find
His complete peace, perfect in everyway.

Sweet sleep came, and with it His perfect peace.

"Tis so sweet to trust in Jesus."

Now Saul was afraid of David,
because the LORD was with him,
but had departed from Saul.

1 Samuel 18:12

The Lord sees our heart
and knows our ways.

Perspective

1 Samuel 18:12

Now Saul was afraid of David,
because the LORD was with him,
but had departed from Saul.

While studying 1 Samuel, I read how David found such favor with Saul that Saul set him over the men of war. All seemed fine until Samuel and David went to war against the Philistines. After a great victory, crowds gathered to welcome them home. As they came into the city, the women began to sing songs of praise toward David.

> Now it had happened as they were coming *home*, when David
> was returning from the slaughter of the Philistine, that the women
> had come out of all the cities of Israel, singing and dancing, to meet
> King Saul with tambourines, with joy, and with musical instruments.

> So the women sang as they danced, and said:
> "Saul has slain his thousands,
> And David his ten thousands."
> Then Saul was very angry, and the saying displeased him;
> and he said, "They have ascribed to David ten thousands,
> to me they have ascribed *only* thousands. Now *what* more can he
> have but the kingdom?"   —1 Samuel 18:6-8

From that point on, because of extreme jealousy, Saul set out to kill David.

As I read this, I couldn't help but wonder how often we see others through a false lense. All is fine until a word spoken, a look given, or an attitude misunderstood takes place, and no longer do we think of that person as we once did. Just as David had no idea why Saul turned on him, I wonder if we have ever allowed a relationship to be destroyed, as did Saul with David. Perhaps someone has turned on you and you have no idea why. It hurts, we become confused. The Lord sees our heart and knows our ways. At times like this we can only rest in Him to make it right.

> But You, O Lord, know me;
> You have seen me,   —Jeremiah 12:3

> Seek good and not evil, that you may live;
> So the LORD GOD of hosts will be with you.   —Amos 5:14

David said furthermore,
"As the LORD lives,
the LORD shall strike him,
or his day shall come to die,
or he shall go out to battle and perish."

1 Samuel 26:10

"As the LORD lives,"
the Lord shall work it out.

Trust

1 Samuel 26:10

David said furthermore, "As the LORD lives,
the LORD shall strike him, or his day shall come
to die, or he shall go out to battle and perish."

As Saul continued in pursuit of David, it happened that Saul camped near David and his army. Finding where Saul and his army lay, David and his men came to the people by night and found Saul sleeping. This was their change to kill Saul and his people and bring this madness to an end.

But David said to Abishai, "Do not destroy him; for who can
stretch out his hand against the LORD'S anointed, and be guiltless?"
—1 Samuel 26:9

As I read this, I couldn't help but marvel at the faith of David. He knew Saul wanted nothing less than to kill him. He also knew his life had become nothing short of a man running for his life. However, David would not kill the LORD'S anointed. He would not have Saul's blood on his hands. Instead, he would trust God.

When we find ourselves in an impossible situation, how hard is it to not take things into our hands, doing all we can to make things right? What if like David, regardless of how impossible the situation may look, we would walk in faith instead, letting God work things out as they should be?

And we know that all things work together for good to those who
love God, to those who are called according to *His* purpose.
—Romans 8:28

The next time we find ourselves fighting for what we think is right, may we remember the faith of David, and just as he chose to trust the Lord, may we be willing to do the same.

"As the LORD lives,"
the LORD shall work it out.

Do not be wise in your own eyes;
Fear the LORD and depart from evil.
It will be health to your flesh,
And strength to your bones.   —Proverbs 3:7-8

*But David strengthened himself
in the LORD his God.*

1 Samuel 30:6

*God desires our obedience
over succumbing to
our own desires.*

Strength in the Lord

1 Samuel 30:6

But David strengthened himself
in the LORD his God.

David and his men, returning to their homes in Ziklag, found the Amalekites had taken the women and children captive. In great distress, the men lifted their voices and wept. Falsely accusing David of the invasion, they threatened to stone him.

When we are falsely accused our human tendency is to strike back, fight for the truth. However, the Scriptures tell us this is not what David did. Instead of fighting back, he strengthened himself by going to the LORD his God.

Impossible situations are not too hard for the Lord. He will fight the battle for us, as He did for David, as we pray for His direction:

> So David inquired of the LORD, saying, "Shall I pursue this
> troop? Shall I overtake them?" And He answered him, "Pursue,
> for you shall surely overtake *them* and without fail recover *all.*"
> —1 Samuel 30:8

God desires our obedience over succumbing to our own desires. When we allow God to lead us through hard places, we will find He has drawn us to Himself and carried us to the other side. There are lessons to be learned, and a purpose for the pain. He is the potter and we are the clay. May we allow Him to mold us into the person He desires for us to be.

> But now, O LORD,
> You *are* our Father;
> We *are* the clay, and You our potter;
> And all we *are* the work of Your hand.   —Isaiah 64:8

> Wait on the LORD,
> Be of good courage,
> And He shall strengthen your heart;
> Wait, I say, on the LORD!   —Psalm 27:14

> I waited patiently for the Lord;
> And inclined to me, and heard my cry.
> He also brought me up out of the horrible pit,
> Out of the miry clay.   —Psalm 40:1-2a

The name of the LORD is strong tower;
the righteous run to it and are safe.

Proverbs 18:10

Why is it we come to
Jesus by faith
than feel we must show our trust
in God in our own strength?

Strong Tower

Proverbs 18:10

The name of the LORD *is* a strong tower;
The righteous run to it and are safe.

I need something stronger than myself to carry me through this day. As I started this journey called cancer, I was determined to be strong, beat it with a smile on my face and a skip in my step. Why? Because I wanted to show the faithfulness of Jesus to those I met along the way.

Not once did I consider what Jesus wanted to do with this giant in my life. Today I understand. He didn't expect me to put up a facade, when inside I was hurting, my bones aching. No, from the beginning, He wanted to use this journey to show me more of Himself. He wanted me to understand I didn't need to be strong for Him, that it's ok to be weak and in need of His strength.

> And He said to me, *"My grace is sufficient for you, for My strength is made perfect in weakness."* Therefore most gladly I will rather boast in my infirmities, that the power of Christ may rest upon me.   —2 Corinthians 12:9

Why is it we come to Jesus by faith, than feel we must show our trust in God in our own strength? Speaking to the Galatians, Paul asked this very question;

> This only I want to learn form you: Did you receive the Spirit by the works of the law or by the hearing of faith? Are you so foolish? Having begun in the Spirit, are you now being made perfect by the flesh?   —Galatians 3:2-3

When I first found out I had cancer the Lord asked me,

> "What is cancer that it should defy the living God?"

What He didn't ask is: "What is cancer that it should defy you?"

There's a big difference in these two questions. Only as Christ has fought this giant, through His grace and love, have I endured the struggles it has brought against my body. It has defied me, but through God's grace I have felt His love bring me through each day.

Today I rejoice in understanding what Christ meant when He spoke those words, *"My grace is sufficient for you, My strength is made perfect in weakness."*

So the LORD said to Cain,
"Why are you angry?
And why has your countenance fallen?
"If you do well, will you not be accepted?
And if you do not do well, sin lies at the door.
And it's desire *is* for you,
but you should rule over it."

Genesis 4:6-7

There is purpose in living
a Godly life.

Why Are You Angry?

Genesis 4:6

So the LORD said to Cain,
"Why are you angry? And why has
your countenance fallen?
"If you do well, will you not be accepted?
And if you do not do well, sin lies at the door.
And it's desire *is* for you but you should rule over it."

The story in Genesis concerning Cain and Abel's offering to the Lord speaks loudly to us today. God required they bring an offering of their very best. Abel brought the firstborn of his flock and of their fat. And the Lord respected Abel and his offering. Cain, however, brought the fruit of the ground to the Lord, but God did not respect Cain, nor his offering.

Have you ever wondered why God didn't accept Cain's offering? I have. Cain was a tiller of the ground and I always assumed he brought the best of his fruits. The problem however, was that God required a blood sacrifice. It was the shed blood for the sins of the people that made the sacrifice acceptable. When Cain found that his offering was not acceptable, he became very angry, and his countenance fell.

We do the same today. We do wrong and face the consequences of our actions, and instead of admitting we are wrong become angry.

Pride *goes* before destruction,
And a haughty spirit before a fall.   —Proverbs 16:18

As God asked Cain, He asks us today:

"If you do well, will you not be accepted?"

There is purpose in living a Godly life.

Do not be wise in your own eyes;
Fear the LORD and depart from evil.
It will be health to your flesh,
And strength to your bones.   —Proverbs 3:7-8

Sin lies at the door of our lives on a daily basis, desiring to take control. It is up to us to rule over it, that we might live in victory instead.

Choose for yourselves this day whom you will serve.
But for me, and my house, we will serve the LORD.
                                        —Joshua 24:15

As he journeyed he came near Damascus,
and suddenly a light shone
around him from heaven.

Acts 9:3

Let's decide this day to
never say never, but instead
walk in what we know is Truth.
When God is in control,
all things are possible.

Suddenly

Acts 9:3

As he journeyed he came near Damascus,
and suddenly a light shone around him from heaven.

Traveling the road to Damascus, Saul was unwavering in his determination to persecute anyone he found proclaiming to be a follower of Christ. To anyone aware of Saul's steadfast mission, any change in his belief looked impossible. As he lived his life with this single-minded quest, he seemed to be unstoppable. That is, until heaven reached down to change his life forever.

> As he journeyed he came near Damascus, and suddenly a light
> shone around him from heaven.
> Then he fell to the ground, and heard a voice saying to him,
> *"Saul, Saul, why are you persecuting Me?"*
> And he said, "Who are You, Lord?", Then the Lord said, *"I am
> Jesus, whom you are persecuting. It is hard for you to kick against the goads."*
> —Acts 9:3-5

In an instant, Saul's life changed from persecuting Christians to falling on his face before Jesus, proclaiming Him as Lord.

As I read this, I couldn't help but think of my loved ones who have yet to accept Jesus as their personal Savior. As I consider their lives, it seems impossible they will ever bend their knee.

But then I remember, Jesus is the same today as He was on that day Saul walked toward Damascus. Saul didn't expect his life to be changed forever, his calling to be one of proclaiming Christ as Lord, as he started walking that morning. And it's just as likely our loved ones don't expect their lives to be changed. But, suddenly, a light shone, and just as quickly the Lord can touch our loved ones' heart. They, too, can be changed forever.

Let's decide this day to never say never, but instead walk in what we know is Truth. When God is in control all things are possible. Let's walk with anticipation for that day when suddenly our loved one sees Christ, proclaiming Him as their Lord and Savior.

> The Lord is not slack concerning *His* promise, as some count
> slackness, but is longsuffering toward us, not willing that any
> should perish but that all should come to repentance.   —2 Peter 3:9

May the God of all grace, who called us
to His eternal glory by Christ Jesus,
after you have suffered a while,
perfect, establish, strengthen and settle you.

1 Peter 5:10

God desires for His children
to be settled, without concern
or frustration for
what troubles them.

Settled

1 Peter 5:10

May the God of all grace, who called us
to His eternal glory by Christ Jesus,
after you have suffered a while,
perfect, establish, strengthen and settle you.

Visiting with my girlfriend, she mentioned how she puts her concerns in a box and hands them to Jesus, only to look inside again and again to see how they are doing. Sadly enough, I'm sure we can all relate.

Recently, we had a certain concern in our life that kept us up at night, it remained first and foremost in our mind during the day, and felt like an impossible situation with no positive solution. As my husband and I discussed this concern, he reminded me we needed to put it in the box, give it to Jesus, and leave it with Him. Wanting peace so badly, this is what we did. We committed our concern to the only One with the answer.

At least that is what I thought I had done. As the day continued, I brought the concern up to my husband once again. His reply to me was: "I guess I nailed my box shut more securely than you did. I can't get my box open." I'll have to admit, that brought a smile to my face. What was I doing opening the box?

The next morning during my devotions, as I read 1 Peter 5:10, the word *"settle"* seemed to jump off the page. Perhaps it spoke to me because I longed to once again feel settled in my soul, to trust God that all would work out. I was weary of the confusion the concern was causing.

Have you ever been there? I'm sure you have. We all have. Allow this Word from God's love letter speak to you today. God desires for His children to be settled, without concern or frustration for what troubles them. He wants nothing more than for us to live in the peace He was nailed on the cross to give us. Give your concern to Jesus. Let Him carry it, deciding today to let go and let God work. Only as we do this will we once again feel settled in our soul.

> Casting all your cares on Him for He cares for You.
>
> —1 Peter 5:7

> Trust in the Lord with all your heart
> And lean not on your own understanding
> In all your ways acknowledge Him,
> And He shall direct your paths.   —Proverbs 3:5-6

"Therefore give to Your servant
an understanding heart to judge Your people
that I may discern between good and evil."

1 Kings 3:9a

Could it be we do not
understand simply because
we do not ask?

Ask!

1 Kings 3:9a

"Therefore give to Your servant
an understanding heart to judge Your people
that I may discern between good and evil."

Following the death of King David, his son Solomon became king over Israel. Solomon loved the LORD, walking in the statues of his father. Because of his faithfulness, at Gibeon the Lord appeared to Solomon in a dream asking a question of him;

> At Gibeon the LORD appeared to Solomon in a dream
> by night; and God said, "Ask! What shall I give you?"
> —1King 3:5

Solomon, realizing he didn't know how to be King, instead of asking for riches and honor, asked the Lord for an understanding heart, that he may discern between good and evil.

As I read this I thought to myself, "That's what I want. I want an understanding heart. I want the wisdom of Solomon that I may walk uprightly before the Lord." Isn't that what we all want?

The Lord told Solomon to ask! Have we ever asked for wisdom or an understanding heart? Could it be we do not understand simply because we do not ask?

> You do not have because you do not ask.   —James 4:2

God said, "Ask! What shall I give you?" May our reply be as Solomon, "Give to me an understanding heart that I may discern between good and evil."

> Wisdom *is* the principal thing;
> *Therefore* get wisdom.
> And in all your getting get understanding.   —Proverbs 4:7

> Happy *is* the man *who* finds wisdom,
> And the man *who* gains understanding;
> For her proceeds *are* better than the profits of silver,
> And her gain than find gold.
> She *is* more precious than rubies,
> And all the things you may desire cannot compare to her.
> —Proverbs 3:13-15

Nevertheless they did not depart from the sins
of the house of Jeroboam,
who had made Israel sin,
but walked in them; and the wooded image
also remained in Samaria.

2 Kings 13:6

I have begged the Lord
For deliverance,
and He has given it without
accusations or judgment.

Nevertheless

2 Kings 13:6

> Nevertheless they did not depart from the sins of the
> house of Jeroboam, who had made Israel sin, but walked
> in them; and the wooden image also remained in Samaria.

As we study the book of 2 Kings, we find king after king over Israel did evil in the sight of the Lord. God ultimately delivered Israel into the hand of Hazael king of Syria. Distressed and without hope, King Jehoahaz, the king of Israel pleaded with the LORD. The Word of God tells us;

> Then the LORD gave Israel a deliverer, so that they
> escaped from under the hand of the Syrians.   —2 King 13:5a

As I read this, I thought of the times the Lord has delivered me. I, too, have cried out to the Lord and found His gracious forgiving hand upon me.

But then I read 2 Kings 13:6. My heart sank as I read but one word. Do you see it? Does it catch your breath as it did mine? *Nevertheless,* they did not depart from the sins of the house of Jeroboam, who made Israel sin, but walked in them.

How I wish I could point my finger and shout with disgust, "How could you do that after the Lord was so gracious and delivered you?" I cannot. Instead I must see myself in this setting. I have begged the Lord for deliverance and He has given it without accusations or judgment.

Nevertheless, instead of turning from my wicked ways I have once again found myself back in the place I begged Him to deliver me from. Why? I did not run from that which brought me to the place of despair in the beginning. I stayed, thinking I was strong enough to not fall once again.

Our Lord is gracious. With each temptation, as we call out to Him, He will make a way of escape that we need not fall back into that from which we were delivered. The question we must ask ourselves; "Will we look for it?" "Will we, unlike the Israelites, remove what brought us to this place in the beginning?" May our answer always be absolutely without reservation, yes!!

> No temptation has overtaken you except such as is common to man;
> but God *is* faithful, who will not allow you to be tempted beyond
> what you are able, but with the temptation will also make the way of
> escape, that you may be able to bear *it*.   —1 Corinthians 1:13

I heard the voice of the Lord, saying:
"Whom shall I send,
And who will go for Us?"

Isaiah 6:8

Who do you know who
needs your prayers
on their behalf?

Standing in the Gap

Isaiah 6:8

I heard the voice of the Lord, saying:
"Whom shall I send,
And who will go for Us?"

Intercessory prayer, what does this mean? According to the Wikipedia, intercessory prayer is the act of praying on behalf of others. This came to my remembrance as I sat in church on Mother's Day. As the Pastor spoke of the importance of mothers, I noticed a precious one who has yet to become a mother, even though this is her heart's desire. I couldn't help but think how her heart must break just hearing these words.

And then I thought of a loved one who lives with an uncertain future. Not knowing where she should move, or what employment she should seek, her future holds more questions than answers.

We have all had times in our life when it becomes hard to hang on to the unknown with faith and anticipation for what the Lord has for us. Time seems to steal our hope in ever realizing answers to our prayers. We know the Lord cares, and we know He hears our prayers, but the enemy lurks in every corner of our life, ready to steal our confidence in walking in what we do not see.

> Now faith is the substance of things hoped for,
> the confidence of things not seen.   —Hebrews 11:1

This is where intercessory prayer comes in. As a Christian brother or sister, we can stand in the gap for that hurting person. When their faith wanes, they feel their prayers are no longer being heard and their hopes will never become a reality, we can be the one who stands on the Word of God on their behalf.

> The eyes of the LORD *are* on the righteous,
> And His ears *are open* to their cry.   —Psalm 34:15

Who do you know who needs your prayers on their behalf? What greater honor could there be than to bring them before the throne of God, asking Him to bless them, giving them the desire of their heart?

> The *righteous* cry out, and the LORD hears.   —Psalm 34:17

For we are to God the fragrance of Christ
among those who are being saved
and among those who are perishing.

2 Corinthians 2:15

Only as I allow Christ
to live through me
will my life diffuse the
sweet fragrance of Christ.

Fragrance of Christ

2 Corinthians 2:15

For we are to God the fragrance of Christ
among those who are being saved
and among those who are perishing.

What does it mean to you to be the fragrance of Christ? Possibly, when you think of fragrance you think of your favorite perfume, or a bouquet of spring flowers. Perhaps it is the fresh fragrance of a morning rain, or the sweet smell of a baby after their bath. Whatever it may be, it is a big order to think God sees us as the fragrance of Christ, His only begotten Son.

To know where I go and what I do is a display of Christ to others causes me to sit up and take notice.

Do I love others as Christ loves me?
Do I forgive others as Christ has forgiven me?
Do I show the mercy and grace Christ showers on me?
Do others see Christ when they see me?

As a child of God these are questions I must consider.

When I want to judge others, do I remember the unconditional love Christ showed me, dying on the cross for my sins, and show His love instead?

But God demonstrates His own love toward us, in that while
we were still sinners, Christ died for us.   —Romans 5:8

When someone offends me, do I remember how Christ forgave me, and diffuse the fragrance of Christ by not holding the offense against them?

And be kind to one another, tenderhearted, forgiving one another,
even as God in Christ forgave you.   —Ephesians 4:32

And remembering where I would be without Christ's grace and mercy bestowed so abundantly upon me, do I extend the same to others?

Let us therefore come boldly to the throne of grace, that we may
obtain mercy and find grace to help in time of need. —Hebrews 4:16

Only as I allow Christ to live through me, living the example set before me, will my life diffuse the sweet fragrance of Christ. Oh, that it might be!

Now thanks *be* to God who always leads us in triumph in Christ,
and through us diffuses the fragrance of His knowledge in every place.
          —2 Corinthians 2:14